UNITED ARAB EMIRATES YEARBOOK
2009

D1664981

This project is undertaken with support and assistance from the National Media Council. It is a multimedia publishing programme involving publication of the UAE *Yearbook* in English, French and Arabic printed and electronic editions; management of UAEINTERACT (www.uaeinteract.com), which contains news updates linked to pages of the *Yearbook*; publication of *UAE at a Glance*, which summarises main data on the UAE; and production of a DVD containing films and e-books on the UAE.

The publishers wish to acknowledge and thank the National Media Council for their valuable encouragement and support for this multifaceted project.

Editor: Paula Vine
Associate Editors: Ibrahim Al Abed, Peter Hellyer, Peter Vine

Photographs ©: Emirates News Agency (WAM), Trident Press Ltd, *The National*, *Gulf News*, Getty Images, Hanne & Jens Eriksen, Photolibrary, Brian McMorrow, Fotosearch, Grapheast, Abu Dhabi Urban Planning Council, BP Photographic Archives, Environment Agency – Abu Dhabi, Peter Vine

English edition design and typesetting: Jane Stark and James Kelly, Trident Press

Yearbook information is, by definition, subject to change. The current volume is based on available information at the time of printing. Whilst every care has been taken to achieve accuracy, the publishers cannot accept any liability for consequences arising from the use of information contained in this book.

Statistics are based on available sources and are not necessarily official or endorsed by the UAE Government.

British Library Cataloguing in Publication Data:
A CIP catalogue record for this book is available
from the British Library.

ISBN 978-1-905486-45-8 (hardback) ISBN: 978-1-905486-46-5 (paperback)

Published by Trident Press Ltd
175 Piccadilly, Mayfair, London W1J 9TB
Tel: 020 7491 8770; Fax: 020 7491 8664
E-mail: admin@tridentpress.com
Website: www.tridentpress.com

For further information please contact:
National Media Council,
Department of External Information,
PO Box 3790,
Abu Dhabi,
United Arab Emirates.
Tel: 00971 2 4452 922
Fax: 00971 2 4450 458
Email: admin@extinfo.gov.ae or info@extinfo.gov.ae

CONTENTS

FOREWORD

THE BUSINESS OF LOOKING-BACK IN TIME IS A PRECISE SCIENCE. Unfortunately none of us knows what will happen tomorrow but we do know what happened yesterday, last week, last month and last year. The recording of recent events, in the form of the United Arab Emirates *Yearbook*, and indeed of the many official reports issued by various government and private organisations on which much of the *Yearbook* data is based, is a valuable tool defining the latest developments in the country. The 2009 UAE *Yearbook* reports on a period of continued rapid development in the UAE.

As I turn these pages, I also have on my desk the UAE *Yearbook* for 1999. What great progress was revealed in that edition and yet what a distance we have travelled in the short period of one decade since then!

Among the many aspects of growth and development that each *Yearbook* portrays there are several consistent threads that do not change. Among these central tenets of what 'makes the Emirates tick' is a spirit of 'openness' that the UAE Government remains very committed towards and which influences almost all areas of its activities and decision making. This embraces many different facets of our national (and individual) psyche, including a willingness to share our views and ideas and to listen to, and respect those of others; a proud acknowledgement of our past and our rich heritage whilst also opening our minds to new developments, new ideas and new technologies; and, perhaps most importantly, a recognition that there are many different ways to consider a particular issue or challenge. We do not claim to have all the answers and do not hold up our record as one that is without flaws. But our openness helps us to learn from the past and to do better in future.

2008 brought many new challenges and significant developments in virtually all fields. The UAE Government Strategy, launched in 2007 with a focus on adopting international best practices in the area of public administration, saw further progress with one of the most important aspects being the enhancement of collaboration between the federal authorities and those in each emirate.

I take this opportunity to thank you for your interest in the United Arab Emirates and hope that you will find this publication assists you in your quest for knowledge and information on our fascinating country.

Saqr Ghobash
Chairman, National Media Council

'He who does not know his past cannot make the best of his present and future, for it is from the past that we learn.'

The arrival of envoys from the Prophet Mohammed in 630 AD heralded the conversion of the region to Islam.

HISTORY

THE UAE HAS A LONG HISTORY, RECENT FINDS in the Hajar Mountains and in the Western Region of Abu Dhabi having pushed the earliest evidence of man in the Emirates back by tens of thousands, perhaps hundreds of thousands, of years. Prior to this, the earliest known human occupation for which there is significant evidence dated from the Neolithic period, 5500 BC or 7500 years ago, when the climate was wetter and food resources abundant. Even at this early stage, there is proof of interaction with the outside world, especially with civilisations to the north. These contacts persisted and became wide-ranging, probably motivated by trade in copper from the Hajar Mountains, commencing around 3000 BC as the climate became more arid and fortified oasis communities focused on agriculture.

A third millennium bronze pedestal chalice from Wadi 'Asimah. Similar to goblets from Baluchistan, it is the only one of its type found so far in south-eastern Arabia.

Foreign trade, the recurring motif in the history of this strategic region, seems to have flourished also in later periods, facilitated by domestication of the camel at the end of the second millennium BC. At the same time, the discovery of new irrigation techniques (*falaj* irrigation) made possible the extensive watering of agricultural areas that resulted in an explosion of settlement in the region.

By the first century AD overland caravan traffic between Syria and cities in southern Iraq, followed by seaborne travel to the important port of Omana (perhaps present-day Umm al-Qaiwain) and thence to India was an alternative to the Red Sea route used by the Romans. Pearls had been exploited in the area for millennia but at this time the trade reached new heights. Seafaring was also a mainstay and major fairs were held at Dibba, bringing merchants from as far afield as China.

The arrival of envoys from the Prophet Mohammed in 630 AD heralded the conversion of the region to Islam with Dibba again featuring, this time as a battleground in the wake of the Prophet's death. By 637 AD Islamic armies were using Julfar (Ra's al-Khaimah) as a staging post for the conquest of Iran. Over many centuries, Julfar became a wealthy port and pearling centre from which great wooden dhows ranged far and wide across the Indian Ocean.

IMPORTANT DATES

c.5500 BC	Evidence of extensive human occupation in UAE.
5500–3000 BC	Occupation by skilled groups of herders using finely made stone tools (so-called 'Arabian bifacial tradition').
3000–2500 BC	Hafit period – era of earliest collective burials first noted on the lower slopes of Jebel Hafit in the interior of Abu Dhabi.
2500–2000 BC	Umm al-Nar period – era of first oasis towns (e.g. at Hili, Tell Abraq, Bidiya, Kalba) dominated by large, circular fortresses; burial of the dead in round communal tombs; wide-ranging trade contact with Mesopotamia, Iran, Indus Valley, Baluchistan, Bactria (Afghanistan); first intensive use of copper resources of Hajar Mountains; area referred to as *Magan* in Mesopotamian sources.
2000–1300 BC	Wadi Suq period and Late Bronze Age – an era which is characterised by fewer towns; change in burial customs to long, generally narrow collective tombs; close ties to Dilmun (Bahrain).
1300–300 BC	Iron Age – introduction of new irrigation technology in the form of *falaj* (pl. *aflaj*), subterranean galleries which led water from mountain aquifers to lower-lying oases and gardens; explosion of settlement; first use of iron; first writing, using South Arabian alphabet; contacts with Assyrian and Persian empires.
300 BC–0	Mleiha period (or Late Pre-Islamic A–B) – flourishing town at Mleiha; beginnings of local coinage; far-flung imports from Greece (black-glazed pottery), South Arabia (alabaster unguent jars); first use of the horse.
0–250 AD	Ed-Dur period (or late Pre-Islamic C–D) – flourishing towns at ed-Dur and Mleiha; extensive trade network along the Gulf linking up the Mediterranean, Syria and Mesopotamia with India; imports include Roman glass, coinage, brass; massive production of coinage by a ruler called Abi'el; first use of Aramaic in inscriptions from ed-Dur and Mleiha.
240 AD	Rise of the Sasanian dynasty in south-western Iran, conquest of most of eastern Arabia.
6th/7th cent. AD	Introduction of Christianity via contacts with south-western Iran and southern Mesopotamia; establishment of monastery on Sir Bani Yas by Nestorian Christian community; Sasanian garrisons in inner Oman and evidence for contact in the UAE shown by coins and ceramics from Kush (Ra's al-Khaimah), Umm al-Qaiwain and Fujairah.
630 AD	Arrival of envoys from the Prophet Muhammad; conversion of the people to Islam.
632 AD	Death of the Prophet Muhammad; outbreak of the *ridda* movement, a widespread rebellion against the teachings of Islam; dispatch of Hudhayfah b. Mihsan by the Caliph Abu Bakr to quell rebellion of Laqit b. Malik Dhu at-Tag at Dibba; major battle at Dibba, collapse of the rebels.

Julfar used as staging post for Islamic invasion of Iran.	637 AD
Julfar used as staging post for Abbasid invasion of Oman.	892 AD
Buyids (Buwayhids) conquer south-eastern Arabia.	963 AD
Geographer Yaqut mentions Julfar as a fertile town.	c. 1220
Close commercial contact between Northern Emirates and kingdom of Hormuz, based on Jarun island in the Straits of Hormuz.	14th–15th cent.
Portuguese circumnavigation of Cape of Good Hope by Vasco da Gama using Arab navigational information.	1498
Portuguese–Ottoman rivalry in the Gulf.	16th cent.
Venetian traveller Gasparo Balbi's description of coast of UAE from Qatar to Ra's al-Khaimah; mention of Portuguese fortress at Kalba; first mention of Bani Yas in Abu Dhabi.	1580
Description of the East Coast of the UAE by a Dutch mariner sailing in the *Meerkat*.	1666
Growth of English trade in the Gulf; increasing Anglo–Dutch rivalry.	1720s
Sharjah and most of Musandam and the UAE East Coast, all the way to Khor Fakkan, under control of Qawasim according to Carsten Niebuhr, German surveyor working with the King of Denmark's scientific expedition.	1764
Repeated English East India Company attacks on Qawasim navy.	1800–1819
General Treaty of Peace between British Government and sheikhs of Ra's al-Khaimah, Umm al-Qaiwain, Ajman, Sharjah, Dubai and Abu Dhabi.	1820
Survey of the Gulf resulting in the publication of the first accurate charts and maps of the area.	1820–1864
Collapse of the natural pearl market; first agreements signed by rulers of Dubai, Sharjah and Abu Dhabi for oil exploration.	1930s
Oil exploration agreements finalised in Ra's al-Khaimah, Umm al-Qaiwain and Ajman.	1945–1951
First export of oil from Abu Dhabi.	1962
British Government announced its intention to withdraw from the Gulf region; discussions begin on formation of a federation of the emirates.	1968
First export of oil from Dubai.	1969
Agreement reached amongst rulers of the emirates to form a union.	10 July 1971
Formation of the State of the United Arab Emirates.	2 Dec 1971
Sheikh Zayed, 1st President of the UAE, died.	2 Nov 2004
Sheikh Khalifa bin Zayed Al Nahyan elected as new President of the UAE.	3 Nov 2004

Foreign trade, hospitality, exploitation of natural resources, an appreciation of nature and the importance of cultural heritage are all recurring motifs in the history of the UAE and continue to be vital building blocks of twenty-first century development.

The Portuguese arrival in the Gulf in the sixteenth century had bloody consequences for the Arab residents of Julfar and east coast ports like Dibba, Bidiya, Khor Fakkan and Kalba. However, while European powers competed for regional supremacy, a local power, the Qawasim, was gathering strength. At the beginning of the nineteenth century the Qawasim had built up a fleet of over 60 large vessels and could put nearly 20,000 sailors to sea, eventually provoking a British offensive to control the maritime trade routes between the Gulf and India.

Inland, the arc of villages at Liwa were the focus of economic and social activity for the Bani Yas from before the sixteenth century. But by the early 1790s the town of Abu Dhabi had become such an important pearling centre that the political leader of all the Bani Yas groups, the sheikh of the Al Bu Falah (Al Nahyan family) moved there from the Liwa. Early in the nineteenth century, members of the Al Bu Falasah, a branch of the Bani Yas, settled by the Creek in Dubai and established Maktoum rule in that emirate.

Following the defeat of the Qawasim in 1820, the British signed a series of agreements with the sheikhs of the individual emirates that, later augmented with treaties on preserving a maritime truce, resulted in the area becoming known as 'The Trucial States'.

The pearling industry thrived in the relative calm at sea during the nineteenth and early twentieth centuries, providing both income and employment to the people of the Arabian Gulf coast. Many of the inhabitants were semi-nomadic, pearling in the summer months and tending to their date gardens in the winter. However, their meagre economic resources were soon to be dealt a heavy blow. The First World War impacted severely on the pearl fishery, but it was the economic depression of the late 1920s and early 1930s, coupled with the Japanese invention of the cultured pearl, that damaged it irreparably. The industry eventually faded away shortly after the Second World War, when the newly independent Government of India imposed heavy taxation on pearls imported from the Gulf. This was catastrophic for the area. Despite their adaptability and resourcefulness, the population faced considerable hardship with little opportunity for education and no roads or hospitals.

Fortunately oil was on the horizon. At the beginning of the 1930s, the first oil company teams carried out preliminary surveys and the first cargo of crude was exported from Abu Dhabi in 1962. With revenues growing as oil production increased, Ruler of Abu Dhabi, Sheikh Zayed bin Sultan Al Nahyan, undertook a massive construction programme, building schools, housing, hospitals and roads. When Dubai's oil exports commenced in 1969, Sheikh Rashid bin Saeed Al Maktoum, *de facto* Ruler of Dubai since 1939, was also able to use oil revenues to improve the quality of life of his people.

FEDERATION

At the beginning of 1968, when the British announced their intention of withdrawing from the Arabian Gulf by the end of 1971, Sheikh Zayed acted rapidly to initiate moves towards establishing closer ties between the emirates. Along with Sheikh Rashid, who was to become Vice President and, later, Prime Minister of the newly formed state, Sheikh Zayed took the lead in calling for a federation that would include not only the seven emirates that together made up the Trucial States, but also Qatar and Bahrain. Following a period of negotiation, however, agreement was reached between the rulers of six of the

The first cargo of crude oil was exported from Abu Dhabi in 1962 and the United Arab Emirates was formally established as a federation on 2 December 1971.

HH Sheikh Zayed bin Sultan Al Nahyan, the late President of the United Arab Emirates.

emirates (Abu Dhabi, Dubai, Sharjah, Fujairah, Umm al-Qaiwain and Ajman) and the federation to be known as the United Arab Emirates (UAE) was formally established on 2 December 1971 with Sheikh Zayed as its President. The seventh emirate, Ra's al-Khaimah, formally acceded to the new federation on 10 February 1972.

A VISIONARY LEADER

The prosperity, harmony and modern development that today characterises the UAE is due to a very great extent to the visionary role played by Sheikh Zayed, both prior to the formation of the federation and in the nearly 33 years that followed until his death in November 2004.

Born around 1918 in Abu Dhabi, Sheikh Zayed was the youngest of the four sons of Sheikh Sultan, Ruler of Abu Dhabi from 1922 to 1926. He was named after his grandfather, Sheikh Zayed bin Khalifa.

As Sheikh Zayed grew to manhood, he travelled widely throughout the country, gaining a deep understanding of the land and of its people. In the early 1930s, when oil company teams arrived to undertake geological surveys, he obtained his first exposure to the industry that was to make possible the development of today.

In 1946, he was chosen as Ruler's Representative in Abu Dhabi's Eastern Region, centred on Al Ain, 160 kilometres east of the island of Abu Dhabi.

He brought to his new task a firm belief in the values of consultation and consensus. Foreign visitors, such as the British explorer Sir Wilfred Thesiger, noted with approbation that his judgements 'were distinguished by their acute insights, wisdom and fairness'.

Sheikh Zayed swiftly established himself as someone who had a clear vision of what he wished to achieve for the people and as someone who led by example. A key task in the early years in Al Ain was that of stimulating the local economy, which was largely based on agriculture. Keen to ensure that the scarce water resources were fairly shared, he surrendered the rights of his own family as an example to others.

Sheikh Zayed also commenced the laying out of a visionary city plan, and ordered the planting of trees that, now mature, have made Al Ain one of the greenest cities in Arabia.

Despite the paucity of government revenues, Sheikh Zayed succeeded in bringing progress to Al Ain, personally funding the

first modern school in the emirate and coaxing others to contribute towards small-scale development programmes. The beginning of oil exports provided the means to fund his dreams.

On 6 August 1966, Sheikh Zayed succeeded his elder brother as Ruler of Abu Dhabi. He promptly increased contributions to the Trucial States Development Fund, and, in February 1968, when the British announced their intention of withdrawing from the Gulf by the end of 1971, he initiated moves to strengthen ties with the other emirates, these leading to the establishment of the UAE. Sheikh Zayed was elected by his fellow rulers as the first President, a post to which he was successively re-elected at five-year intervals.

The new state emerged at a time of political turmoil in the region. A couple of days earlier, Iran had seized the islands of Greater and Lesser Tunb, part of Ra's al-Khaimah, and had landed troops on Abu Musa, part of Sharjah (see section on Foreign Policy).

Sheikh Zayed bin Sultan Al Nahyan and Sheikh Rashid bin Saeed Al Maktoum touring the country in the early days of the federation.

www.uaeinteract.com/zayed

An aerial view of Abu Dhabi in the 1960s.

Foreign observers predicted that the UAE would survive only with difficulty, pointing to disputes with its neighbours and to the wide disparity between the seven emirates. Sheikh Zayed was more optimistic and the predictions of those early pessimists were shown to be unfounded.

During his years in Al Ain, Sheikh Zayed had developed a vision of how the country should progress. Once Ruler of Abu Dhabi, and then President, he spent over three and a half decades making that vision a reality.

One foundation of his philosophy as a leader was that the resources of the country should be used to the benefit of the people. He saw them not as a means unto themselves, but as a tool to facilitate the development of what he believed to be the country's real wealth – its people, and, in particular, the younger generation.

All citizens have a role to play in its development, he felt, and, recognising that in the past a lack of education and development had prevented women from participating fully in society, he took rapid action to promote women's education. Under his leadership, the country's women came increasingly to play their part in political and economic life.

Sheikh Zayed also believed in the need to preserve the traditional culture of the people, in order to familiarise the younger generation with the ways of their ancestors. In his view, it was crucial that the lessons and heritage of the past were remembered.

He who does not know his past cannot make the best of his present and future, for it is from the past that we learn. We gain experience and we take advantage of the lessons and results [of the past].

He was also a firm proponent of the conservation of the UAE's environment, deriving this belief from his own upbringing where a sustainable use of resources required man to live in harmony with nature. Here, as in other areas of national life, Sheikh Zayed believed that there was a role not only for government, but also for individuals, both citizens and expatriates, and non-governmental institutions.

An abundant supply of water enabled development.

Sheikh Zayed imbibed the principles of Islam in his childhood and they remained central to his beliefs throughout his life. He firmly opposed those who pervert the message of Islam to justify harsh dogmas, intolerance and terrorism. In his view, such an approach was not merely a perversion of the message but is in direct contradiction of it. Extremism, he believed, has no place in Islam. In contrast, he stressed that:

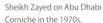

Sheikh Zayed on Abu Dhabi Corniche in the 1970s.

Islam is a civilising religion that gives mankind dignity. A Muslim is he who does not inflict evil upon others. Islam is the religion of tolerance and forgiveness, and not of war, of dialogue and understanding . . . To treat every person, no matter what his creed or race, as a special soul is a mark of Islam. It is just that point, embodied in the humanitarian tenets of Islam, that makes us so proud of it.

Sheikh Zayed was an eager advocate of tolerance and a better understanding between those of different faiths and was an ardent advocate of dialogue between Muslims and Christians.

In foreign policy, his firmly held belief in eschewing rhetoric in the search for solutions led the UAE to adopt an approach of seeking

Sheikh Zayed with Sheikh Maktoum and Sheikh Khalifa.

to find compromises, and to avoid, wherever possible, a resort to the use of force, whether in the Arab arena or more widely. Under his leadership, the country became a major donor of overseas aid, both for infrastructural development and for humanitarian relief, whether provided through civilian channels or, occasionally, by sending units of the UAE Armed Forces as international peacekeepers, such as to Kosovo in the late 1990s.

The UAE, under his leadership, also showed its preparedness to fight to defend justice, as was seen by its participation in the war to liberate Kuwait from occupation in 1990/91.

Sheikh Zayed died in November 2004, being succeeded as the UAE's President and as Ruler of Abu Dhabi by his eldest son, HH Sheikh Khalifa bin Zayed Al Nahyan. The principles and philosophy he brought to government, however, remain at the core of the state, and of its policies, today.

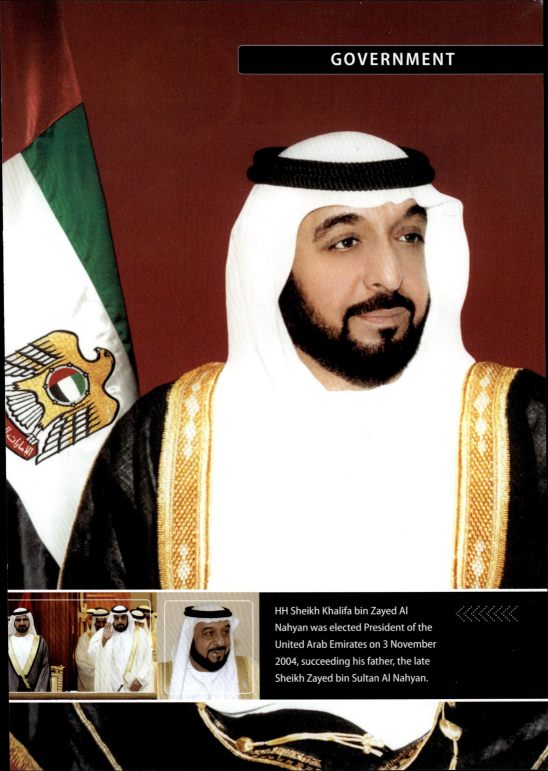

HH Sheikh Khalifa bin Zayed Al Nahyan was elected President of the United Arab Emirates on 3 November 2004, succeeding his father, the late Sheikh Zayed bin Sultan Al Nahyan.

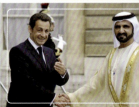

HH Sheikh Mohammed bin Rashid Al Maktoum, Vice President and Prime Minister of the UAE and Ruler of Dubai.

GOVERNMENT

POLITICAL SYSTEM

SINCE THE ESTABLISHMENT OF THE FEDERATION IN 1971, the seven emirates that comprise the United Arab Emirates (UAE) have forged a distinct national identity through consolidation of their federal status and enjoy an enviable degree of political stability. The UAE's political system, a unique combination of the traditional and the modern, has underpinned this success, enabling the country to develop a modern administrative structure while, at the same time, ensuring that the best of the traditions of the past are maintained, adapted and preserved.

Over the course of the last three years, major steps have been taken, both at a federal and at a local level, in terms of reforming the structure of government, these steps being designed both to make it more responsive to the needs of the country's population and to ensure that it is better equipped to cope with the challenges of development, in all spheres, in a manner that is in keeping with current best practices in administration and the delivery of services, as well as being more cost-effective.

The process has been directed at a federal level by the country's President, HH Sheikh Khalifa bin Zayed Al Nahyan, and has been devised and guided at an executive level by the Vice President and Prime Minister, HH Sheikh Mohammed bin Rashid Al Maktoum, who was appointed in early 2006, following his succession as Ruler of Dubai.

Both leaders have also overseen major reforms in the structures of government in Abu Dhabi, ruled by Sheikh Khalifa, and Dubai, ruled by Sheikh Mohammed, these being implemented by the Executive Councils of each emirate, chaired respectively by HH Sheikh Mohammed bin Zayed Al Nahyan, Crown Prince of Abu Dhabi, and by HH Sheikh Hamdan bin Mohammed Al Maktoum, Crown Prince of Dubai.

The most important recent development was the formal launching in early 2007 of a UAE Government Strategy for the years ahead. Covering 21 individual topics, in the six sectors of social development, economic development, public sector development, justice and safety,

Over the course of the last three years, major steps have been taken, both at a federal and a local level , in terms of reforming the structure of government.

infrastructure and rural areas development, the strategy was based upon the National Programme unveiled by President HH Sheikh Khalifa in December 2005. Drawn up after extensive consultation between the federal ministries, as well as other bodies, the strategy was launched by HH Sheikh Mohammed bin Rashid, who noted that it 'sets the foundations for a new era of public administration. The changing times and the nature of the challenges prompt us to think in a different way and to adopt international best practices in the area of public administration. This strategy unifies efforts within a strategic framework with clear objectives, based on detailed studies (and). . . clearly identifies and integrates federal and local efforts.'

Implementation of the strategy continued in 2008, with one of the most important aspects being the enhancement of collaboration between the federal authorities and those in each emirate.

Other general principles in the strategy include the revitalisation of the regulatory and policy-making role of the ministries and the improvement of their decision-making mechanisms, and increasing of the efficiency of governmental bodies and upgrading of the level of the services provided, in accordance with customer needs.

Other principles include an improvement of the civil service, based on competence, effective Emiratisation and leadership training, empowering the ministries, in accordance with public and joint policies, and reviewing and upgrading of existing legislation.

A separate policy agenda for Abu Dhabi was announced in August 2007, covering that year and 2008. This included independent policy statements providing details of plans in areas such as planning and economy, energy, tourism, health, education, labour, civil services, culture and heritage, food control, urban planning, transport, health and safety, environment, municipal affairs, police and emergency services, electronic government, women, and legislative reform.

The UAE flag was first raised on 2 December 1971.

The agenda is expected to enhance the spirit of teamwork among government departments, improving government performance and improving the quality of services delivered to residents of the emirate, as well as enhancing Abu Dhabi's ability to attract inward investment.

It was swiftly followed by a more detailed Plan Abu Dhabi 2030, covering the city of Abu Dhabi, the UAE's federal capital, and adjacent areas. Work began in late 2008 on a new Plan 2030 for the Western Region of Abu Dhabi, now called Al Gharbia, in an effort to ensure that this area receives its full share of economic and social development.

One major initial step in the process of reform that was designed to enhance public participation in government was the introduction of indirect elections to the country's parliament, the Federal National Council (FNC). First announced by HH Sheikh Khalifa bin Zayed Al Nahyan in his statement on the occasion of National Day on 2 December 2005, it provided for half of the FNC members for each emirate to be elected by members of electoral colleges established by each ruler, rather than being appointed by the ruler, as had previously been the case. The 40 seats in the FNC are allocated to the individual emirates on the basis of population and size, (eight each for Abu Dhabi and Dubai, six each for Sharjah and Ra's al-Khaimah, and four each for Fujairah, Ajman and Umm al-Qaiwain).

Abu Dhabi, capital city of the United Arab Emirates.

The elections were held in late 2006, seeing a respectably high turnout and with one woman among the successful candidates. Once the remaining seats for each emirate had been filled by nomination from the rulers, the new Federal National Council had nine women amongst its 40 members, representing 22.2 per cent of the total, an indication of the way in which the UAE's women are expanding their participation in all levels of government and political society. The system of indirect elections now in operation is perceived as being only a first stage in the reforming of the FNC's role in government, while further reforms being considered are an expansion of the number of FNC members, to reflect the increase in the number of the country's citizens, now many times larger than it

The system of indirect elections to the FNC, which was instituted in 2006, is perceived as being only a first stage in the reforming of the FNC's role in government.

was when the UAE was founded in 1971. Consideration is also being given to the introduction of an electoral process at local level, although no timetable has yet been announced for this.

THE FEDERAL SYSTEM

The UAE Constitution specifies the powers that are allocated to the federal institutions, all others remaining the prerogative of the individual emirates.

The philosophy behind the federal state, officially entitled *Dawlat al Imarat al Arabiyya al Muttahida* (State of the United Arab Emirates), was explained in a statement that was released on 2 December 1971 as the new state was formally established:

The United Arab Emirates has been established as an independent state, possessing sovereignty. It is part of the greater Arab nation. Its aim is to maintain its independence, its sovereignty, its security and its stability, in defence against any attack on its entity or on the entity of any of its member Emirates. It also seeks to protect the freedoms and rights of its people and to achieve trustworthy co-operation between the Emirates for the common good. Among its aims, in addition to the purposes above described, is to work for the sake of the progress of the country in all fields, for the sake of providing a better life for its citizens, to give assistance and support to Arab causes and interests, and to support the charter of the United Nations and international morals.

Each emirate already had its own existing institutions of government prior to 1971 and, to provide for the effective governing of the new state, the rulers agreed to draw up a provisional Constitution specifying the powers that were to be allocated to the new federal institutions, all others remaining the prerogative of the emirates.

Areas of responsibility assigned to the federal authorities, under Articles 120 and 121 of the Constitution, were foreign affairs, security and defence, nationality and immigration issues, education, public health, currency, postal, telephone and other communications services, air traffic control and licensing of aircraft, in addition to a number of other topics specifically prescribed, including labour relations, banking, delimitation of territorial waters and extradition of criminals. The Constitution also stated in Article 116 that 'the Emirates shall exercise all powers not assigned to the Federation by this Constitution'. This was reaffirmed in Article 122, which stated that 'the Emirates shall have jurisdiction in all matters not assigned to the exclusive jurisdiction of the Federation, in accordance with the provision of the preceding two Articles'.

The UAE's Federal National Council in session.

In May 1996, the UAE Federal Supreme Council approved two amendments to the provisional Constitution, making it permanent and naming Abu Dhabi as the capital of the state.

The federal system of government includes a Supreme Council, a Cabinet, or Council of Ministers, a parliamentary body, the Federal National Council, and an independent judiciary, at the apex of which is the Federal Supreme Court. The Supreme Council comprises the rulers of each of the emirates, who elect a president and a vice president from amongst their number, to serve for a five-year, renewable, term.

The Federal Supreme Council has both legislative and executive powers. It ratifies federal laws and decrees, plans general policy, approves the nomination of the prime minister and accepts his resignation. It also relieves him of his post upon the recommendation of the president.

The Council of Ministers or Cabinet, described in the Constitution as 'the executive authority' for the federation, includes the usual complement of ministerial portfolios and is headed by a prime minister, chosen by the president in consultation with his colleagues on the Supreme Council. The prime minister, currently the vice president (although this has not always been the case), then proposes a list of ministers, these then being ratified by the president. The current Cabinet was appointed on 17 February 2008, according to the proposal of Vice President and Prime Minister HH Sheikh Mohammed

The federal system of government includes a Supreme Council, a Cabinet, or Council of Ministers, a parliamentary body, the Federal National Council, and an independent judiciary.

THE GOVERNMENT OF THE UNITED ARAB EMIRATES

SUPREME COUNCIL MEMBERS

HH President Sheikh Khalifa bin Zayed Al Nahyan, Ruler of Abu Dhabi

HH Vice President and Prime Minister Sheikh Mohammed bin Rashid Al Maktoum, Ruler of Dubai

HH Dr Sheikh Sultan bin Mohammed Al Qasimi, Ruler of Sharjah

HH Sheikh Saqr bin Mohammed Al Qasimi, Ruler of Ra's al-Khaimah

HH Sheikh Hamad bin Mohammed Al Sharqi, Ruler of Fujairah

HH Sheikh Saud bin Rashid Al Mu'alla, Ruler of Umm al-Qaiwain

HH Sheikh Humaid bin Rashid Al Nuaimi, Ruler of Ajman

CROWN PRINCES

HH General Sheikh Mohammed bin Zayed Al Nahyan, Crown Prince of Abu Dhabi and Deputy
   Supreme Commander of the UAE Armed Forces

HH Sheikh Hamdan bin Mohammed Al Maktoum, Crown Prince of Dubai

HH Sheikh Sultan bin Mohammed bin Sultan Al Qasimi, Crown Prince and Deputy Ruler of Sharjah

HH Sheikh Saud bin Saqr Al Qasimi, Crown Prince and Deputy Ruler of Ra's al-Khaimah

HH Sheikh Mohammed bin Hamad Al Sharqi, Crown Prince of Fujairah

HH Sheikh Ammar bin Humaid Al Nuaimi, Crown Prince of Ajman

HH Sheikh Rashid bin Saud bin Rashid Al Mu'alla, Crown Prince of Umm al-Qaiwain

DEPUTIES OF THE RULERS

HH Sheikh Hamdan bin Rashid Al Maktoum, Deputy Ruler of Dubai, Minister of Finance and Industry

HH Sheikh Maktoum bin Mohammed Al Maktoum, Deputy Ruler of Dubai

HH Sheikh Ahmed bin Sultan Al Qasimi, Deputy Ruler of Sharjah

HH Sheikh Khalid bin Saqr Al Qasimi, Deputy Ruler of Ra's al-Khaimah

HH Sheikh Sultan bin Saqr Al Qasimi, Deputy Ruler of Ra's al-Khaimah

HH Sheikh Hamad bin Saif Al Sharqi, Deputy Ruler of Fujairah

HH Sheikh Abdullah bin Rashid Al Mu'alla, Deputy Ruler of Umm al-Qaiwain

MEMBERS OF THE CABINET

Prime Minister: Vice President HH Sheikh Mohammed bin Rashid Al Maktoum

Deputy Prime Minister: HH Sheikh Sultan bin Zayed Al Nahyan

Deputy Prime Minister: HH Sheikh Hamdan bin Zayed Al Nahyan

Minister of Finance: HH Sheikh Hamdan bin Rashid Al Maktoum

Minister of Interior: Lt Gen. HH Sheikh Saif bin Zayed Al Nahyan

Minister of Presidential Affairs: HH Sheikh Mansour bin Zayed Al Nahyan

Minister of Foreign Affairs: HH Sheikh Abdullah bin Zayed Al Nahyan

Minister of Higher Education and Scientific Research: Sheikh Nahyan bin Mubarak Al Nahyan

Minister of Public Works: Sheikh Hamdan bin Mubarak Al Nahyan

Minister of Foreign Trade: Sheikha Lubna Al Qasimi

Minister of Cabinet Affairs: Mohammed Abdullah Al Gargawi

Minister of Energy: Mohammed Dhaen Al Hamili

Minister of Economy: Sultan bin Saeed Al Mansouri

Minister of Social Affairs: Maryam Al Roumi

Minister of Education: Dr Hanif Hassan Ali

Minister of Health: Humaid Mohammed Obaid Al Qattami

Minister of Culture, Youth and Community Development: Abdul Rahman Mohammed Al Owais

Minister of Justice: Dr Hadef bin Juaan Al Dhahiri

Minister of Environment and Water: Rashid Ahmed bin Fahad

Minister of Labour: Saqr Ghobash Saeed Ghobash

Minister of State for Foreign Affairs: Dr Mohammed Anwar Gargash

Minister of State for Financial Affairs: Obaid Humaid Al Tayer

Minister of State: Dr Maitha Salem Al Shamsi

Minister of State: Reem Ibrahim Al Hashimi

bin Rashid Al Maktoum, He had previously formed his first Cabinet in 2006, following his accession as Ruler of Dubai and election as Vice President.

Following the death of the Ruler of Umm al-Qaiwain, HH Sheikh Rashid bin Ahmed Al Mu'alla on 2 Januray 2009, he was succeeded by his son and Crown Prince HH Sheikh Saud bin Rashid Al Mu'alla.

Constitutional amendments agreed by the Federal Supreme Council in December 2008 granted the FNC new powers to debate foreign policy matters, extended its term from two to four years and extended its annual session from six to seven months.

FEDERAL NATIONAL COUNCIL

The Federal National Council (FNC) is drawn from the emirates on the basis of their population. As noted above, this body, initially wholly appointed, has, since late 2006, had half of its members chosen through a process of indirect elections.

Day-to-day operation of the FNC is governed by standing orders based on the provisions of Article 85 of the Constitution, first issued in 1972 and subsequently amended by Federal Decree No. 97 of 1977. The FNC plays an important role in consolidating the principles of *shura* (consultation) in the country. Presided over by a speaker, or either of two deputy speakers, elected from amongst its members, the FNC has both a legislative and supervisory role under the Constitution. It is responsible for examining, and amending, if necessary, all proposed federal legislation, and may summon and question any federal minister regarding ministry performance. The current FNC is chaired by Abdul Aziz Abdullah Al Ghurair who was elected in 2006.

With its membership now partially elected, the FNC is currently adopting a more pro-active role. In the long term, the objective is that it will become a wholly elected body, although here, as elsewhere, a cautious approach is being followed in the process of reform.

FEDERAL JUDICIARY

The federal judiciary, whose total independence is guaranteed under the Constitution, includes the Federal Supreme Court and Courts of First Instance. The Federal Supreme Court consists of five judges appointed by the Supreme Council of Rulers. The judges decide on the constitutionality of federal laws and arbitrate on inter-emirate disputes and disputes between the Federal Government and the emirates.

LOCAL GOVERNMENT

Parallel to, and interlocking with, the federal institutions, each emirate also has its own local government. All have expanded significantly

HH General Sheikh Mohammed bin Zayed Al Nahyan, Crown Prince of Abu Dhabi, Deputy Supreme Commander of the UAE Armed Forces.

as a result of the country's growth over the last 37 years, though they differ in complexity from emirate to emirate, depending on factors such as population, area, and degree of development.

The largest and most populous emirate, Abu Dhabi, has its own central governing organ, the Executive Council, chaired by the Crown Prince, HH Sheikh Mohammed bin Zayed Al Nahyan, under which there are a number of separate departments, equivalent to ministries. A number of autonomous agencies, such as the Environmental Agency – Abu Dhabi (EAD), the Abu Dhabi Tourism Authority (ADTA) the Abu Dhabi Authority for Culture and Heritage, (ADACH) and the Health Authority – Abu Dhabi (HAAD) also exist, with clearly specified powers.

The emirate is divided into two regions, Al Gharbia (previously known as the Western Region) and the Eastern Region, headed by Ruler's Representatives. The main cities, Abu Dhabi and Al Ain, are administered by municipalities, each with a nominated municipal council, these coming under the Department of Municipalities and Agriculture, while an additional municipal authority has also been created for Al Gharbia.

Abu Dhabi's National Consultative Council, chaired by a Speaker, and with 60 members selected from among the emirate's main tribes and families, undertakes a role similar to that of the FNC on a country-wide level.

The Dubai Executive Council, established in 2003, has similar functions for the UAE's second-largest emirate. In late 2006, Sheikh Hamdan bin Mohammed bin Rashid Al Maktoum, now also Crown Prince of Dubai, was appointed as the Council's new Chairman, since which time it has overseen a drive by local departments to improve their efficiency and the coordination between their various activities, as well as efforts to upgrade the level of services offered to the public. It is also responsible for assisting the Ruler, Vice President and Prime Minister HH Sheikh Mohammed bin Rashid, in preparation of development plans for the emirate and in formulation and implementation of both federal and local legislation. Key recent developments have included a strengthening of Dubai's Roads and Transport Authority and of the Land Department, both key players in the management of the emirate's rapid development.

Sharjah and Ajman also have Executive Councils, and Sharjah has a Consultative Council that covers the whole emirate. In addition, Sharjah, with three enclaves on the country's east coast, has adopted

HH Sheikh Hamdan bin Mohammed bin Rashid Al Maktoum, Crown Prince of Dubai.

the practice of devolving some authority on a local basis, with branches of the Sharjah Emiri Diwan (Court), headed by deputy chairmen, in both Kalba and Khor Fakkan. A similar pattern of municipalities, departments and autonomous agencies can be found in each of the other emirates. In smaller or more remote settlements, the ruler of each emirate may choose a local representative, an emir or wali, to act as a conduit through which the concerns of inhabitants may be directed to government. In most cases, these are the leading local tribal figures, whose authority derives both from their fellow tribesmen and from the confidence placed in them by the ruler, an example of the way in which leaders within the traditional system have become involved with, and lend legitimacy to, the modern structures of government.

FEDERAL AND LOCAL GOVERNMENT

New systems of government have not replaced the traditional forms which coexist and evolve alongside them.

The powers of the various federal institutions and their relationship with the separate local institutions have evolved and changed since the establishment of the state. Under the terms of the Constitution, rulers may relinquish certain areas of authority to the Federal Government, one significant such decision being that to unify the armed forces in the mid-1970s.

The relationship between the federal and local governments continues to evolve. As a result of the country's rapid economic and social development since 1971, including an increasing population and rising educational standards, local governments in each emirate now seek to assume, or to re-assume, functions that had previously been assigned to the Federal Government, although not a federal responsibility under the terms of the country's constitution. This process is likely to continue, in part because many well-qualified Emiratis prefer, naturally, to perform governmental tasks in their home emirate. These new systems of government have not, however, replaced the traditional forms that coexist and evolve alongside them.

TRADITIONAL GOVERNMENT

Traditionally, the ruler of an emirate, the sheikh, was the leader of the most powerful, though not necessarily the most populous, tribe, while each tribe, and often its sub-sections, also had a chief or sheikh. These maintained their authority only insofar as they were able to retain the support of their people, in essence a form of direct democracy. Part of that process was the unwritten but strong principle that the people should have free access to their sheikh, and that he should hold a frequent and open *majlis*, or council, in which his fellow tribesmen could voice their opinions.

A continuing aspect of life in the UAE today, and one that is essential to an understanding of its political system, is the way in which the institution of the *majlis* maintains its relevance. In larger emirates, not only the ruler, but also a number of other senior family members, continue to hold open majlises (or *majalis*), in which participants may raise a wide range of topics, both of personal interest and of broader concern. In smaller emirates, the *majlis* of the ruler himself, or of the crown prince or deputy ruler, remains the main focus. To these majlises come traditionally minded tribesmen who may have waited months for the opportunity to discuss with their ruler directly, rather than pursuing their requests or complaints through a modern governmental structure. Through such means, the well-tested traditional methods of government in the United Arab Emirates have been able to retain both their essential relevance and unique vitality, and they continue to play an important role in the evolution of the state today.

A BALANCED APPROACH

When the rulers of the emirates met 37 years ago to agree on the forms of government for their new federal state, they deliberately chose not simply to copy from others but, instead, to work towards a society that would offer the best of modern administration, while retaining the traditional forms of government, that, with their inherent commitment to consensus, discussion and direct democracy, offered the best features of the past.

With the benefit of hindsight, it is evident that they made the correct choice. For, despite the massive economic growth and the social dislocation caused by an explosion in the population, the state has enjoyed political stability. During the last few decades there have been numerous attempts to create federal states, both in the Arab world and elsewhere. The UAE is the only one in the Arab world to have stood the test of time, proof of that being the smooth transition that occurred, in government and throughout the country, following the death of the federation's founder, Sheikh Zayed bin Sultan Al Nahyan.

Despite the massive economic growth and the social dislocation caused by an explosion in the population of the UAE, the state has enjoyed an enviable degree of political stability, largely due to the marrying of traditional and modern forms of government.

www.uaeinteract.com/governmentaffairs

SHEIKH KHALIFA BIN ZAYED AL NAHYAN

HH Sheikh Khalifa bin Zayed Al Nahyan was elected as President of the United Arab Emirates on 3 November 2004, to succeed his father, the late HH Sheikh Zayed bin Sultan Al Nahyan, UAE President from 1971 to 2004, from whom, he has said, he learned 'the need for patience and prudence in all things'.

Over the course of the last year, HH Sheikh Khalifa has continued to demonstrate, both at home and in terms of the country's external relations, that he is strongly committed not only to the secure and stable development of the UAE but also to its active participation in the international community.

Of particular importance at a local level was his decision late in 2008 to take swift and decisive action to support the local economy, then being buffeted by the global economic crisis. Although the UAE's banking institutions are generally well-funded, problems elsewhere were causing a worrying erosion of consumer confidence. In September and October, the President ordered that the UAE Central Bank should make a total of Dh120 billion (US$32.7 billion) available to local banks, to help them maintain adequate levels of liquidity. His initiative had an immediate effect in terms of restoring confidence. By the end of the year, it was apparent that the UAE had succeeded in weathering at least the worst aspects of the storm.

At an international level, the President met regularly with visiting leaders and statesmen (see Foreign Affairs) and also oversaw the expansion of the country's programme of development aid and humanitarian assistance (see Foreign Aid), as well as continuing to be a generous private donor. Recent donations have included millions of US dollars for relief of flood victims in Yemen and in Pakistan's Baluchistan province.

Issues related to developments in the Arab world have, of course, continued to be a major concern. In a statement on the occasion of the twentieth Arab Summit in Damascus in March 2008, the President noted:

The circumstances through which the Arab Nation is currently passing require a unified Arab stance, deeper consultations to eventually produce collective visions and decisions in order to overcome serious challenges facing the present and future of our Arab Nation, in particular the current situation in the occupied Palestinian Territories, the ongoing Israeli siege on Gaza Strip, the situation in Lebanon and in Iraq, in addition to the dangers that loom over other Arab countries threatening their stability and security.

Despite all the difficult situations facing our Nation, we are completely confident that a unified and one stance by the Arab Nation which already has the needed capabilities would enable Arabs to overcome each and every obstacle as well as achieve our common interests and goals.

Within the context of Arab affairs, Sheikh Khalifa has continued to emphasise the country's commitment to the six-member Gulf Co-operation Council (GCC) which is seen as a fundamental building bloc for the long-term development of greater co-operation throughout the region.

One wider focus of the President's attention has been the challenges posed by globalisation and the consequent necessity to devote resources to tackling poverty and to spreading knowledge. In a message to the third Global Knowledge Conference, held in Malaysia at the end of 2007, he noted that the Arab world had, over the centuries, been a major contributor to the dissemination of practical and science-based knowledge.

Among today's key issues, he said, 'there is perhaps none as important for the future of our globe than the transmission of knowledge in an efficient and equitable manner . . . We, in the Arab world, are anxious to participate in these decisions and to engage others in taking the right path toward peace and justice.'

Referring to the UAE's own growth since it was formed in 1971, he went on:

we understand that if we hope to continue this progress we must continue to focus on the transmission of knowledge for the sake of human development. . . All of us have a stake in human development across the globe and we must carve out a path to deliver the knowledge that will enhance the quality of life for our fellow men and women . . .'

I know there are some who view globalisation as a negative and they point out the distinct possibility that it will lead to greater inequities between the 'haves' and the 'have-nots' of the globe . . . This, however, can be avoided if we make careful decisions regarding the transmission of knowledge and if we do so with an eye toward equity and the good of all mankind. . . We must make wise decisions now to bring about a better world for future generations.

Since becoming President, Sheikh Khalifa has overseen dramatic changes in the structure of government, both at a federal level and in the Emirate of Abu Dhabi. In the latter, particular attention has been paid to two aspects – improvements in terms of efficiency and cost for services provided to the public and the opening up of much of the economy to provide greater scope for direct private investment and for public-private partnerships. During the

SHEIKH KHALIFA BIN ZAYED AL NAHYAN

Sheikh Khalifa with President Nicolas Sarkozy of France.

early years of the federation, he believes, it was appropriate for government to play the leading role, but now, with a burgeoning private sector and with a well-educated population, the time is right for government to concentrate on its core areas of responsibility. Now, the people of the UAE must take upon themselves the task of contributing effectively. He noted in 2005 that:

It is high time for our political, religious, cultural, information, educational and civil society institutions to take up their responsibilities to instil in our society the values of love of work, to change the negative perceptions about vocational work. It is high time to make them understand the true meaning of work – that it means responsibility and reflects human, civil and religious values. These institutions also need to work hard to diversify the skills of the national human resources, to raise productivity, encourage investment in human resources development, improve voluntary work and create awareness of this noble work and its significance to individuals and society in general.

His character and performance as President, of course, can only be properly understood in the context of his earlier life. He assumed his posts as Ruler of Abu Dhabi and President of the United Arab Emirates in 2004 after many decades working closely with his father, Sheikh Zayed bin Sultan Al Nahyan, the founder of the federation.

Born in the inland oasis-city of Al Ain in 1948, Sheikh Khalifa was educated in the local school. On 18 September 1966, following his father's assumption of the post of Ruler of Abu Dhabi, Sheikh Khalifa was appointed as Ruler's Representative in the Eastern Region of Abu Dhabi and as Head of the Courts Department in Al Ain.

On 1 February 1969 Sheikh Khalifa was nominated as Crown Prince of Abu Dhabi, this being followed on 2 February 1969 by his appointment as the Head of the Abu Dhabi Department of Defence, in which post he oversaw the building up of the Abu Dhabi Defence Force (ADDF), which later became the nucleus of the UAE Armed Forces.

On 1 July 1971, Sheikh Khalifa was appointed Prime Minister of Abu Dhabi and Minister of Defence and Finance. On 23 December 1973, he assumed the post of Deputy Prime Minister in the second UAE Federal Cabinet. Shortly afterwards, when the Cabinet of Abu Dhabi was dissolved, as part of the process of strengthening the institutions of the UAE Federation, Sheikh Khalifa was appointed, on 20 January 1974, as the first Chairman of the Abu Dhabi Executive Council, which replaced the emirate's Cabinet. He was succeeded in this post in

November 2004 by Crown Prince HH Sheikh Mohammed bin Zayed Al Nahyan.

Under Sheikh Khalifa's direction, and in accordance with the instructions of HH Sheikh Zayed, the Executive Council oversaw the implementation of a wide-ranging development programme in Abu Dhabi.

Of particular importance in terms of ensuring that citizens benefited from the country's increasing wealth was the establishment by Sheikh Khalifa in 1981 of the Abu Dhabi Department of Social Services and Commercial Buildings, charged with the provision of loans to citizens for construction.

The establishment of the Department, popularly known as the 'Khalifa Committee', followed another decision taken by Sheikh Khalifa in 1979 to alleviate the burden on citizens of the repayment of loans from the commercial banks.

A further step to ensure that citizens were able to build the properties that they needed, both for residential and for investment purposes, came with the creation by Sheikh Khalifa of the Private Loans Authority, early in 1991.

President HH Sheikh Khalifa has also been involved extensively in other areas of the country's development. In May 1976, following the unification of the armed forces of the Emirates, Sheikh Khalifa was nominated as Deputy Supreme Commander of the UAE Armed Forces. In this capacity, he devoted much attention to the building up of the country's defensive capability, through the establishment of many military training institutions and through the procurement of the latest military equipment and training.

Sheikh Khalifa has held a number of other top posts in the Abu Dhabi government. Since the late 1980s, for example, he has been Chairman of the Supreme Petroleum Council, responsible for oversight of Abu Dhabi's upstream and downstream oil and gas industries, although he has also actively encouraged diversification of the country's economy away from dependence on its depletable reserves of hydrocarbons.

He is also Chairman of the Abu Dhabi Investment Council, which oversees management of the emirate's financial reserves and investments and was until 2006 the Chairman of the Abu Dhabi Fund for Development (ADFD), which handles the country's international development assistance programme, and Honorary Chairman of the Environment Agency – Abu Dhabi (EAD).

He has stated that his key objectives as President of the United Arab Emirates will be to continue on the path laid down by his father, whose legacy, he says, 'will continue to be the beacon guiding us into the future, a prosperous future where security and stability will reign.'

www.uaeinteract.com/sheikh_khalifa

SHEIKH MOHAMMED BIN RASHID AL MAKTOUM

HH Sheikh Mohammed bin Rashid Al Maktoum, Vice President and Prime Minister of the UAE and Ruler of Dubai, was born in 1949, the third of the four sons of Sheikh Rashid bin Saeed Al Maktoum, Ruler of Dubai (1958–1990) and UAE Vice President (1971–1990).

Having finished secondary school in Dubai in 1966, HH Sheikh Mohammed enrolled in the Bell School of Languages in Cambridge and then attended Mons Officer Cadet School. In November 1968, he was appointed as Head of Dubai Police and Public Security.

In addition to his academic education, HH Sheikh Mohammed acquired a considerable amount of knowledge through being close to his father, Sheikh Rashid, and frequently attending his *majlis*, which was always crowded with intellectuals, politicians, businessmen and Dubai's high-profile guests.

He grew up to witness important developments in the region, including the creation of the federation between Abu Dhabi and Dubai, which launched the establishment of the United Arab Emirates on 2 December 1971. He was subsequently appointed as the UAE's first Minister of Defence.

HH Sheikh Mohammed gained deep knowledge of the regional and global situation and of international affairs. The late Sheikh Zayed bin Sultan Al Nahyan trusted Sheikh Mohammed and relied on him, taking him to Arab, Gulf and Islamic summits and involving him in following up on the important regional events since the early 1970s.

Sheikh Mohammed enjoying one of his favourite pastimes, endurance racing.

Sheikh Mohammed with Chinese Premier Wen Jiabao on a state visit to China in 2008.

HH Sheikh Mohammed also took part in the building of Dubai, being assigned by Sheikh Rashid major responsibilities in the economic sector, in addition to his responsibilities for police and public security.

When Sheikh Rashid passed away in October 1990, his oldest son, Sheikh Maktoum, succeeded him as Dubai Ruler and UAE Vice President. On 4 January 1995, Sheikh Maktoum appointed his brother Mohammed as Crown Prince of Dubai and assigned him the tasks of governing Dubai. In only a few years, HH Sheikh Mohammed succeeded in establishing the emirate as a tourism destination and a global hub for business, trade, media, information technology, aviation and financial services.

HH Sheikh Mohammed has always shown interest in the Arab world and has voiced support for Arab causes. His aid and support have extended to all parts of the Arab and Islamic worlds.

Following the death of his brother, Sheikh Maktoum, HH Sheikh Mohammed bin Rashid Al Maktoum became the Ruler of Dubai on 4 January 2006.

HH Sheikh Khalifa bin Zayed Al Nahyan, President of the United Arab Emirates subsequently nominated HH Sheikh Mohammed as UAE Prime Minister, and the Supreme Council approved this nomination on 5 January 2006, also electing HH Sheikh Mohammed as UAE Vice President. HH Sheikh Mohammed then launched a campaign of administrative and legislative reforms that has resulted in the first proper strategy for the UAE Federal Government and institutional and ministerial restructuring. Under his premiership, the Government also succeeded in carrying out the first elections for the Federal National Council.

HH Sheikh Mohammed has explained his extensive experience of the development process in his book *My Vision – Challenges in the Race for*

SHEIKH MOHAMMED BIN RASHID AL MAKTOUM

Excellence. In this, he stresses leadership and pioneering as the most important factors for a successful development process and as being the two necessary conditions for excellence.

In this context, HH Sheikh Mohammed says:

The UAE experience represents a role model for what a country can achieve when it is blessed by a leadership that cares about people and works in the interests of the whole community. Credibility in this drive is achieved by actions not sayings. This makes the big difference between a leadership that considers people as the real wealth of the nation and another that considers them as the real burden.

To overcome challenges of a new century in a new millennium, we need a new way of thinking and innovative approaches that help us achieve social development and accelerate the development process. We need to change our thinking patterns, to be able to understand the world's language, to convey our mission and stances clearly and simply so that the whole world can understand us. This will help deepen cooperation and eliminate misunderstanding among nations and will give the chance to direct all efforts towards development.

HH Sheikh Mohammed believes that Arabs share the same destiny. He says in his book: 'This continuous division is not normal. What is normal is for all of us to be united. I wish for all the Arab brothers the same as I do for the UAE. I hope they will be at the same level of the developed countries. I expect them to reign, to lead, to achieve excellence in all fields.'

He also believes in the ability of the Arabs to achieve development. 'Our accomplishments are not just for us but for our Arab brothers. Dubai's projects are for all the Arabs, and I will never stop sharing our experience with whoever can gain from them. In addition, we are committed to offer our brothers all the possible support.'

HH Sheikh Mohammed has launched a number of initiatives to enhance the key role played by the UAE on the regional and global arenas. In 2007, he established the 'Mohammed bin Rashid Al Maktoum Foundation' to participate in the development of knowledge in the Arab world (see Media & Culture). In the same year, he launched the 'Dubai Cares' campaign to improve children's access to primary education in developing countries. In its first year, Dubai Cares succeeded in helping four million children in 13 countries in Asia and Africa. In 2008, he launched Noor Dubai initiative for the prevention and treatment of blindness and impaired vision (see Foreign Aid).

Sheikh Mohammed enjoys horse-riding, shooting and hunting. He is also fond of Arabic poetry, being a master of the local style Nabati poetry.

FOREIGN POLICY

The foreign policy of the United Arab Emirates is based upon a set of guiding principles laid down by the country's first President, Sheikh Zayed bin Sultan Al Nahyan. These are based upon a belief in the need for justice in international dealings between states, including the necessity of adhering to the principle of non-interference in the internal affairs of others and the pursuit, wherever possible, of peaceful resolutions of disputes, together with a support for international institutions, such as the United Nations.

Within the Arabian Gulf region, and in the broader Arab world, the UAE has sought to enhance cooperation and to resolve disagreement through dialogue. Thus one of the central features of the country's foreign policy has been the development of closer ties with its neighbours in the Arabian Peninsula. The Arab Gulf Cooperation Council (AGCC), grouping the UAE, Kuwait, Saudi Arabia, Bahrain, Qatar and Oman, was founded at a summit conference held in Abu Dhabi in May 1981, and has since become, with strong UAE support, an effective and widely respected grouping.

President HH Sheikh Khalifa sees the promotion of intra-GCC ties as being a fundamental element in the UAE's foreign policy. 'I strongly believe that the Gulf region is one entity and one area,' he has said. 'Unity is strength. It is my hope that we would be able to forge a greater union or federation, across the Gulf, not just in the UAE, and the success of our federation in the UAE is a cause for hope. Unity is a conviction and a belief.'

In its desire to work with other members of the international community to promote the search for a just and lasting peace in the Middle East, the UAE continued to urge other governments to become pro-active on the issue throughout 2008. Leading UAE officials, including the President, the Vice President and the Foreign Minister have held discussions, both in the UAE and elsewhere, with other global leaders, on ways to revitalise the peace process. The election of a new US President in November 2008 brought the hope that a new approach might be adopted in Washington during 2009.

At the same time, the UAE frequently reaffirmed its support for the Palestinian people and for the Palestine Authority, while calling on the Palestinians to unite so as to face effectively the challenges before them.

The foreign policy of the UAE is based upon a belief in the need for justice in international dealings between states, including the necessity of adhering to the principle of non-interference in the internal affairs of others and the pursuit of peaceful resolutions of disputes.

President Sheikh Khalifa bin Zayed Al Nahyan confers during the opening session of the Arab Summit in Damascus.

www.uaeinteract.com/foreign_policy

In a speech to the United Nations in October, in which he noted the UAE's concerns 'about Israel's growing lack of interest in negotiations', Foreign Minister HH Sheikh Abdullah bin Zayed Al Nahyan repeated the call for the world community to act.

We call upon the International Community and, in particular, the United Nations Security Council and the Middle East Quartet of powers, to exert further pressure on Tel Aviv, so that it lifts the siege it has imposed on the Palestinian people, and implements the international resolutions related to the ending of its occupation of all those Palestinian and Arab territories seized in 1967, including the Holy City of Jerusalem, the Golan Heights and Lebanese territory. Such an ending of occupation would be in compliance with legitimate international resolutions and with the Arab Peace Initiative, which constitutes a sincere and practical option for a solution of the Arab-Israeli conflict in such a way as to guarantee both Israeli security and self-determination for the Palestinians, through their exercising of their inalienable right to establish their own independent state with Jerusalem as its capital, in conformity with the Road Map for the peace process.

The UAE was an active participant in the decision of the March 2008 Arab summit, held in Damascus, to continue to promote the initiative agreed by an earlier Beirut summit as a practical and real solution to the Middle East crisis, noting that it took into account the fundamental factors that must be included in any settlement.

The UAE continued throughout 2008 to provide support to the Government of Iraq. Addressing a conference of Arab Foreign Ministers in April, the UAE Foreign Minister said that the UAE would continue to work through existing bilateral and collective frameworks to serve the interests of Iraq and its people in order to sustain efforts for peace, security and stability in the region and the world at large. 'The states of the Gulf Co-operation Council all share the hope that our whole region may become stable and prosperous. As part of that aspiration, we all look forward to Iraq being a full and active partner, both contributing to the process of development and benefiting from it as this will contribute to maintaining security, stability and prosperity in our region', he said.

Support for the Government in Iraq was not confined simply to the political sphere. During 2008, the UAE was among the first Arab countries to re-open its diplomatic mission in Baghdad while in August, on the instructions of President HH Sheikh Khalifa bin Zayed Al

Former British Prime Minister and Middle East Quartet Representative, Tony Blair.

Nahyan, a decision was taken to write off debts and interest of over US$7 billion owed by Iraq to the Emirates.

In the UAE's view, it is essential that all Iraqi parties should agree on a comprehensive political formula and that all parties must get involved in the plan to strengthen security. There is also a need, the UAE believes, to disarm all militias and restrict weapons only to the security forces, so as to stop violence and chaos, and to resume the political process with the objective of repairing Iraq's economic and social fabric while all groups should be encouraged to participate actively in the political process and to engage in dialogue.

The UAE also continued to offer support to the Government of Lebanon and the Foreign Minister attended the session of the Lebanese Parliament in May during which the country's new President was elected after a long impasse.

During the year, no visible progress was made on resolving the long-running dispute with neighbouring Iran on the question of the three UAE islands of Abu Musa and Greater and Lesser Tunb. Indeed, in August, the UAE sent a letter of protest to the United Nations over a move by Iran to set up two offices on Abu Musa in contravention of the 1971 Memorandum of Understanding on the island.

Sheikh Khalifa attends the opening of the Arab Summit on 29 March 2008 in Damascus, Syria.

In August 2008, the UAE sent a letter of protest to the United Nations over a move by Iran to set up two offices on Abu Musa in contravention of the 1971 Memorandum of Understanding on the island.

'Iran's illegitimate actions on the Abu Musa Island violate the provisions of the Memorandum and are a bid by Iran to change the legal status on the Island', the letter said. 'Although the Memorandum does not give Iran sovereignty over the island or even parts of it, nor did it give Iran the right to take any security measures on it, Iran has been violating the provisions of the Memorandum ever since 1980.'

In his UN General Assembly speech in October, Foreign Minister HH Sheikh Abdullah bin Zayed Al Nahyan noted:

we adhere to our position of demanding a full restoration of the UAE's sovereignty over the three occupied islands, their territorial waters, their air space, their continental shelf and their Exclusive Economic Zone. These islands and their surrounding waters and air space are integral parts of our national sovereignty and patrimony. We reiterate that all actions, whether military or administrative, undertaken by Iran with regards to these three islands since their occupation are void, illegitimate, in breach of the United Nations Charter and of the provisions of international law and the principles of good neighbourliness. There is not, and cannot be, any legal effect related to the Iranian actions, regardless of how much time may pass.

At the end of October, however, following an earlier visit to the UAE by Iran's President, the Foreign Minister visited Iran and signed a Memorandum of Understanding with his Iranian colleague to establish a joint commission between the two countries, which, it is hoped, may lead to some steps to resolve the dispute.

The UAE has also continued to express concern about Iran's nuclear power programme, and has sought reassurances that the programme is for peaceful purposes only.

Beyond the Arab world, the UAE has pursued a policy of seeking, wherever possible, to build friendly relations with other nations, both in the developing and in the industrialised world. While this policy is implemented at a bilateral level, another important feature of UAE policy has been its support for international bodies, like the United Nations and its various agencies. Through its support for such bodies, it seeks to reinforce the rule of international law, and to support the implementation of internationally agreed conventions, so as to protect the interests of the small, the weak and the powerless.

Relations have also been strengthened with other parts of the world through conferences attended by regional groupings of which the UAE is a member, such as a joint meeting between Arab and

UAE Foreign Minister Sheikh Abdullah bin Zayed Al Nahyan signing an agreement with Kuwait.

Latin American states early in the year, followed by another between Arab states and members of the European Union.

In October 2008, the UAE hosted the fourth in a series of Forums for the Future, following earlier meetings in Morocco, Bahrain and Jordan. Attended by senior officials from the Arab world, Turkey and members of the G8 group of industrialised nations, the Forum focused on ways of promoting political and social progress in the region.

The UAE also hosted a major conference of parliamentarians from the North Atlantic Treaty Organisation (NATO) for discussions on regional security.

During the year, there was the usual steady flow of high-ranking visitors from other countries to the Emirates, both from within the Gulf and Arab world, and from further afield. Senior UAE officials, including President HH Sheikh Khalifa, Vice President HH Sheikh Mohammed bin Rashid and the Crown Prince of Abu Dhabi and Deputy Supreme Commander of the UAE Armed Forces, HH Sheikh Mohammed bin Zayed, made numerous visits abroad.

(From L to R) Omani Foreign Minister Yussef bin Alawi, Japanese Deputy Foreign Minister Seiko Hashimoto, UAE Foreign Minister Sheikh Abdullah bin Zayed Al Nayhan, Syrian Foreign Minister Walid Muallem, Arab League Secretary General Amr Mussa and Foreign Minister of Bahrain Sheikh Khaled bin Ahmad Al Khalifa at the opening session of the Forum For The Future conference in Abu Dhabi on 19 October 2008.

Sheikh Mohammed bin
Zayed Al Nahyan with
George W. Bush.

In November 2008, the
UAE became a member
of the Permanent Court
of Arbitration (PCA)
following its ratification
of the Convention for
the Pacific Settlement
of International
Disputes.

Throughout the year, the UAE continued to extend all possible support to the international fight against terrorism, while emphasising the necessity both of a clear definition of terrorism and of ensuring that terrorism perpetrated by states should not be overlooked. Support has been offered to countries suffering from terrorism, including collaboration in terms of exchanges of information designed to help law enforcement authorities track down and arrest suspects.

The United Arab Emirates believes, however, that the prevailing climate of misunderstanding between different faiths and cultures is used by terrorists and those who harbour them. It firmly supports, therefore, the promotion of intercultural and interfaith dialogue.

The country took part in the Interfaith Dialogue initiated during the year by King Abdullah bin Abdul Aziz of Saudi Arabia. Supreme Council member HH Sheikh Hamad bin Mohammed Al Sharqi led the UAE delegation, which also included Foreign Minister HH Sheikh Abdullah bin Zayed Al Nahyan, to the November 2008 conference on 'The Culture of Peace and Dialogue among Religions and Cultures' held at the United Nations.

At the same time, the UAE has continued to argue that there is a need for different societies and cultures to avoid acts which can further deepen misunderstandings. Thus, referring to a decision by a Dutch film-maker to release a film that was perceived as being insulting to Islam and to the Prophet Mohammed, the Foreign Minister noted that it was necessary to show respect for the religions of others and to refrain from instigating hatred under the pretext of practicing freedom of expression.

As noted at the beginning of this chapter, the UAE has always sought to work with and to support the United Nations and its agencies.

During 2008, the UAE signed or ratified a number of international conventions. Among these were the Protocol to the Convention on the Rights of Persons with Disabilities, while preparations were nearing completion at the end of the year for the signing of the Convention against Torture and Other Cruel, Inhuman or Degrading Treatment or Punishment.

The UAE also signed the UN Convention for Suppression of Nuclear Terrorism, as part of measures designed to ensure that its own programme to develop peaceful uses of nuclear energy, within the guidelines of the International Atomic Energy Agency (IAEA) fully complied with all applicable global agreements.

While specific political issues, naturally, attracted much attention during 2008, the United Arab Emirates has continued to maintain its focus on a range of topics with a global relevance. Among these has been the issue of human trafficking, which came to prominence early in 2008 with the holding of a special UN forum in Vienna to launch the UN Global Initiative to Fight Trafficking, UN.GIFT.

The UAE anti-human trafficking law Federal Law 51 of November 2006 was the first of its kind to be introduced in the Arabian Gulf region (see Social Development). As noted in the inaugural edition of what will become an annual series of reports on efforts to combat trafficking to and in the UAE, human trafficking is a crime that crosses national borders, and the UAE is working closely with international and regional law enforcement agencies, as well as the authorities in other countries, to apprehend those engaged in trafficking.

In terms of the UAE itself, the country is particularly affected because of its dynamic growth, which has prompted an inflow of economic migrants from throughout the Arab world and the Asian continent. This, in turn, increases the risk of trafficking, and the Government expended considerable effort during 2008 in developing strategies with the source countries of migrant labour to help to stamp out trafficking in the countries of origin. A conference of Labour

FNC Speaker Abdul Aziz Al Ghurair meets with Pope Benedict in Rome.

The UAE is working closely with international and regional law enforcement agencies to apprehend those engaged in human trafficking.

The Abu Dhabi Declaration, an agreement between source and host countries on ways of regulating the flow of contractual labour, was signed in Abu Dhabi early in 2008.

Ministers from source and host countries for migrant labour was held in Abu Dhabi early in the year, at which an Abu Dhabi Declaration on ways of regulating the flow of workers was agreed. This was followed in late October by another major conference in Manila, Philippines, attended by the UAE Minister of Labour (see Social Development).

Another issue of global concern was economic in nature, rather than political, following the depression that hit the world like a tsunami in the latter part of the year. While moving to ensure that, as far as possible, the local economy was insulated (see Economy), the Government moved to work with multilateral institutions like the International Monetary Fund (IMF) as well as on a bilateral basis, to help to shore up the economies of the countries most seriously affected.

During the year, the United Arab Emirates established diplomatic relations with Montenegro and Kosovo, two of the successor states to the former Yugoslavia, continuing its active involvement in this area of south-eastern Europe. UAE forces earlier took part in peace-keeping activities in Kosovo.

FOREIGN AID

Boxes of dates donated to Muslims in the Philippines during the holy month of Ramadan.

Since the establishment of the United Arab Emirates, the country has played an active role in the provision of aid to developing countries and has been a major contributor of emergency relief to regions affected by conflict and natural disasters. The philosophy behind the aid policy is two-fold – first, a belief that help for the needy is a duty incumbent on all Muslims and, second, that part of the country's wealth from oil and gas should be devoted to helping other countries which have been less well-endowed. The philosophy was well-described by former UAE President Sheikh Zayed bin Sultan Al Nahyan:

Foreign aid and assistance is one of the basic pillars of our foreign policy. For we believe that there is no true benefit for us from the wealth that we have unless it does not also reach those in need, wherever they may be, and regardless of their nationality or beliefs. That is why we have ensured that our brothers and our friends have shared in our wealth.

The main UAE governmental agency for foreign aid is the Abu Dhabi Fund for Development (ADFD) which was established in 1971, before the creation of the UAE Federation. Its key priority is to contribute to the economic development of developing countries through the extension of loans to finance projects that help to reduce poverty and to improve living conditions and quality of life. Since its establishment, the ADFD has provided over Dh12.6 billion (US$3.45 billion) in soft loans and grants to countries around the world. Of this amount, Dh12 billion (US$3.27 billion) has been provided as soft loans, for a total of 197 projects, with a further 23 grants, worth Dh666 million (US$181.5 million) also being made. Dh612 million (US$166.7 million) has been provided as capital investment in 12 companies in developing countries. In addition, the ADFD also manages 61 loans and grants provided directly by the Abu Dhabi government. Since 1971, these have accounted for a further Dh10 billion (US$2.72 billion), bringing the total amount of the loans, grants and investments provided by the fund or the Abu Dhabi government, and managed by the fund, to around Dh24 billion (US$6.54 billion), covering 258 different projects in a total of 52 countries.

Red Crescent collection of donations in a UAE shopping mall.

In November 2008, the Abu Dhabi Fund announced a long term loan of around US$278 million for rehabilitation of agricultural land in the Central Asian state of Uzbekistan. The loan will be used for three projects to improve management of water resources and to repair dams and irrigation systems.

Other assistance has also been provided through commitments made at various multilateral donor conferences. Between 1994 to mid-2008, for example, around Dh15.4 billion (US$4.2 billion) has been provided for the Palestinians, including, most recently, US$300 million pledged at a donor conference in Paris and an annual commitment of US$43 million to support the Palestine National Authority. The UAE Federal Government also participates in a number of other multilateral aid-giving institutions, including the International Development Agency (IDA), and other bodies like the OPEC Fund for International Development, the Arab Gulf Fund for the UN (AGFUND), the Arab Bank for Economic Development in Africa (BADEA), the Abu Dhabi-based Arab Monetary Fund (AMF) and the Islamic Development Bank (IDB). In recent years, however, increasing attention has been paid to various forms of humanitarian aid, destined for those in need because of natural disasters or conflict and for those in such poverty and urgent need that longer-term development projects will, quite simply, not deliver help in time.

The ADFD has provided over Dh12.6 billion (US$3.45 billion) on soft loans and grants to countries around the world.

www.uaeinteract.com/aid

Red Crescent Authority

Over the last few years, the Red Crescent has spent in excess of Dh2 billion (US$545 million) on relief operations in a total of 95 countries throughout the globe, with a special emphasis on those in need in Palestine, Iraq, Lebanon, Afghanistan, Sudan and the Horn of Africa countries.

A key body in this process is the UAE Red Crescent Authority, chaired by the country's Deputy Prime Minister, Sheikh Hamdan bin Zayed Al Nahyan. The philosophy of the Red Crescent was spelt out in a major speech given by Sheikh Hamdan on the occasion of World Refugee Day in June. Referring specifically to the issue of refugees, he noted that there was a growing problem of refugees throughout the world, caused both by natural disasters and by conflict. This, he said, 'poses a great challenge to the international community, humanitarian organisations and other philanthropic bodies. What these refugees are facing worldwide as a result of their exceptional situation requires a concerted effort by the international community and the strengthening of partnership among humanitarian organisations to try to improve their situation,' he said. 'That is why the UAE continues to provide humanitarian support, execute development programmes to help alleviate the sufferings of those weak and innocent people,' he added.

Over the last few years alone, the Red Crescent has spent over Dh2 billion (US$545 million) on relief operations in a total of 95 countries throughout the globe, with a special emphasis on those in need in Palestine, Iraq, Lebanon, Afghanistan, Sudan and the Horn of Africa countries. In some cases, countries need a continuing programme of assistance. The countries of the Horn of Africa, for example, particularly Ethiopia and Somalia, but also Djibouti, Eritrea, Sudan and Kenya, have been suffering from drought for several years. During the course of the last year, over 2000 tonnes of foodstuffs were delivered to these African states. Overall, since 1994, the Red Crescent has provided Somalia with nearly Dh100 million (US$27.2 million) in emergency food supplies. Afghanistan is another country that has needed a continuing programme of support, not just because of the impact of natural calamities but also because many of its people have suffered from and are continuing to suffer from conflict. Between 1997 and 2008, the Red Crescent supplied over Dh104 million (US$28.3 million) in aid, while other UAE government and non-governmental agencies have also contributed very substantial sums.

The Asian countries hit by the devastating tsunami in December 2004 and Pakistan, hit shortly afterwards by a major earthquake, have also needed continuing assistance, since, once the initial needs of survivors for food, medical assistance and shelter have been met, there is a continuing need to help them rebuild their shattered communities.

Clothes being sorted for distribution at UAE Red Crescent depot.

Over the course of the last year, the Red Crescent has continued to be the country's premier emergency relief agency, at least in terms of the number of countries in which it operates, even though some of the larger privately funded charitable foundations have disbursed more money. During 2007, it provided a total of around Dh281 million (US$76.5 million) in relief, humanitarian and development aid, 50 per cent higher than in the previous year. Victims of natural disasters and armed conflicts in 40 countries benefited. In the first half of 2008, a further Dh170.2 million (US$46.4 million) was disbursed. It also handled the distribution and administration of funds allocated by government and other private foundations, which amounted to a substantially larger sum.

UAE Red Crescent relief programmes during 2008 included further aid to the Palestinians. Following the closure of the Egyptian–Gaza border early in the year for example, there were major food shortages in Gaza, to which the Red Crescent responded by donating Dh367,000 (US$100,000) to UNRWA to purchase food. Other support included the supply of polio vaccines for children. Further help for UNRWA included a donation of Dh18.35 million (US$5 million) to fund the rehabilitation of the Palestinian refugee camp at Neirab in Syria and a separate agreement to sponsor Palestinian orphans.

The UN Agency has described the UAE Red Crescent as 'our best partner in the Arab region over the last ten years', in terms of support for aid for its programmes. The Agency's Commissioner-General has also singled out the Zayed bin Sultan Al Nahyan Charitable and Humanitarian Foundation for its help for the refugee camps, in particular in terms of helping children and providing them with access to education.

In May, following the earthquake which devastated Sichuan province in China, the Red Crescent rushed emergency aid and medical supplies to the area, while UAE President HH Sheikh Khalifa bin Zayed Al Nahyan personally donated US$50 million to help the work. Other Red Crescent help went to victims of a major earthquake in Kyrgyzstan, cyclone victims in Madagascar, Burma and Bangladesh, those affected by a disaster in Cairo, Egypt, in which part of a large hill collapsed on a heavily populated area, orphans in the Indian state of Kerala, those affected by conflict in Iraq and by famine in Mauritania and flood victims in Algeria and Sudan, as well as to other countries. Wherever possible, the Red Crescent seeks to establish

The UAE Red Crescent now ranks in the top-ten member organisations of the ICRC in terms of the amount of relief assistance provided.

UAE relief for victims of cyclone Sidr in Dhaka.

The 'Generous Heart Initiative', a partnership between the Red Crescent and the Emirates World Heart Group, brings together top cardiac surgeons from all over the world to give their services for free to those suffering from heart problems in developing countries.

partnerships with other agencies, including, of course, other Red Crescent and Red Cross Societies from around the world. It now ranks in the top ten member organisations of the International Committee of the Red Cross in terms of the amount of relief assistance provided – an impressive achievement for a country as small as the Emirates. Other partners include the United Nations Development Programme (UNDP) the UN High Commission for Refugees, (UNHCR) the United Nations Children's Fund (UNICEF), the UN Office for Coordination of Humanitarian Affairs (OCHA), the United Nations Relief and Works Agency for Palestine Refugees in the Near East (UNRWA), and the World Food Programme (WFP).

Two important global partnership initiatives have, however, had their origins in the UAE itself. One is between the Red Crescent and the Emirates World Heart Group, which brings together top cardiac surgeons from all over the world to give their services for free to those suffering from heart problems in developing countries, with particular attention being paid to children with congenital heart problems. The 'Generous Heart Initiative', set up in July 2008, has been equipped with mobile cardiac centres and provided help to over 400 people within the first few months of its operation, with patients coming from the Emirates, Eritrea, Sudan, Yemen, Iraq and the Philippines. The Emirates World Heart Group also undertook heart operations, free of charge, in Tanzania, within the framework of the Zayed Charity Initiative, originally launched by the UAE's former President. Another UAE initiative to go global during 2008 was the

'Generous Hands' campaign, launched by HH Sheikha Fatima bint Mubarak, widow of the former UAE President and Chairwoman of the UAE's General Women's Union. This offers a special medical treatment programme for those who cannot afford to pay for treatment and is being managed by the UAE Red Crescent.

Those who suffer the most from natural disasters, as well as from conflict, are often women and children, who may find it difficult to compete for scarce supplies. A further new initiative during 2008 was specifically designed to address their needs. The Sheikha Fatima bin Mubarak Fund for Refugee Women, established on the initiative of HH Sheikha Fatima, was launched during Ramadan by the UAE Red Crescent, acting in partnership with the Office of the UN High Commissioner for Refugees. The proceeds of fund-raising will be used to support the UNHCR's projects in girls' education, livelihood, health and nutrition for some of the most vulnerable displaced women and children around the world.

PRIVATE HUMANITARIAN EFFORTS

Besides the overseas aid and relief assistance provided by bodies like the UAE Red Crescent, the private humanitarian efforts of the UAE's leading figures have also been active during the course of the year. The Khalifa bin Zayed Charity Foundation, established by President HH Sheikh Khalifa bin Zayed Al Nahyan, made several major donations, including Dh200 million (US$54.5 million dollars) to Afghanistan, to fund sustainable social, economic, health, educational and utilities projects and Dh184 million (US$50 million) in emergency assistance for China, following the Sichuan earthquake. Other assistance included help in August for residents of areas in Pakistan hit by floods, while in May, in a move designed to help those suffering from the world shortage of wheat and consequent rising prices, the President donated a million tonnes of wheat to Egypt and half a million tonnes to Yemen.

A wide range of private humanitarian organisations provide both long-term and emergency assistance to the needy at home and abroad.

The Zayed bin Sultan Al Nahyan Charitable and Humanitarian Foundation, established by the former President, focused its attention during 2008 on projects inside the UAE, but still spent around 30 per cent of its budget overseas. In Africa, projects included a child care centre in Niger, a college for management sciences in Burkino Faso, a scientific institute in Liberia and a eye centre in The Gambia, with other projects in the Philippines, Afghanistan, Indonesia, Pakistan, Bangladesh, Tajikistan and Thailand and schools and Islamic Centres

www.uaeinteract.com/aid

in Australia, New Zealand, Canada, Sweden and Britain. Over the last few years, the foundation has spent nearly Dh1,25 billion (US$340 million) on projects at home and abroad.

A lead in terms of generosity in giving has also been shown by HH Sheikh Mohammed bin Rashid Al Maktoum, UAE Vice President and Prime Minister and Ruler of Dubai. His Mohammed bin Rashid Charity and Humanitarian Foundation has provided assistance for, amongst others, hospitals in Palestine and earthquake victims in China and has also worked successfully to encourage Dubai-based institutions to donate lavishly to its projects.

Much more significant are two initiatives taken in the last couple of years by HH Sheikh Mohammed that are designed to have a global reach. In 2007, he launched the Dubai Cares campaign, with the initial goal of providing primary education to one million underprivileged children around the world. Within its first year of operations, Dubai Cares had provided education to over four million children in 13 countries across Africa and Asia, far exceeding its original targets. In a speech launching the campaign, HH Sheikh Mohammed noted:

The worst disease in this world is the unbreakable partnership between ignorance and poverty. This partnership is the source of all evil from which many countries suffer and it is the root of persecution, and the main reason for divisions in the world between a wealthy North and a poor South, between advanced countries and deprived countries, between societies that know, and societies that do not know. The only way to break this partnership between ignorance and poverty is by relentlessly attacking ignorance and by exerting every effort to spread education. We are doing our duty, regardless of the fact that many countries have resigned from playing their role in combating illiteracy worldwide and the international community is not able to fulfill its promises.

With well over Dh1 billion (US$273 million) raised to support its work, Dubai Cares is already making a major impact on child illiteracy worldwide. This was followed in 2008 by another project, the 'Noor Dubai' (Light of Dubai) initiative, launched in September. Its objective is to help at least one million people around the world who are suffering from blindness and eye disease. Within a few weeks, hundreds of patients, from over a dozen countries in Africa, the Arab world and South Asia, arrived in Dubai for treatment, with top eye surgeons being specially flown in from the United States and Europe.

Within its first year of operations, Dubai Cares provided education to over four million underprivileged children in 13 countries across Africa and Asia.

دبي العطاء

Dubai Cares

With well over Dh1billion (US$273 million) raised to support its work, Dubai Cares is already making a major impact on child illiteracy worldwide.

UAE Red Crescent distributes
relief to labourers.

During 2008, a new
body, the External Aid
Liaison Bureau, was set
up in collaboration
with OCHA to
coordinate the
country's many relief
programmes
worldwide.

Noor Dubai, which is being administered by the Dubai Health Authority, is collaborating closely with the World Health Organisation (WHO) and the International Agency for the Prevention of Blindness (IAPB), to help them achieve their goals. It is also working with Lions Clubs International, the world's largest volunteer organisation with an international network of 1.3 million members in 202 countries, and ORBIS International, a global development organisation whose mission is to treat and prevent blindness by strengthening the capacity of local eye health partners. It is not possible in a summary of a year's events to give details of all the humanitarian assistance provided by all public and private bodies and by individuals, both UAE citizens and expatriates, throughout the Emirates. A further initiative that should be recorded, however, was one designed to raise funds specifically for Palestinian children, launched by HH Dr Sheikh Sultan Al Qasimi, Ruler of Sharjah, and his wife, HH Sheikha Jawaher. Over Dh55 million (US$15 million) was raised in the fund-raising drive, with Sheikh Sultan saying that support for the campaign was a humanitarian duty. The non-governmental Sharjah Charity Association also sent relief supplies to Sri Lanka following heavy floods there in March, with much of the assistance being funded by donations from the public.

HUMANITARIAN COORDINATION

As will be apparent from this review of the UAE's involvement in overseas aid, there are a number of important organisations within the country engaged in the effort. During 2008, a new body was set up to coordinate the country's relief programmes, both governmental and non-governmental. Called the External Aid Liaison Bureau and set up in collaboration with the UN Office for the Coordination of Humanitarian Affairs (OCHA), the new body is also chaired by Sheikh Hamdan bin Zayed. Its main task, he said, will be to 'seek to prevent overlapping by combining efforts made by government and non-government organisations in the humanitarian fields and to coordinate with international relief agencies in a way that will enable quicker intervention to ease the plight of people affected by natural disasters and emergencies.' The long-term objective is to see the unification of all humanitarian aid being provided by the UAE, and to fully document the country's contributions to humanitarian projects worldwide. The aid programme, Sheikh Hamdan has stressed, is designed to help all those in need as a result of natural or man-made disasters, irrespective of their geographical, religious and racial affiliations.

ECONOMIC DEVELOPMENT

Despite the steadying of economic growth to 5.2 per cent in 2007, the UAE remained one of the fastest growing economies in the world.

As financial turmoil rocked world markets, the UAE Government moved quickly to ensure that there was sufficient liquidity in the UAE's banking system.

ECONOMIC DEVELOPMENT

THE ECONOMY

GIVEN THE WIDESPREAD TURMOIL THAT IMPACTED the global financial system in 2008, it is somewhat reassuring to look at the UAE's economic performance before the credit crisis took central stage and also to study statistics indicating how well it weathered the storm in 2008.

For many years the UAE's Central Bank, like national monetary agencies throughout the world, has been able to rely on a well-established set of parameters to predict economic growth, money supply and financial stability. By mid-2008 it seemed as if someone had rewritten the rule book!

One of the main lessons learnt from the crisis was the intricate connectivity of global markets: events in New York, Japan or London reverberated throughout the world, even affecting economies such as that of mainland China which were previously thought to enjoy some degree of immunity from global financial turbulence. The UAE, as one of the world's largest suppliers of crude oil, had initially benefited from high oil prices but, as the recessionary cycle took hold and demand for hydrocarbons fell, the price of oil nose-dived from its peak levels at nearly US$150 per barrel and it was clear that there were no winners in a crisis that was continuing to unfold as this review was being finalised.

The UAE's real economic growth rate in 2007 was 5.2 per cent compared to 11.5 per cent in 2006. Meanwhile, nominal GDP (based on current prices) grew by 16.8 per cent in 2007 compared with 28.7 per cent in 2006 and 25.6 per cent in 2005, GDP at current prices in 2007 reaching Dh729.73 billion compared with Dh624.62 billion in 2006. Despite the steadying of economic growth, the country remained one of the fastest growing economies on a global scale. This was not solely due to a rise in value of the oil and gas sectors, which increased by 18.2 per cent in 2007, related in part to a 13.1 per cent hike in average oil prices. The non-oil sector also performed impressively, reaching Dh467.9 billion, equivalent to 64.1 per cent of overall GDP.

UAE GDP, at current prices, reached Dh729.73 billion in 2007, up from Dh624 billion in 2006

Key factors influencing growth in the economy were (based on Central Bank statistics) increases in the construction and building

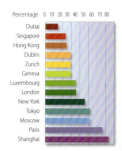

Total corporate tax rate index – selected cities (percentage).

Dubai............14.4	London.........35.7
Singapore.......23.2	New York........46.2
Hong Kong......24.4	Tokyo............52.0
Dublin..........28.9	Moscow.........51.4
Zurich..........29.1	Paris.............66.3
Geneva.........29.1	Shanghai.......73.9
Luxembourg.....35.3	

Source: World Bank

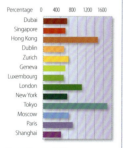

Annual cost of office space – selected cities (euro per m²).

Dubai............552	London...........901
Singapore.......517	New York........564
Hong Kong.....1,271	Tokyo...........1,493
Dublin..........486	Moscow.........602
Zurich..........592	Paris.............694
Geneva.........518	Shanghai.......423
Luxembourg.....480	

Source: Cushman & Wakefield, 2007

sector (25.6 per cent), along with significant growth in manufacturing and industry (19.8 per cent); real estate (16.9 per cent); the financial sector (11.5 per cent); transportation and communications (8.3 per cent); and tourism, which continued its steady growth at a rate of 6.4 per cent. Added to these positive influences, the state maintained its strongly supportive role through investment in government services, electricity and agriculture. Indeed, the government services sector output actually increased by 22.7 per cent in 2007, reaching a figure of Dh49.27 billion.

Notwithstanding a strong performance by the non-oil sector, there is no escaping the importance of oil and gas to the UAE's economic performance. The UAE's trade balance, for example, increased by 11.8 per cent in 2007 (despite a large increase in imported goods) as a result of a 20.4 per cent increase in the value of exported hydrocarbons (at Dh309.92 billion) along with a more or less similar jump in non-oil exports. The 12.9 per cent average increase in oil price over the year meant that the country was in positive growth territory regardless of any increase in the volume exported. In actual fact the value of oil exports (including condensates) jumped by 22.5 per cent to reach Dh261.42 billion in 2007, while gas exports rose by 9.3 per cent in value, to reach Dh28.5 billion.

But diversification remains the key to achieving sustainable growth in the UAE and the Government is firmly focused on encouraging the non-oil sector to maintain its major role in the country's economy. As mentioned above, at Dh467.9 billion, the UAE's non-oil sector contributed around 64 per cent of total GDP in 2007.

The visible signs of massive economic activity throughout the country are apparent to even the most casual of observers. One of the highest concentrations of cranes in the world speaks volumes about the incredible rate of construction taking place, particularly in Dubai and Abu Dhabi, but also in other emirates. It is no surprise, therefore, that the construction sector grew by a massive 25.6 per cent in 2007, compared to 2006. Projects such as Jumeirah Beach Residences, one of the world's largest synchronised real estate developments; the Jumeirah Palm, one of the world's largest man-made islands; Aldar's massive Abu Dhabi Central Market project; Burj Dubai (destined to be the world's tallest building); the truly magnificent Sheikh Zayed Grand Mosque; together with a seemingly unlimited number of skyscrapers and ongoing development work

EXPENDITURE ON GDP 2004–2007 (millions AED, at current prices)

	2004	2005	2006*	2007**
Gross domestic product	386,535	513,089	624,623	729,732
Private consumption	205,882	242,176	271,793	319,867
Gross fixed capital formation	81,255	93,798	120,999	148,479
Net exports of goods & services	51,720	119,847	167,209	177,761
Public consumption	44,286	51,544	57,961	76,190
Variation in the inventory	3,392	5,724	6,663	7,435

Source: Ministry of Economy   * Adjusted   ** Preliminary

By the end of 2008, the Dubai property sector was undergoing a transitional phase, companies were reviewing their project strategies, several mega-developments were being reviewed and developers were more cautious with their investments on projects.

on mega-projects such as Saadiyat Island, Al Reem, Jebel Ali Palm, Deira Palm; Al Maktoum International Airport, Dubai World Central and Dubailand, to mention only a few, leave one in little doubt that the country is in a phase of rapid development and change.

Government has also maintained its focus on investing in its people, placing a high priority on investment in education, health and social services. The government services sector, which grew at 22.7 per cent, represented 7 per cent of GDP in 2007 compared with 6 per cent in the previous year.

Meanwhile, the UAE balance of payments estimates issued in the Central Bank Report for 2007 reported a surplus of Dh183.24 billion compared with Dh23.88 billion in 2006.

ECONOMIC REPORTING

The main official sources of economic information on the United Arab Emirates are contained in regular reports issued by the UAE Central Bank and by the Ministry of Economy. The Central Bank (www.uaecentralbank.ae) issues an Annual Report along with annual

Burj Dubai rises above the city.

www.uaeinteract.com/economicdevelopment

Economic Bulletins and quarterly *Statistical Bulletins.* Central Bank figures for the national economy are derived from a number of sources, including the Ministry of Economy (www.economy.ae), which issues an Annual Social and Economic Report each year. Individual emirates also publish statistical reports, while some banks produce economic studies covering particular aspects of the UAE economy.

FIXED CAPITAL FORMATION

Fixed investment in the UAE is one of the main drivers of economic growth and employment creation. There are three main sources of fixed capital investment, i.e. government investment, investment by public institutions and investment by private entities. Almost Dh150 billion of fixed investment was made in 2007 (actual figure Dh148.5 billion), an increase of 22.7 per cent over 2006. Investments were made across a wide range of sectors with private sector investment accounting for 56.8 per cent of total investment, at Dh84.3 billion. Meanwhile, public sector investment reached Dh43 billion and accounted for 29 per cent of the total. Government investment in major infrastructure projects such as roads, ports, airports, water and electricity, government housing, schools, hospitals and healthcare centres accounted for Dh21.2 billion or 14.2 per cent.

The four primary sectors attracting investment and providing the main driving force for moving the economy forward are hydrocarbons, manufacturing, transport and communications, and real estate.

There are four primary sectors attracting investment and providing the main driving force for moving the economy forward. These are hydrocarbons, manufacturing, transport and communications, and real estate. Approximately 11.1 per cent of investment in 2007 was in the oil industry; 17 per cent in manufacturing; 18.3 per cent in transport and communications and 14.6 per cent in the real estate sector. Additional sectors include water and electricity, hotels and restaurants.

BALANCE OF TRADE

Balance of trade figures achieved a surplus in 2007 of Dh236.15 billion compared with Dh211.30 billion in 2006. Total exports FOB (including re-exports) reached Dh664.34 billion in 2007 as against Dh534.66 billion in 2006, while total imports (FOB) rose to Dh428.19 billion in 2007, compared with Dh323.36 billion in 2006. Increase in oil production, and a higher average oil price of US$71.7 compared with US$63.50, helped to boost the value of oil exports (including condensates) to Dh261.42 billion, compared with Dh213.37 billion

GDP BY SECTOR (in millions of dirhams)

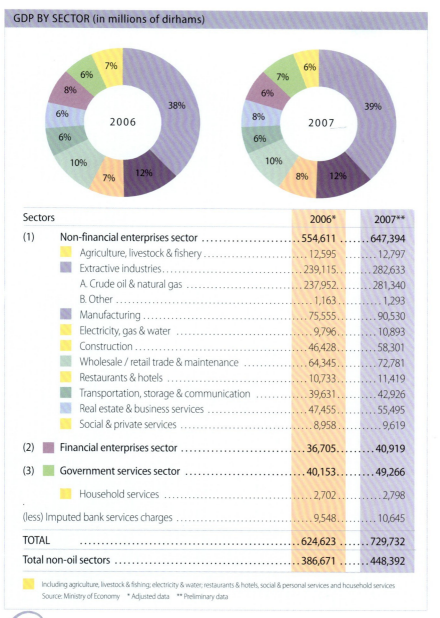

Sectors		2006*	2007**
(1)	Non-financial enterprises sector	554,611	647,394
	Agriculture, livestock & fishery	12,595	12,797
	Extractive industries	239,115	282,633
	A. Crude oil & natural gas	237,952	281,340
	B. Other	1,163	1,293
	Manufacturing	75,555	90,530
	Electricity, gas & water	9,796	10,893
	Construction	46,428	58,301
	Wholesale / retail trade & maintenance	64,345	72,781
	Restaurants & hotels	10,733	11,419
	Transportation, storage & communication	39,631	42,926
	Real estate & business services	47,455	55,495
	Social & private services	8,958	9,619
(2)	Financial enterprises sector	36,705	40,919
(3)	Government services sector	40,153	49,266
	Household services	2,702	2,798
	(less) Imputed bank services charges	9,548	10,645
	TOTAL	**624,623**	**729,732**
	Total non-oil sectors	**386,671**	**448,392**

Including agriculture, livestock & fishing; electricity & water; restaurants & hotels, social & personal services and household services

Source: Ministry of Economy   * Adjusted data   ** Preliminary data

ESTIMATE OF UAE BALANCE OF PAYMENTS 2006–2007 (in millions of dirhams)

	2006	2007*
Current Account Balance	132,375	135,936
Trade Balance (FOB)	211,302	309,922
Total Exports of Hydrocarbon	257,442	257,442
Oil Exports	213,372	261,422
Petroleum Products Exports	17,995	20,000
Gas Exports	26,075	28,500
Total Goods Exports	104,518	125,729
Free Zone Exports	75,286	83,661
Other Exports [1]	29,232	42,068
Re-Exports [2]	172,706	228,694
Total Exports and Re-Exports (FOB)	534,666	664,345
Total Imports (FOB)	-323,364	-428,194
Total Imports (CIF)	-367,459	-486,580
Other Imports [3]	-291,050	-395,718
Free Zone Imports	-76,409	-90,866
Services (NET)	-66,226	-87,614
Travel	-14,157	-19,174
Transport	-8,086	-10,165
Government Services	112	115
Freight and Insurance	-44,095	-58,390
Investment Income (NET)	17,400	21,500
Banking System [4]	8,800	8,150
Private Non-Banks	-600	-1200
Enterprises of Public Sector	30,000	41,100
Foreign Hydrocarbon Companies in UAE	-20,800	-26,550
Transfers (NET)	-30,101	-34,111
Public Transfers	-2,025	-2,159
Workers Transfers	-28,076	-31952

[1] Including estimates of other exports from all emirates.
[2] Including re-exports of non-monetary gold.
[3] Including estimate of imports from all emirates and imports of non-monetary gold.
[4] Central Bank and all banks.

* Adjustable figures and preliminary estimates
Source: Central Bank Annual Report, 2007

ESTIMATE OF UAE BALANCE OF PAYMENTS, continued

	2006*	2007*
Capital and Financial Account (Net)	**-58,987**	**41,524**
Capital Account [5]	–	–
Financial Account	-58,987	41,524
Enterprise of Private Sector	87,593	217,324
Direct Investment	7,030	-1,400
Outward	-40,000	-53,500
Inward	47,030	52,100
Portfolio Investment	4,400	5,300
Banks	35,563	178,324
Securities	-12,715	-1,157
Other Investment	48,278	179,481
Private Non-Banks	40,600	35,100
Enterprises of Public Sector	-146,580	-175,800
Net Errors and Omissions	-49,503	5,788
Overall Balance: Surplus (+) or Deficit (-)	**23,885**	**183,238**
Change in Reserves (- indicates an increase)	**-23,885**	**-183,238**
Net Foreign Assets with Central Bank	-24,034	-183,127
Reserve Position with I.M.F.	149	-111

[5] Data not available at time of report.

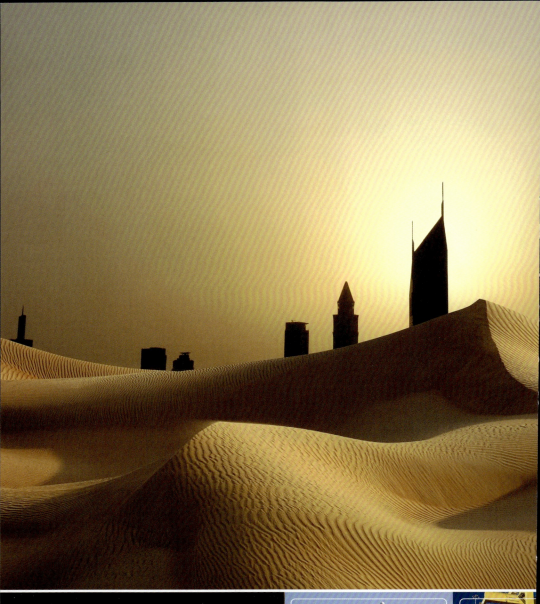

 The UAE is a contracting party to GATT and
one of the original members of the WTO.

in 2006. Non-hydrocarbon exports, including those from free zones and elsewhere, reached Dh125.73 billion compared with Dh104.52 billion in 2006. The above figures made the UAE the second largest trading nation in the Arab world in 2007.

STRUCTURAL FRAMEWORK

Economic policy approved by the Federal Supreme Council is administered by the UAE Ministry of Economy, under its Minister, Sultan bin Saeed Al Mansouri, and the Ministry of Foreign Trade, under its Minister, Sheikha Lubna Al Qasimi. Whilst these federal ministries set economic guidelines and provide the essential administrative framework, individual emirates exercise a high degree of direct control over their own economies and frequently play significant roles in local business development.

The UAE is a contracting party to the General Agreement on Tariffs and Trade (GATT) and one of the original members of the World Trade Organisation (WTO). Its Constitution, Commercial Companies Law and Trade Agencies Law (see below) form the main structure of federal legal instruments under which business and commerce operate. Within this framework, additional laws, decree-laws, ordinary decrees, and regulations are promulgated from time to time to deal with specific issues affecting how business is conducted in the UAE.

'Doing Business in the Arab World 2008', a joint report by the International Finance Corporation and the World Bank, has ranked the UAE fourth in the Arab world and forty-sixth globally in terms of ease of doing business.

STRATEGIC PLANNING

As outlined in the chapter on Government, both federal and local governments recently released strategic planning documents. The major economic policies listed within the federal strategy were aimed at stimulating economic growth, strengthening the competitiveness of the UAE economy, and upgrading regulations and legislation to match current and expected economic growth. Implicit within this policy is the Government's participation in empowering UAE citizens to take the lead in developing the economy and the labour market. In order to achieve this the Government has adopted a comprehensive nationalisation policy to include leadership development and project management.

Initiatives under the national strategy included establishment of a National Competitiveness Council, a National Statistics Office, and a Vocational Training Unit, with the collaboration of the private sector. The strategy also contains commitments to formulate federal policies

for small and medium-sized enterprises in cooperation with local governments; and to prepare a federal framework for minimum regulations for both free zones and special economic zones that would encompass labour rights, conservation of the environment and other issues.

Abu Dhabi Strategic Plan

Abu Dhabi's strategic five-year plan indicated that the emirate will develop more liberal economic policies, boost its industrial infrastructure and provide additional support to small and medium scale businesses.

In May 2008 the Abu Dhabi Council for Economic Development (ADCED) issued its strategic plan for 2008–2012. The five-year plan indicated that the emirate will develop more liberal economic policies, boost its industrial infrastructure and provide more support to small and medium scale businesses enabling them play a more proactive role in the development of the emirate.

An announcement at the launch of the five-year plan stated that: 'the legal regime will be revamped in order to encourage inward investment. This overhaul will include aspects such as licensing, transparency, free competition and incentives. In other words, the entire business climate will be made investor-friendly'.

Abu Dhabi's economic strategy may be summarised as follows:

- Premium education, health care and infrastructure assets
- A large empowered private sector
- Creation of a sustainable knowledge-based economy
- An optimal transparent regulatory environment
- Complete international and domestic security
- A continuation of strong and diverse international relationships
- Emirate resource optimisation
- Maintenance of Abu Dhabi's values, culture and heritage
- A significant and ongoing contribution to the federation of the United Arab Emirates.

A central core of Abu Dhabi's economic policy is to leverage the emirate's strong hydrocarbon sector to stimulate and support broader economic diversification by strengthening downstream production capabilities and expanding the proportion of value-added exports, as well as diversifying into new industries on the back of ongoing performance in the hydrocarbon sector.

CONSUMER PRICE INDEX BY MAJOR GROUPS (2000=100)

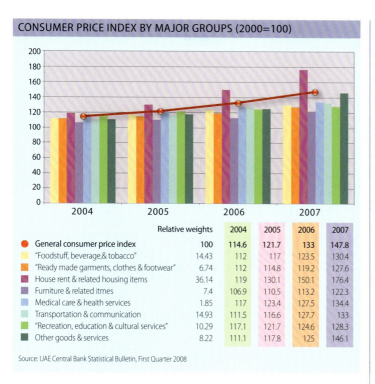

	Relative weights	2004	2005	2006	2007
● General consumer price index	100	114.6	121.7	133	147.8
"Foodstuff, beverage,& tobacco"	14.43	112	117	123.5	130.4
"Ready made garments, clothes & footwear"	6.74	112	114.8	119.2	127.6
House rent & related housing items	36.14	119	130.1	150.1	176.4
Furniture & related itmes	7.4	106.9	110.5	113.2	122.3
Medical care & health services	1.85	117	123.4	127.5	134.4
Transportation & communication	14.93	111.5	116.6	127.7	133
"Recreation, education & cultural services"	10.29	117.1	121.7	124.6	128.3
Other goods & services	8.22	111.1	117.8	125	146.1

Source: UAE Central Bank Statistical Bulletin, First Quarter 2008

Dubai's Strategic Plan

In contrast to Abu Dhabi's strategic plan, that of Dubai downplays the importance of oil revenues. In fact, HH Sheikh Mohammed bin Rashid stated in his introductory remarks: 'Oil's contribution to GDP is a mere three per cent today. Our economic development is now supported by an infrastructure that is not directly affected by oil'. Looking forward to 2015, the plan, based on expected future global trends, has as its objective the sustaining of real economic growth at a rate of 11 per cent per annum to reach a GDP of US$108 billion in 2015, and to increase GDP per capita to US$44,000. In order to achieve this, Dubai will focus on economic sectors where it holds a strong competitive advantage and ones that are expected to grow globally. The emirate's key strengths are tourism, transport, trade, construction and financial services. At the same time, according to Sheikh Mohammed, growth enablers must not be ignored and he

Dubai is focusing on economic sectors where it holds a strong competitive advantage and ones that are expected to grow globally.

www.uaeinteract.com/economicdevelopment

highlighted human capital, productivity, innovation, cost of doing business and living, quality of life, policy and institutional frameworks, and laws and regulations.

GLOBAL COMPETITIVE INDEX

The United Arab Emirates has consolidated its position as one of the most competitive economies in the region, moving up by six positions to thirty-first place in the Global Competitiveness Report 2008–2009, released by the World Economic Forum.

Overall, the country improved its ranking across all pillars of the Growth Competitiveness Index (GCI), experiencing a more stable macroeconomic environment and a better assessment of the quality of the educational system.

The country's institutional environment provides competitive advantage, characterised by a low regulatory burden (fifth), high public trust in politicians (eighth), and reliable police services, positioning the country at seventy-ninth in the global index. In addition, the use and penetration of ICT and other advanced technologies are widespread and are increasingly catching up with the rest of the world, allowing the country to move up in the rankings to twenty-eight position in this area.

INFLATION

The Nielsen Global Consumer Confidence survey showed that out of 52 countries surveyed, UAE consumers ranked the third most optimistic as regards their local job prospects and the state of their personal finances.

Dubai was the thirty-fourth most expensive city in the world in 2007, but this rating was adjusted in July 2008 to the fifty-second most expensive city, just ahead of Perth in Australia. The survey of all the world's major cities by Mercer Consulting takes into consideration monetary value, consumer confidence, investment, interest rates, exchange rates of the country's currency, and housing costs. Abu Dhabi, meanwhile, was rated sixty-fifth in March 2008, a significant improvement on its previous rating of forty-fifth most expensive country in 2007. These rankings are worth comparing with the situation in 2006 when Dubai was rated as the thirtieth most expensive city in the world, ahead of Barcelona, Berlin, Singapore, Lisbon, Istanbul, Mexico, Auckland, Athens, Moscow, Rio de Janeiro and Manama, among many others. Mercer issued a report in July 2008 stating that Dubai had the third highest quality of living standards in the Middle East and Africa, whilst Abu Dhabi is the best city in this region for personal safety, followed by Dubai. The Government's

BANK CREDIT (GROSS) TO RESIDENTS BY ECONOMIC ACTIVITY

Economic sector	millions AEDs	
	2006	2007
🟥 Agriculture	1,403	1,664
🟨 Mining & industry	30,072	42,108
🟨 Electricity & water	11,091	12,536
🟩 Construction	54,344	68,417
🟩 Trade	92,637	106,191
🟦 Transportation, storage & communication	19,416	21,987
🟦 Other financial institutions	18,594	36,941
🟦 Government	47,885	58,402
🟪 Others	198,719	299,236
Total	474,161	647,482

Source: UAE Central Bank Annual Report

measures to curb inflation have thus borne some fruit but the problem has not gone away.

UAE citizens spend on average the equivalent of US$27 per day, reported to be one of the highest daily per capita consumer spending rates in the world in 2008. This high consumer spending, accounting for almost half of the UAE's GDP, has been fuelled in part by the ease of obtaining credit from banks. The Abu Dhabi Department of Planning and Economy, concerned about social and economic impacts of this situation, called for 'stringent measures to limit the ceiling of personal loans'.

The prime driving force of the inflationary pressure in the UAE continues to be rental costs, which recorded a 17.5 per cent increase, closely followed by 'Other Goods and Services' at 16.8 per cent. The increase in average prices of other expenditure groups ranged from 3 to 8 per cent. Not only did house rentals and related costs register the highest rate of increase but they also represent the most important element in the basket of living costs, at 36 per cent.

The official inflation rate is calculated by measuring the percentage change in prices of a representative basket of goods and services consumed by the average household throughout the UAE. In 2007 the rate was calculated at 11.1 per cent: a figure that is considered relatively high in global economies. This is a matter of key concern to the Government, which has taken a number of measures to control

> UAE citizens spend on average the equivalent of US$27 per day, reported to be one of the highest daily per capita consumer spending rates in the world.

www.uaeinteract.com/economicdevelopment

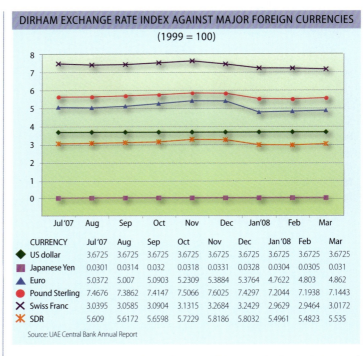

DIRHAM EXCHANGE RATE INDEX AGAINST MAJOR FOREIGN CURRENCIES
(1999 = 100)

CURRENCY	Jul '07	Aug	Sep	Oct	Nov	Dec	Jan '08	Feb	Mar
◆ US dollar	3.6725	3.6725	3.6725	3.6725	3.6725	3.6725	3.6725	3.6725	3.6725
■ Japanese Yen	0.0301	0.0314	0.032	0.0318	0.0331	0.0328	0.0304	0.0305	0.031
▲ Euro	5.0372	5.007	5.0903	5.2309	5.3884	5.3764	4.7622	4.803	4.862
● Pound Sterling	7.4676	7.3862	7.4147	7.5066	7.6025	7.4297	7.2044	7.1938	7.1443
✕ Swiss Franc	3.0395	3.0585	3.0904	3.1315	3.2684	3.2429	2.9629	2.9464	3.0172
✳ SDR	5.609	5.6172	5.6598	5.7229	5.8186	5.8032	5.4961	5.4823	5.535

Source: UAE Central Bank Annual Report

Throughout 2007 and early 2008 the rate of inflation was influenced by a disadvantageous dirham-dollar rate. However, a long-awaited reversal in the US dollar's international valuation brought some relief to the inflationary cycle in the second half of the year

the rising cost of living. Throughout 2007 and early 2008 the rate of inflation was influenced by a disadvantageous dirham-dollar rate since the latter fell against the currencies that account for the major portion of UAE imports, making those goods more expensive in terms of the national currency.

Whilst the dollar's value was beyond the control of the UAE authorities, some effective measures were introduced to dampen inflation. These included capping annual increases on existing rental agreements at 5 per cent (in 2008) and controlling prices of certain basic commodities. In terms of the construction industry, which reported very steep cost increases in 2007 and early 2008, the Government supported increased cement production and exempted both cement and steel from import duties.

However, these efforts only partially solved the situation and living costs continued to rise. The construction industry faced the biggest cost-control challenges with steel and concrete both showing large price hikes in the first half of 2008. A report by the Abu Dhabi

Department of Planning and Economy, issued in August 2008, stated that steel prices in the emirate leapt by 91 per cent from 1 January to the end of June 2008, while those of cement rose 46 per cent. Abu Dhabi's very substantial development programme, with projects worth at least US$54 billion under way in mid-2008, added to the pressure on essential building supplies. Despite its own expanding steel production, Abu Dhabi was still importing at least 60 per cent of its requirements during 2008.

A long awaited reversal in the US dollar's international valuation did however bring real relief to the inflationary cycle in the UAE. By mid-2008 it was clear that the dollar had been strengthening against other major currencies and the Governor of the Central Bank reaffirmed that there was no change in the region's exchange rate policy. 'We are firm on the peg, there's no revaluation . . . We see that inflation is causing the United States to raise interest rates in the near future and that is going to take the dollar up. So why do anything opposite to what is good for us?', he stated.

Accurate data on UAE inflation rates was a prime target of UAE regulatory bodies since certain media reports quoting inflationary figures for the UAE were based on inadequate studies. This led to a degree of confusion regarding actual inflation rates. In early September 2008, the Abu Dhabi Department of Planning and Economy (DPE) stated that it was working on a new index to cover the whole UAE. The revised methodology used to calculate the CPI

The Aquarium and Discovery Centre in The Dubai Mall, which opened its doors on 4 November, has clinched the Guinness World Record for the 'World's Largest Acrylic Panel'.

By mid-2008 it was clear that the dollar had been strengthening against other major currencies and the Governor of the Central Bank reaffirmed that revaluation was not imminent.

figure, based on the results of a recent survey on household income and expenditure, will provide a more accurate basis for inflation calculations. Previously the 'consumer basket' comprised 500 items of goods and services whereas the aim of the revised system was to produce a unified basket for the whole of the UAE that includes more than 1100 goods and services, divided into major categories. Instead of the eight categories used in the past, the improved method, in accordance with the Classification of Individual Consumption by Purpose (COICOP), recognises twelve groups.

The IMF regional report issued in late October 2008 suggested that the UAE's inflation rate for 2008 would reach 12.9 per cent, a 16 per cent increase on the 2007 figure of 11.1 per cent.

DIVERSIFICATION

Economic diversification has been a key plank of UAE Government policy since the founding of the state in 1971.

Diversification of the economy has been a key plank of UAE policy ever since the founding of the state in 1971. Funded from oil and gas sales, new investments were made initially in hydrocarbon and energy-related industries such as aluminium and petrochemicals. However, times are changing and dependence on oil and gas has fallen significantly. As previously mentioned, Dubai's vibrant economy only receives a 3 per cent input from oil and gas. Its main businesses are in tourism, transport, trade, construction and financial services.

Meanwhile, as mentioned above, Abu Dhabi, with over 90 per cent of the UAE's oil reserves, set forth its own plans for creating a more diversified economy, both in its Policy Agenda 2007–2008 and in its Strategic Plan 2008–2012. These two documents refer to diversifying into 'a raft of new areas.' In addition to exporting raw materials in the form of oil and gas, Abu Dhabi is adding further value to these by increasing production of refined and semi-refined products.

On the broader economic front, the strategy document states that: 'it is important to stress that the Abu Dhabi government's strategy of economic diversification is not misunderstood as simply 'moving away from oil and gas'. On the contrary, the continued significance of hydrocarbons to the economy is the means by which a broader diversification will be achieved and supported, and not the reason it is necessary.' It is the Abu Dhabi government's stated intention to further develop its energy sector both in terms of productivity and efficiency.

Another area of economic growth that Abu Dhabi is fostering is tourism. The emirate has recently re-branded itself and has made a

The continued significance of hydrocarbons to the economy is the means by which a broader diversification will be achieved and supported.

series of strong moves to boost its tourism development. Tourism has already proved to be an important driver of Dubai's economy. The UAE is expecting to attract 11.2 million tourists by 2010, underlining its successful efforts to boost investment in the development of the hotel and hospitality industry throughout the country.

Manufacturing continues to be an essential component of economic development in the UAE. The latest technologies and state-of-the-art facilities are now a feature of the UAE's manufacturing base, which includes, among other sectors, food and beverages; chemicals, metals and minerals; cement and blocks; ceramics; textiles and clothing; pharmaceuticals; gold and jewellery. The UAE has pumped nearly Dh29 billion into manufacturing projects over the past four years in support of more than 1000 projects. National investors controlled nearly 85 per cent of the cumulative industrial capital of around Dh72 billion at the end of 2007. Excluding the oil sector, the manufacturing industries sector contribution to nominal GDP touched 20.2 per cent in 2007. But it is the services sector that now plays the major role in terms of its GDP contribution at 61.4 per cent in 2007.

> A strong focus on transport in terms of ports and airports, shipping companies and airlines, together with efficient road networks, has underpinned a strategic plan aimed at establishing the UAE as a major transport hub between Europe and South-East Asia.

A strong focus on transport in terms of ports and airports, shipping companies and airlines, together with efficient road networks, has underpinned a strategic plan aimed at creating a major transport hub between Europe and south-east Asia.

The financial sector also played a valuable role in boosting the UAE economy in 2007 when banks continued to benefit from profits associated with financing applications for oversubscribed IPOs. Islamic banking has also blossomed in the UAE, while the insurance sector has shown robust growth. Projects like Dubai International Financial Centre and the country's stock exchanges in Abu Dhabi and Dubai have provided a framework for growth in the financial sub-sector.

THE 'E' WORD

The 'Internet Age', embracing electronic communications, digital data storage and wireless networks offers huge opportunities for both governments and corporations in terms of enabling administrative and commercial procedures. The UAE has been quick to recognise the opportunity and has embraced the 'E' word in almost every area of its activities. In so doing it has earned both national and international recognition for the professionalism of its approach to establishing both E-government and E-commerce.

The United Nations Department of Economic and Social Affairs' eGovernment Survey ranked the UAE in fifth position in terms of transactional services, just behind developed countries such as Sweden, Denmark, Norway and the US. The survey also placed the UAE in thirty-second position among 192 United Nations member states in the 2008 eGovernment Readiness Index.

The United Arab Emirates also received two awards at the thirteenth Middle East eGovernment and eServices Excellence Awards. Organised by the Middle East Excellence Awards Institute, the 'eService Provider Organisation of the Year' award went to Abu Dhabi's Department of Planning and Economy, while the Dubai Police were winners of the 'Information and Knowledge Portal of the Year' award.

The creation of an 'eCouncil', a digital electronic system to support the members of the Abu Dhabi Executive Council and employees of the General Secretariat, was announced in 2008. It provides such time-saving facilities as electronic agendas, click access to resolutions and instant updating or signing of online documents along with an intranet. Meanwhile, the Abu Dhabi Systems and Information Committee (ADSIC) has been engaged with enhancing electronic communications between local government bodies and the federal government. In mid-2008 ADSIC was leading more than 75 e-government projects including the Abu Dhabi Government Network, the Abu Dhabi Portal (www.abudhabi.ae), and the Government Data Centre.

Electronic services provided by the portal include paying of traffic fines, obtaining IDs for residents, applying for residency cancellation, obtaining a fishing licence, accessing information about vacant properties and their locations, and filing a complaint about hospital services in Abu Dhabi. In addition, the Abu Dhabi Business Gateway, also part of the government portal, provides useful information to businesses and simplifies their access to, and interaction with government agencies and services.

Dubai has been a leader in E-government and E-commerce since the advent of the internet, with pioneering projects such as Tejari having earned top recognition for their professionalism and excellence.

One of the more recent additions to the emirate's E-status is its integrated electronic payment system (E-pay), which was expected to record revenues of Dh1 billion by the end of 2008. E-pay acts as a payment gateway between Dubai residents and the government. Revenues collected go directly to various government departments without any physical interaction.

A UN eGovernment survey ranked the UAE in fifth position, just behind developed countries such as Sweden.

www.uaeinteract.com/economicdevelopment

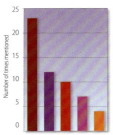

Top 5 financial centres that might become significant

■ Dubai	23
■ Shanghai	12
■ Singapore	10
■ Malta	7
■ Beijing	4

Source: The Global Financial Centres Index

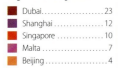

Top 5 financial centres where organisations may open new operations in the next two or three years.

■ Dubai	22
■ Luxembourg	11
■ Singapore	9
■ Mumbai	6
■ Malta	5

Source: The Global Financial Centres Index

Beginning in 2003 with 205 transactions amounting to Dh120,000 (US$32,697), the number of transactions had reached 555,562 by the end of August 2008, amounting to more than Dh602 million (US$164 million). By the end of 2007 such non-conventional channels provided residents with quick access to 91 per cent of Dubai government services.

FINANCIAL SECTOR

FINANCIAL MARKETS

Despite the turmoil that gripped world stock markets in 2008, the UAE's financial markets have played an important role in the UAE's economic growth. There is also growing evidence that the UAE is rapidly climbing up the global ladder of financial centres. London's Global Financial Centres Index (GFCI) for March 2008 ranked Dubai twenty-fourth, ahead of cities like Shanghai, Stockholm, Brussels, Mumbai and Madrid. Outside Europe and North America, Dubai was ranked fifth in the world and as a destination where businesses are thinking of opening in the next few years, Dubai ranked in first place in the overall GFCI Index.

ADX (FORMERLY ADSM)

Abu Dhabi Securities Market (ADSM) continued its impressive growth in 2007 with trading volume expanding by 148 per cent; traded shares in the exchange's 64 listed companies growing by 360.9 per cent and executed deals by 54.1 per cent over 2006 levels. Share prices of 53 companies advanced, eight declined and three remained unchanged. Market capitalisation of listed companies reached Dh445.14 billion and the general share price index rose by 34 per cent to reach 4,551.80 on 31 December 2007. The lion's share of the equity market was dominated (in terms of the traded shares) by real estate, at 36.4 per cent. Banking and financial services accounted for almost exactly a quarter of the total value of traded shares; followed by construction (14.8 per cent), energy (14.7 per cent) and telecommunications (4.8 per cent).

In May 2008 the Abu Dhabi Securities Exchange (ADX) was adopted as the new name for ADSM. The renaming and accompanying

re-branding reflected the increasing diversity and sophistication of the types of securities to be traded on the exchange. A new corporate logo, featuring the abbreviation ADX in blue and grey, accompanied the name change. The ADX announced plans to add exchange-traded funds and foreign listings to its existing offering of share trading in publicly listed companies.

Soon after the name change ADX announced its new strategic plan for 2008–2012, under the slogan 'Excellence among Regional Stock Markets'. The new plan emphasised ADX's commitment to transparency and high standards of governance, and promised to involve the community with the market's effort to develop and improve. One of the plan's key objectives is to encourage more institutional participation in the ADX market, making it a preferred destination for international investment.

Following the impressive growth of 2007, there was another giant leap in terms of the growth of ADX in the first half of 2008 when the value of traded securities trebled compared to the first half of 2007. From 1 January to 30 June 2008, Dh163 billion (US$44 billion) worth of shares were traded compared to Dh51 billion (US$14 billion) in the same period of 2007. The number of shares traded and the number of individual trades also increased dramatically, by 93 per cent and 60 per cent respectively.

Investors at DFM follow stock market activity as global equities tumbled.

The ADX index was up by 9 per cent in the first half of 2008, reflecting the quality of companies trading through the exchange. Meanwhile, the exchange was actively encouraging foreign investors into the market as well as UAE citizens, since a broader and more international investor base is important for long-term sustainability. After UAE citizens, UK investors were the most active in trading on ADX. In fact, by mid-2008, UK investors owned Dh18.2 billion (US$5 billion) worth of ADX traded shares – an increase of Dh15 billion (US$4.1 billion) in the first half of 2008. Among ADX priorities are plans to develop the debt market, list Exchange Traded Funds (ETFs) on ADX, and develop a derivatives market.

The financial crisis that hit world markets in the autumn of 2008 severely impacted UAE stock markets. In the case of the Abu Dhabi market, by late December 2008, the Abu Dhabi index had fallen by 49.9 per cent from the year's opening figure and the volatility was continuing.

Dubai Financial Market (DFM)

DFM also grew in 2007 with value of traded shares reaching Dh379 billion, an increase of Dh31.44 billion over 2006 figures. Over 100 billion (105.26 billion) shares in 58 listed companies were traded during the year, a massive increase of 265 per cent compared to the 2006 figure. The number of transactions actually fell however, reaching 2.25 million compared with 2.42 million the previous year. Twelve new companies were added to the DFM list during the year and their market capitalisation reached Dh499.72 billion (US$136.16 billion), an increase of 60.5 per cent over the 2006 figure. Once again the lion's share of the market was taken up by real estate and construction, at 38.3 per cent, and other major sectors were investment and financial services (21.7 per cent), banking (17 per cent) and transportation (14.6 per cent).

As of the end of December 2008, DFM had recorded a fall of 73 per cent from the beginning of the year.

Dubai International Financial Centre (DIFC)

DIFC is an onshore hub for global finance, bridging the time zone disparity between the financial centres of Hong Kong and London. It also services a region with the largest untapped emerging market for financial services. Possibly the fastest-growing financial centre in the world, the DIFC is home to over 600 companies that include the

British Prime Minister Gordon Brown and Director General of DIFC Omar bin Suleiman in front of the main gate of the DIFC.

Stock markets in the UAE were not immune to the financial turmoil experienced around the world in the second half of 2008.

world's leading financial services companies and banks. Over the last four years, DIFC has emerged as a gateway to the growing financial market in the Middle East region and a key player in the global financial industry. The DIFC offers its member institutions incentives such as 100 per cent foreign ownership, zero tax on income and profits and no restrictions on foreign exchange.

Corporate governance along with transparency are cornerstones of confidence building in equity markets and the UAE has continued to raise standards on these issues, helping to underpin growth in their stock markets. Central to all business agreements is an effective means to settle disagreements. In early September 2008 DIFC announced its plans to offer state-of-the art facilities for arbitration. Working under a new Arbitration Law, the DIFC-LCIA Arbitration Centre provides neutral, efficient and reliable dispute resolution services to companies worldwide and enables DIFC to position itself as a world-class centre for arbitration.

Cognisant of the fact that the vast majority of regional companies in the UAE and the surrounding region are owned by single family groups, DIFC announced in September 2008 a new programme to enable such groups, known as SFOs (Single Family Offices) to establish holding companies at DIFC in order to assist them with managing private family wealth. The DIFC Single Family Office (SFO) regulations specifically address the needs of family-run institutions. In contrast to conventional financial institutions, SFOs have no direct public liability as all their shareholders are bloodline descendants of a common ancestor. As such, their regulatory requirements differ significantly. The enactment of the regulations followed a period of consultation where companies were invited to comment on the proposed regulations. The new regulations came into effect on 2 September 2008.

The UAE has continued to raise standards of corporate governance and transparency, thereby helping to underpin confidence in equity markets.

NASDAQ Dubai

NASDAQ Dubai (formerly called Dubai International Financial Exchange or DIFX) is the international stock exchange between Western Europe and East Asia (see www.nasdaqdubai.com). In late November 2007, DP World, the international ports operator, selected DIFX to launch the Middle East's largest initial public offering (IPO) valued at US$4.96 billion. It was also the first IPO to be listed exclusively on the DIFX and its offering to a wide range of institutional and retail investors was oversubscribed more than 15 times.

DEPOSITS ACCORDING TO OWNERSHIP

Sectors	millions AEDs	
	2006	2007
Total deposits	518,806	716,021
A) Residents' deposits	469,322	651,338
Government	93,680	114,579
Public sector*	38,142	36,196
Private sector*	176,046	272,241
Individuals	142,321	202,780
Others	19,133	25,542
Non-residents' deposits	49,484	64,683

Source: UAE Central Bank Annual Report

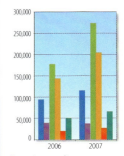
Deposits according to ownership.

DEPOSITS ACCORDING TO TYPE & CURRENCY

Items	millions AEDs	
	2006	2007
A) Type:		
Current deposits	123,886	188,859
Savings deposits	22,170	30,234
Time deposits	272,367	371,865
Total	418,423	590,958
B) Currency:		
Deposits in local currency	282,166	454,229
Deposits in foreign currency	136,257	136,729
Total	418,423	590,958

Source: UAE Central Bank Annual Report

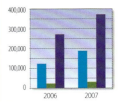
Deposits according to type.

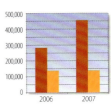
Deposits according to currency.

The chairman of Borse Dubai, the holding company for the Dubai NASDAQ, commented at the time: 'This step is in line with Borse Dubai's strategy to attract leading local companies, which will act as a catalyst to attract further substantial equity listings from regional and international companies.'

NASDAQ Dubai recently announced plans to establish a derivatives trading market that will offer investors the option to trade on individual stocks or derivative stocks representing the whole index,

www.uaeinteract.com/economicdevelopment

as well as future contracts. The initial derivatives were to be futures and options on equities listed on GCC stock markets, as well as futures and options on selected equity indices.

BANKING

The UAE banking and finance sector enjoyed an extremely active year in 2007 with the aggregated balance sheet of banks operating in the UAE increasing by 42.3 per cent to reach Dh1223.07 billion against Dh859.57 billion at the end of 2006. Cash and deposits with the Central Bank increased by 273.5 per cent to reach Dh236.85 billion. Net foreign assets of banks reversed during the year, with a 15.1 per cent decrease in assets and an 80.6 per cent increase in liabilities resulting in a negative figure of Dh124.04 billion.

As already noted above, credit issued to residents increased quite sharply, by 36.6 per cent, mainly in the form of loans, advances and overdrafts. Credit issued to all other sectors also increased: the trade sector by 21.6 per cent, the construction sector by 25.09 per cent, the government sector by 22 per cent, mining and industry sector by 40 per cent, to other financial institutions by 98.7 per cent, transportation, storage and communications by 13.2 per cent, agriculture by 18.6 per cent, and water and electricity by 13 per cent. Finally, credit to other sectors increased by 50.6 per cent.

The total value of deposits with banks operating in the UAE at the end of 2007 amounted to Dh716.02 billion or 38 per cent more than

The UAE banking sector enjoyed an extremely active year in 2007 with the aggregated balance sheet of banks operating in the UAE increasing by 42.3 per cent. However, by August 2008 it was clear that UAE banks that had experienced strong profit growth in recent years would be affected by signs of cooling in the property sector.

at the end of 2006. The rise was mainly due to sharp increases in deposits by both residents and non-residents. Meanwhile, private sector deposits from business, industries and financial institutions increased by 54.6 per cent. Excluding government deposits and commercial prepayments, bank deposits increased in all categories: current account deposits by 52.4 per cent; time deposits by 36.5 per cent and savings deposits by 36.4 per cent.

The capital position at the end of 2007 indicated that the total of capital and reserves accounts at these banks reached Dh130.88 billion, an increase of 25.7 per cent compared to the position at the end of 2006. As a result the position of capital and reserves to total assets reached 10.7 per cent. Meanwhile, unclassified liabilities fell by just over 41 per cent.

The first half of 2008 saw a continued growth and strong profitability of many UAE banks. In fact, net profits of UAE banks were up by nearly 40 per cent. This was due to a surge in credits and investments resulting in net earnings of the country's 24 national banks and 28 foreign units reaching Dh16 billion in the first six months of 2008 compared with Dh11.4 billion in the first half of 2007.

But the UAE's banking sector is not immune from global forces or from the general downturn in the financial sector that was triggered by the sub-prime mortgage crisis in the US and the subsequent downturn in property values. Investor sentiment, influenced by the recessionary trends that began to hit western economies in 2008, fed through to UAE investors and affected many local companies despite their strong fundamentals. This, in turn, fed through to the banking sector, resulting in a lowering of expectations for regional banks performances during 2008.

By August 2008 it was clear that UAE banks that had experienced strong profit growth in recent years would be affected by signs of cooling in the property sector. Strong loan growth, due largely to the increased spending on public and private infrastructure and construction projects, and the boost they have given to the property market, left some banks potentially vulnerable to any reversal of these trends. Concerned that banks could find themselves in dangerous territory, the Central Bank enforced regulations limiting the amount that banks can lend against their deposits. It was hoped that this would ease inflation and prevent banks from overexposure to the property market. At the same time, a tightening of available credit avenues in

LIQUIDITY MEASURES

22/09/08
UAE sets up Dh50 billion emergency facility for banks operating in the UAE.

08/10/08
Central Bank lowers its repo rate to 1.5% from 2.0%.

12/10/08
UAE guarantees deposits of local banks and foreign banks with core operations in UAE

14/10/08
UAE announces it will inject Dh70 billion into banking system as long term deposits

www.uaeinteract.com/economicdevelopment

CENTRAL BANK STATEMENT

In early October 2008 the Governor of the UAE Central Bank H.E. Sultan bin Nasser Al Suwaidi visited Washington DC to attend the IMF/WB Annual Meetings. A considerable amount of time at the meetings was dedicated to discuss the liquidity crisis and the financial markets turmoil especially in the advanced industrial countries. The discussion included analysis of reasons that led to these crises and solutions or what is called policy response, i.e. changes in monetary policies and those relating to capital markets.

In late November, Islamic mortgage lenders Amlak Finance and Tamweel, both of which were struggling due to a downturn in the Dubai property market, were merged under the Abu Dhabi-based Real Estate Bank. The UAE's Ministerial Council for Services also approved the merger of the Real Estate Bank and the Emirates Industrial Bank to form the Emirates Development Bank.

The Central Bank took advantage of the occasion, on 11 October 2008, to comment on the status of UAE Banks:

. . . national banks and foreign banks enjoy a strong financial position, as the ownership of deposits are distributed as follows:

– Nationals 75 per cent

– Arab 8 per cent

– Other nationalities 17 per cent

and the ownership of nationals and Arabs of deposits at national banks is higher. Also banks financing from the European Commercial Paper issues (ECP) and Medium-Term Notes (MTN) to the total bank assets is 9.9 per cent only.

As for the inter-bank deposits percentage, it is 12.7 per cent to the total assets and most of these are owned by banks in the UAE.

For the assets side, the majority of assets of national and foreign banks operating in the UAE are in the UAE and their parties are known and sound, contrary to what is there in other economies where most parties in these countries are unknown.

And for capital of banks and their reserves, they represent 11.02 per cent of bank assets, which is considered high according to Basel II standards.

Thus, national banks and branches of foreign banks operating in the UAE are constructed on safe and sound foundations of 77.4 per cent of secure financing recourses.

The Central Bank also pointed out that local governments in the UAE already had substantial shareholdings in local banks so the situation that had arisen in countries where such shareholdings formed part of a rescue package did not occur in the UAE.

international markets, linked to the global slowdown, made borrowing more difficult for local banks. Meanwhile, the Dubai government issued new regulations requiring property buyers to have paid at least 30 per cent of the price of a property before they can sell it.

In September and October 2008 the Ministry of Finance set the terms for two tranches of emergency funding of up to Dh120 billion that was made available to local banks to enable them to tide over the inter-bank liquidity squeeze, but warned them not to use the cash being made available for speculative activity. The Government funding was provided on the basis of interest payable every three months calculated on the prevailing interest rate for five-year US Treasury bonds, plus 120 basis points or 4 per cent, whichever is higher.

The move was targeted at underpinning the stability of the UAE's financial model and banks were required to use the money to participate in the inter-bank loan market and ensure credit facilities were available to small and medium enterprises at reasonable cost. Banks were also told to invest in their risk management practices to ensure they meet the requirements of the Central Bank.

On 13 October 2008 the UAE Cabinet made a momentous decision to guarantee banking deposits held in the UAE for three years. The decision covered national banks and foreign banks that 'have significant operations in the UAE'. Despite such measures, the global financial roller-coaster placed considerable pressures on UAE markets.

In December 2008, the UAE Central Bank set up a task force, the Financial Stability Unit, to 'keep an eye' on potential threats to the UAE's financial system. Proposals on the table include the introduction of 'financial vehicles' to underpin real estate loans.

FOREIGN INVESTMENT

OUTWARD INVESTMENT

Overseas investments have been a critical component of the UAE's economic development strategy for decades as the country has consistently made an effort to diversify where and how it invests its financial assets. The UAE Government regards such investment as a security net for future generations who will one day face a depletion of the country's energy resources. During the period of review (2007–2008) there was intense discussion amid global financial and political circles regarding the impact of SWFs or sovereign wealth funds. Readers of this *Yearbook* may already be familiar with the difficulties that followed Dubai Ports Authority's purchase of P&O

Line, leading to it being pressured to sell the US ports management division that formed part of the original deal. This, along with other major international investments by SWFs, led to a series of meetings aimed at calming political nerves and strengthening economic bonds between SWF investors and the countries where they invest.

But, despite the alarmist views of some reactionary commentators, SWFs play a very valuable role in maintaining stability in world markets. Their strategic investments, creating modest and passive holdings that tend to be held for significant periods, contrast sharply with many of the disruptive and exploitative computer trading mechanisms that have helped to create turmoil in world markets.

Abu Dhabi alone has at least eight such SWFs and is a major investor on the international stage with several investments attracting international attention. In response to re-emerging concerns about SWFs, in the USA in particular, the director of international affairs in the Diwan of the Abu Dhabi Crown Prince, Yousef Al Otaiba, subsequently appointed as UAE Ambassador to the United States, wrote an open letter to the US treasury secretary and other Western financial officials, in which he stated: 'It is important to be absolutely clear that the Abu Dhabi Government has never and will never use its investment organisations or individual investments as a foreign policy tool.'

The debate that followed led to establishment of a working group at the IMF in order to create a set of voluntary principles for sovereign wealth funds. In late April 2008, representatives of ADIA and 24 other SWFs met at the International Monetary Fund (IMF) headquarters in Washington, D.C. and formally established an International Working Group (IWG), co-chaired by senior representatives from ADIA and the IMF. The objective of the IWG was to arrive at a common set of voluntary principles for SWFs that properly reflects their investment practices and objectives.

The Abu Dhabi Fund for Development (ADFD)

The oldest of Abu Dhabi's government funds was launched in 1971 and manages approximately Dh4 billion in assets. ADFD is essentially part of Abu Dhabi's international aid programme and is covered in more detail within the Foreign Affairs section of this book. It gives grants and loans to small projects in developing countries that promote poverty reduction, social equality or sustainable growth. It also makes direct equity investments and has so far invested in 52 countries in Africa, the Middle East, central and south Asia.

Abu Dhabi Investment Authority (ADIA)

ADIA's mission is to secure and maintain the current and future prosperity of the Emirate of Abu Dhabi through prudent management of the emirate's investment assets. Established in 1976, ADIA is a premier global institutional investor, and for the past 32 years the institution has built a strong reputation across global financial markets as a trusted and responsible investor and a leading provider of capital.

Over 1100 people and 40 different nationalities work in ADIA's head office on Abu Dhabi's Corniche. ADIA manages a substantial global diversified portfolio of holdings across different sectors, regions and asset classes, including public listed equities, fixed income, real estate, and private equity. With a long tradition of prudent investing, ADIA's decisions are based on its economic objectives of delivering sustained long-term financial returns and it does not seek active management of the companies it invests in.

ADIA has been active for many years. Included among its more prominent early investments were a 9 per cent stake in Reuters in 1984 and a 5 per cent stake in the French oil company Total in 1987. In 2008, ADIA made an investment in Citigroup.

Established in 1976, ADIA's mission as a premier global institutional investor is to secure and maintain the current and future prosperity of the Emirate of Abu Dhabi.

Abu Dhabi Investment Company (ADIC)

ADIC is one of the leading financial services firms in the region. Established in 1977, ADIC is involved with providing treasury services, loan syndication, equity and debt underwriting, financial advice, asset management and brokerage across a range of asset classes, industries and regions.

ADIC leverages its investment expertise across four strategic areas: asset management, private equity, infrastructure and real estate. It offers targeted products and services designed to meet specific client requirements. In 2007 ADIC celebrated its thirtieth anniversary and was issued with a new mandate, i.e. to use its decades of experience, knowledge and relationships to move from primarily proprietary investing to primarily managing third-party investments. One of its first moves in this area was launch of its first multi-strategy hedge fund. In 2008 it created a joint venture with UBS to create funds investing in infrastructure in the Middle East and North Africa.

International Petroleum Investment Company (IPIC)

The UAE is a country with a hard-earned experience of finding, developing, marketing and transporting oil and gas. It is taking this experience to overseas locations where a combination of investment and expertise has helped to bring added value to existing natural resource projects. It is a long-term strategy that has worked well in the past and in which the main proponents have reasserted their belief for future activities.

IPIC, which was established in 1984, is wholly owned by the Abu Dhabi government. The company is run by an independent board of directors, whose Chairman is HH Sheikh Mansour bin Zayed Al Nahyan. IPIC has been established to invest in the hydrocarbons and related sectors outside of Abu Dhabi. This broad investment mandate includes the crude oil downstream sector, petrochemicals, oil, product and gas pipelines, the oil services sector, the hydrocarbons shipping sector, the hydrocarbon-based power sector, and other hydrocarbon-intensive process industries, including nitrogenous fertilisers and aluminium smelting.

IPIC's 80 employees oversee a substantial and diversified portfolio of petroleum assets that includes exploration and production rights in 11 countries and an estimated US$1.35 billion from the downstream sector, including six refineries. IPIC does not participate in the day-to-

The UAE is taking its hard-earned experience of finding, developing, marketing and transporting oil and gas to overseas locations where a combination of investment and expertise has helped to bring added value to existing natural resource projects.

day management of companies it invests in, except in exceptional circumstances. Though it has 65 to 70 per cent controlling shares in its largest investments (Borealis OMV and Hyundai Oilbank), it typically targets a significant minority equity participation level of 25 to 40 per cent, accompanied by appropriate minority shareholder protections. Meanwhile, one of its longest standing investments is its 9.5 per cent shareholding in Spain's Cepsa.

Buoyed by a 28 per cent surge in its net earnings in 2007, IPIC stepped up its investment drive with plans to set up multi-billion dollar refineries and other projects. They include the construction of a major refinery in Fujairah and two refineries in Morocco and Pakistan. The company was expected to invest between Dh22 billion and Dh37 billion in the Fujairah refinery

One of its strategic investments has been the Abu Dhabi crude oil pipeline (ADCOP). When completed, this will pipe crude from Abu Dhabi's port at Habshan across 370 kilometres of desert and mountain terrain to the east coast port of Fujairah, enabling Abu Dhabi's oil exports to bypass the Straits of Hormuz, a chokepoint of the global oil trade.

In August 2008 IPIC and Borealis signed a Memorandum of Understanding (MoU) with Uzbekistan's State Joint-Stock Company (Uzkimyosanoat) to conduct a feasibility study for the construction of a world-scale fertiliser complex in Uzbekistan. Borealis is Europe's second largest manufacturer of plastics, and IPIC owns 65 per cent of the company. Scheduled to start up in 2012, the new plant will be the largest fertiliser complex in Central Asia and will include ammonia and urea production units.

IPIC acquired a majority share in Aabar Petroleum Investments on 16 September 2008 and also created, on 10 September 2008, a US$1 billion investment fund, the Falah Fund, in conjunction with Kazakhstan.

Abu Dhabi National Energy Company (Taqa)

Taqa was founded in 2005 with the objective of becoming a global leader in the energy sector. Today, it has a workforce of 2800 drawn from 38 nationalities working in nine markets across the world, from India to Canada and Abu Dhabi to the United Kingdom.

Taqa's business is spread across the global energy sector and the company is fully integrated with operations from wellhead to wall

Taqa's net profits amounted to Dh1.6 billion in the first nine months of 2008 compared with Dh381 million in the same period in 2007.

www.uaeinteract.com/economicdevelopment

socket. It has interests in power generation, desalination, upstream oil and gas, pipelines, services and structured finance.

Taqa is incorporated as a public joint stock company, 51 per cent of which is owned by Abu Dhabi Water and Electricity Authority (Adwea) and is listed on the Abu Dhabi stock exchange with a combined total of over Dh68 billion in assets and revenues in excess of Dh8.3 billion annually. Taqa owns six businesses in the UAE that between them produce nearly 7500 MW of power and 600 million imperial gallons of desalinated water a day. The operations are spread throughout the UAE, although the majority are based in Abu Dhabi.

The company has also made substantial investments in the energy field internationally. It has invested US$200 million into the Carlyle Infrastructure Fund, bought US$550 million worth of Talisman Energy's North Sea oilfields, and paid another US$694 million for BP's Dutch exploration and production subsidiary, BP Nederland, now called Taqa Energy. Taqa also paid US$900 million for the African, Middle Eastern and South Asian assets of CMS Energy and ABB, has invested US$2 billion in Canada's Northrock Resources, owner of one of Canada's ten largest natural gas reserves, paid US$540 million for the oil driller, Pioneer Canada, and US$5 billion for the Canadian oil and gas producer, PrimeWest Energy Trust.

Mubadala Development Company

Mubadala, with headquarters in Abu Dhabi, is a public joint stock company whose sole shareholder is the Abu Dhabi government. Mubadala's focus is on developing and managing an extensive and economically diverse portfolio of commercial initiatives, operating either independently or in partnership with leading international organisations. Mubadala's commercial strategy is built on long-term, capital-intensive investments delivering strong financial returns.

The company manages a multi-billion dollar portfolio of local, regional, and international investments, projects and initiatives. Through its investment and development projects, Mubadala is both a catalyst for, and a reflection of, the Abu Dhabi's drive for economic diversification. Its impact is evident domestically and internationally in sectors such as energy, aerospace, real estate, health care, education, technology, infrastructure, and services.

With approximately US$10 billion under management, recent investments include an 8.1 per cent stake in computer chip maker,

Mubadala's focus is on developing and managing an extensive and economically diverse portfolio of commercial initiatives, operating either independently or in partnership with leading international organisations.

AMD, for US$622 million in 2007, a US$1.35 billion payment for a 7.5 per cent stake in private equity giant Carlyle Group and a commitment of US$500 million to a Carlyle investment fund.

Unlike ADIA, Mubadala may take controlling interests in companies in which it invests. In addition to its growing list of international investments, Mubadala is a strong force in local projects such as port operator, Abu Dhabi Terminals, the Abu Dhabi Future Energy Company, the company behind the clean-energy Masdar Initiative, Yahsat satellite company, and a planned resort with MGM Mirage. It also owns 51 per cent of Dolphin Energy, which pipes natural gas to Abu Dhabi from Qatar; and 50 per cent of Emirates Aluminium, which is building what is expected to become the world's largest aluminium smelter in Al Taweelah. Mubadala also became a significant oil producer in early 2008 with the purchase of the Pearl Energy subsidiary of Aabar Petroleum Investments, itself later taken over by IPIC. Pearl has extensive production and exploration interests in several South-East Asian countries.

In mid-2008 General Electric Company (GE) and Mubadala entered into a framework agreement on a global partnership encompassing a broad range of initiatives including commercial finance, clean energy research and development, aviation, industry and corporate learning. The agreement provides for shared capital commitments to new joint ventures and investment funds. The expectation was that Mubadala

In mid-2008 General Electric and Mubadala entered into a framework agreement on a global partnership encompassing a broad range of initiatives including clean energy research and development, aviation, industry and corporate learning.

www.uaeinteract.com/economicdevelopment

will become one of GE's top ten institutional investors and that investments under the cooperation arrangement will begin in Q1 2009.

Mubadala has been awarded AAA-long-term credit ratings by three global ratings agencies.

Abu Dhabi Investment Council (ADIC)

ADIC is responsible for investing part of Abu Dhabi government's surplus financial resources. The council employs a globally diversified investment strategy targeting positive capital returns to accumulate an expansive portfolio comprising highly diversified asset classes and active investment management strategies.

Abu Dhabi Retirement Pensions & Benefits Fund (ADRPBF)

ADRPBF manages funds allocated as retirement pensions and end-of-service benefits for UAE nationals employed by the Abu Dhabi government, or by any other organisation that is registered with the fund. The fund collects pension contributions from employees and employers, whilst the Abu Dhabi government also makes substantial contributions to the fund. Contributions are then managed by the fund, and converted into stable and secure investments for the future.

The Investment Corporation of Dubai

This body invests in order to create further diversification and long-term stability. It owns 60 per cent of Borse Dubai, a holding company which in turn acts as holding company for Dubai Financial Market and NASDAQ Dubai.

Dubai Holdings

Dubai Holdings is one of Dubai's major investment vehicles. It is divided into a number of subsidiaries, including Dubai International Capital and Dubai Group.

Dubai International Capital (DIC)

Established in October 2004 as the international investment arm of Dubai Holding, DIC, while focused on the private equity asset class, operates through three divisions: firstly global buy-outs specialising in secondary LBOs, primarily in Europe, but also in North America and Asia; secondly MENA investments including LBOs, funds and co-investments, infrastructure, growth and development capital; and thirdly equity investments in publicly quoted companies large class

Dubai International Capital, while focused on the private equity asset class, operates through three divisions: global buy-outs, MENA investments, and equity investments in large publicly quoted companies

companies such as HSBC Holdings Plc; EADS (Europe's largest aircraft and defence manufacturer and Airbus parent company); and Sony, in which it acquired a 3 per cent stake for US$1.5 billion.

DIC had assets under management totalling more than US$12 billion in 2008 and is aiming to double this figure by 2010. The company's key objectives are to achieve above average risk-adjusted returns on its investments in both established and developing private equity markets and to help diversify Dubai Holding's portfolio, thus acting as a catalyst for economic growth.

Dubai Group

Dubai Group is the diversified financial services company of Dubai Holdings, focusing on banking and insurance investment both regionally and globally. Dubai Group plays a pivotal role in the realisation of the Dubai Strategic Plan 2015, which is a road map to steer the emirate to the next level of development. Dubai Group was first created in 2000 under the name The Investment Office but was renamed Dubai Investment Group in 2004 and then again, in January 2007, when it was restructured and re-branded as Dubai Group.

The ever-expanding portfolio of Dubai Group currently includes a diverse collection of six companies, each of which has a specific sector and geographic area of operation as its focal point; i.e. Dubai Investment Group; Dubai Capital Group; Dubai Financial Group; Dubai Banking Group; Dubai Insurance Group and Noor Investment Group.

Through its subsidiaries and affiliates, Dubai Group has business interests in 26 countries, with 1000 branches employing 16,000 individuals and serving over four million customers around the world.

Dubai Group is the leading diversified financial services company of Dubai Holdings, focusing on banking and insurance investment both regionally and globally. Each of its six companies has a specific sector and geographic area of operation.

Dubai World

Dubai World is a prominent and active contributor to Dubai's global investment programme. As a holding company it operates in a highly diversified spectrum of industrial segments and plays a major role in the emirate's rapid economic growth. Its investments span four strategic growth areas, i.e. transport and logistics, drydocks and maritime, urban development, and investment and financial services. Its portfolio comprises some of the world's best-known companies and a number of outstanding projects. These include DP World, one of the largest marine terminal operators in the world; Drydocks World and Dubai Maritime City, designed to turn Dubai into a major

www.uaeinteract.com/economicdevelopment

shipbuilding and maritime hub; Economic Zones World (EZW), which operates several free zones around the world, including Jafza and TechnoPark in Dubai; Nakheel the property developer behind iconic projects such as The Palm Islands and The World among others; Limitless the international real estate master planner with current development projects in various parts of the world; Leisurecorp a global sports and leisure investment group that is reshaping the industry; Dubai World Africa, which oversees a portfolio of investments in the African continent; and Istithmar World, the group's investment arm that has a global footprint in finance, capital, leisure, aviation and various other business ventures.

In mid-2008 Dubai World purchased Wal-Mart-owned property developer Gazeley Ltd as part of the global expansion of its subsidiary EZW. Gazeley built Wal-Mart's distribution warehouses in Britain and China and is helping the world's biggest retailer with its expansion into India and Latin America. Meanwhile, Limitless LLC was linked to a takeover of London office developer Minerva, while Leisurecorp bought the Scottish golf resort of Turnberry. Dubai World's other recent international projects include the London Gateway Terminal, V&A Waterfront in Cape Town, South Africa and Vancouver Terminal. Istithmar World and Nakheel bought a 20 per cent stake in Cirque du Soleil, the world's leading live entertainment company and Nakheel and Cirque du Soleil announced a 15-year partnership in May 2007 to develop a permanent show on Palm Jumeirah.

Tatweer

Tatweer's portfolio comprises energy and health care, tourism and entertainment, industry, knowledge and real estate.

Launched in December 2005, Tatweer is the strategic and operational driver of a selected group of Dubai Holding entities that will develop new markets to serve the development of Dubai. Its portfolio is divided into energy and health care, tourism and entertainment, industry, knowledge and real estate. Tatweer has been a key contributor to Dubai's transformational growth, providing energy to industries, moulding ultra-luxurious enclaves from barren desert, and creating world-class facilities that enhance living standards. Market-leading entities include The Tiger Woods Dubai, DreamWorks, Dubailand, Dubai Healthcare City, Dubai Energy, Universal Studios, Bawadi, Global Village, Dubai Industrial City, Mizin, Tatweer Lammtara Joint Venture and the Dubai Mercantile Exchange (DME).

The Burj al-Arab, the first and arguably the most famous iconic building in Dubai, is a symbol of Dubai's transformation in recent years.

In August 2008 DME concluded the sale of equity stakes in the exchange to a number of leading global financial institutions and energy trading firms, including, among others, Goldman Sachs and Morgan Stanley.

Meanwhile, Dubai Industrial City (DI) launched its headquarters in July 2008, creating a one-stop customer service centre offering ten UAE government departments' transactions under one roof. The centre is the largest facility of its kind in the country.

Other International Investments

Etisalat, the Abu Dhabi-based telecommunications giant, has continued to be very active on the international front. In 2007 it invested in projects in Nigeria and Indonesia, locations with large populations and relatively low telecom penetration. Meanwhile, its Mobily network reaches 93.7 per cent of the population in the Kingdom of Saudi Arabia and Mobily had over 11 million subscribers there by the end of December 2007, a growth of over 60 per cent in comparison to 2006. In terms of revenue, Mobily grew by 44 per cent year on year, with net profit growing by 97 per cent. The company already has major investments in mobile networks in Afghanistan, Egypt, Pakistan and Singapore. Thuraya, the Etisalat majority-owned satellite telecommunications corporation also continues to invest in global expansion of its services (see section on Telecommunications).

Etisalat is now the sixteenth largest telecommunications firm in the world, and the corporation aims to be among the top ten in the world by 2010. Etisalat is also ranked at two hundred and nineteenth place in the 2008 Global 500 Financial Times list of leading companies in the world, by market capitalisation, having risen in the list from four hundred and forty-fourth place in 2007. Indeed *Global Mobile*, a newsletter published by Informa Telecoms & Media, ranked Etisalat as the fastest growing telecommunications company in the world according to proportionate subscription growth during the first quarter of 2008, based on their percentage ownership of mobile operators.

In recognition of its outstanding record, Etisalat received Superbrand status in 2008 from the Superbrand Council, the independent body that honours branding excellence in various sectors across the world.

INWARD INVESTMENT

Although, for the UAE, FDI is the highest in the region at around US$19 billion, the government has been active in its efforts to improve

> Etisalat is now the sixteenth largest telecommunications firm in the world, and the corporation aims to be among the top ten in the world by 2010. Etisalat is also ranked at two hundred and nineteenth place in the 2008 Global 500 Financial Times list.

conditions to meet with the aspirations of international, regional, and local investors. Among key incentives to investors is the very favourable tax environment especially in the free zones where in most cases there are no corporate and income taxes. It helps that the UAE per capita income is one of the highest in the region. Coupled with this, its population growth rate is among the highest worldwide. These factors create a 'virtuous cycle': i.e. a market with very high, and rapidly growing, purchasing power, which attracts further FDI.

A survey of more than 800 foreign companies in the UAE, conducted by the Ministry of Economy (MoE) in 2008, investigated conditions for FDI. It identified a range of pluses and minuses in terms of the country's FDI attractiveness. Among major attractions were the UAE's political stability, its excellent access to regional markets, its favourable geographical position and the convenience of access to world markets. Among significant negative factors were rising operating costs, fuel prices and tough foreign competition. However, smooth investment procedures, sufficient space for activity, strategic assets, high market value of shares, low cost of finance, and appropriate commercial values of investments bolstered the argument for investing in UAE based companies.

The value of foreign direct investment (FDI) in Abu Dhabi was predicted to reach Dh27 billion (US$7.35 billion) in 2008 compared to Dh17 billion (US$4.63 billion) in 2007. Abu Dhabi's share of foreign investment in the UAE as a whole is relatively low at around 24 per cent of total foreign investment in the UAE, contrasting with its 58 per cent contribution to GDP. The primary aim of attracting FDI is not so much to do with money but more to do with expertise, technology and experience, contributing to the improved production methods and enhanced infrastructure. Among measures being considered by the Abu Dhabi government were plans to pass legislation revising ownership rights for foreign investors, allowing up to 100 per cent in many sectors.

TRADE

The UAE was the second largest trading nation in the Arab world in 2007. Trade for the year totalled Dh1.01 trillion (US$275.1 billion) in 2007, accounting for 22.2 per cent of the total Arab commercial exchange of US$1.234 trillion, despite the fact that its population

UAE trade in 2007 totalled Dh1.01 trillion, accounting for 22.2 per cent of all Arab trade, despite the fact that the UAE population is only 1.4 per cent of the total Arab population.

www.uaeinteract.com/economicdevelopment

accounts for just 1.4 per cent of the total Arab population. Economists attributed the surge in trade to an increase in crude oil and gas exports, higher non-oil exports by free zones and other areas, and a sharp rise in imports as a result of strong domestic demand and a steady increase in re-export.

Trade figures throughout the UAE showed impressive increases. For example, Dubai's non-oil direct foreign trade jumped by 54.3 per cent during the first half of 2008, reaching Dh296.6 billion (around US$80.8 billion), compared to Dh192.2 billion (US$52.3 billion) achieved during the same period in 2007. India topped the list of Dubai's main trading partners, followed by China, and in third place, the USA. India was also the UAE's largest exports destination in the first half of 2008, with Switzerland making a sudden leap from fifty-fourth to second place. Dubai's bilateral trade with Switzerland grew from Dh24.7 million to Dh1.5 billion! In terms of Dubai's re-export trading during first half of 2008, India was the top partner with Iran in second place, while Switzerland came third.

The UAE is negotiating eight FTAs with key economic blocs that will significantly impact trade. Whilst the potential benefits of such agreements are clear, final deals have proven to be somewhat elusive. Agreements with the European Union and the US are particularly important for exports, economic diversification and attracting foreign investment into the region.

> Trade figures throughout the UAE continued to show impressive increases in 2008. At the same time, the UAE is negotiating eight free trade agreements with key economic blocs that will significantly impact trade.

CUSTOMS LAW AND REGULATIONS

The UAE's Unified Customs Law is expected to come into force by the end of 2009. The Federal Customs Authority (FCA) will oversee standardising of all the UAE's customs tariffs and regulations and will issue a unified executive list that is binding for the entire UAE. Steps are being taken to complete the process as soon as possible, especially in Abu Dhabi, Dubai and Sharjah, which together account for 95 per cent of the UAE's customs transactions. The FCA completed an electronic link between the different customs departments and set up information and intelligence units in all customs departments to intensify the fight against counterfeit goods and drugs.

Among the functions of these customs regulations is the prevention of trade in fake goods. A special section equipped with modern technology to effectively track shipments has been set up by Dubai Customs. In the first five months of 2008, Dubai Customs destroyed

293 tons of counterfeit, smuggled and illegal products. These were destroyed in coordination with other governmental bodies. Such actions are likely to become more frequent through implementation of the unified GCC customs law, which gives customs authorities the full right to seize and destroy illegal goods.

Goods imported into the United Arab Emirates from countries with most favoured nations (MFN) status are subject to the GCC Common External Tariff (CET), which averaged around 5 per cent in 2007. Over 400 basic food items and pharmaceuticals are duty free. Tobacco products, on the other hand, attract up to a 100 per cent tax rate, depending on the item.

With the exception of oil, gas and petrochemicals, the primary export centres in the UAE are free zones that provide logistical, administrative and financial advantages for exporting or re-exporting companies. These free zones are exempt from the licensing, agency, emiratisation, and national majority-ownership obligations that apply in the domestic economy. There are many success stories among the companies operating from the UAE's free zones, with major enterprises using the UAE as a base to compete efficiently in the international market place.

According to figures released by the Ministry of Finance and Industry in the latter half of 2008, the total cumulative industrial capital value of all non-oil and gas industrial projects in the UAE now exceeds US$20 billion, creating 290,000 jobs.

INDUSTRIAL DEVELOPMENT

The cumulative industrial capital of the country at the beginning of 2008 was around Dh72 billion, with Dh38.9 billion of that total accounted for by Abu Dhabi; Dh17.1 billion by Dubai; Dh6.4 billion by Fujairah; Dh4.03 billion by Sharjah; Dh4.2 billion by Ra's al-Khaimah; Dh1.49 billion by Ajman; and Dh483 million by Umm al-Qaiwain.

By early 2008 almost 44 per cent (i.e. around Dh32.1 billion) of the total manufacturing capital of the UAE was in food, beverages and tobacco. Other sectors in order of size were chemicals, mineral products, metal products, equipment, paper products, textiles and garments, and wood products. Abu Dhabi's industrial base is dominated by a few large-scale projects, in contrast to some other emirates where there are many smaller enterprises.

In addition to contributing to economic diversification programmes, industrial projects created a large number of jobs, standing at

288,180 at the end of 2007. Mineral products emerged as the largest job provider, employing nearly 54,000 people; followed by chemical projects with nearly 36,800 employees, textile and garments with 31,700 and food and beverage with 29,130.

The last few years have been a time of considerable innovation and adjustment in the UAE's industrial profile. There has been an increased focus on high technology and knowledge-based industries, opening up new frontiers in terms of the country's economic profile. Who would have thought, a few years ago, that the UAE would emerge as a centre for alternative energy research and development, a favoured location for movie production, or an aircraft manufacturer? These are just a few of the industries that are taking a hold in twenty-first century UAE.

> The last few years have been a time of considerable innovation and adjustment in the UAE's industrial profile, with an increased focus on high technology and knowledge-based industries.

AEROSPACE INDUSTRY

Mubadala has been a leading UAE investor in the aviation industry, with companies such as Abu Dhabi Aircraft Technologies, Gulf Aircraft Maintenance Company (Gamco) and Horizon International Flight Academy in its stable. It is creating a new global aerospace industry for Abu Dhabi – focused on an integrated approach, including manufacturing, maintenance, repair and overhaul (MRO). Mubadala's purchase of a 35 per cent stake in Piaggio Aero Industries in 2006 opened the way for aircraft to be manufactured within the UAE. Another recent venture is Abu Dhabi UAV Investments (AD UAVI), which is 95 per cent owned by Mubadala, and specialises in design and manufacture of unmanned aerial vehicle systems. Mubadala also owns 40 per cent of SR Technics, an independent provider of technical services in the aircraft, component and engine areas. Other partners are Dubai Aerospace Enterprise (DAE) and Istithmar.

DAE, whose shareholders include Emaar, Istithmar, Dubai Airport Free Zone Authority, Dubai International Capital, Dubai International Financial Centre, the Dubai government and Amlak Finance, has been establishing a global aerospace manufacturing and services corporation based in Dubai. It has established subsidiaries in six key sectors: research and development, manufacturing, maintenance, repair and overhaul, aircraft leasing and aerospace services. The group is forming international partnerships at the highest level of industry with the aim of establishing one of the most innovative and successful businesses in the global aerospace industry inside the next decade. DAE is expected to grow through a series of phased developments to produce an integrated aerospace cluster, located at Dubai World Central – the new airport and logistics city being constructed by Jebel Ali.

With both Abu Dhabi and Dubai developing their aerospace capabilities, the aviation industry is seen as an important plank in the country's industrial diversification.

AVIATION

Emirates Airline

There can be no disguising Emirates' impressive expansion plans, which are vividly illustrated by the fact that, in autumn 2008, it had 244 new aircraft on order, with a total value of approximately US$60 billion! In the financial year ending March 2008, Emirates recorded an impressive 54 per cent increase in group net profit amounting to Dh5.3 billion (US$1.45 billion), following an increase of 23.5 per cent in 2006. Airline profits were a record Dh5 billion (US$1.36 billion), up from Dh3.1 billion (US$844 million) a year earlier, an increase of over 62 per cent. These results were achieved despite continuing high oil prices.

Thomas Enders, Chief Executive of Airbus, and Sheikh Ahmed bin Said Al Maktoum, Chief Executive of Emirates, sign contracts following the delivery of Emirates' first Airbus A380.

With a fleet of 113 aircraft, Emirates flies to over 100 destinations in 62 countries around the world, and its network is expanding constantly. Nearly 800 Emirates flights depart Dubai each week on their way to destinations on six continents. In fact, Emirates' flights account for nearly 40 per cent of all flight movements in and out of Dubai International Airport, and the airline aims to increase this market-share to 70 per cent by 2010.

At the Dubai Airshow in November 2007, Emirates announced a historic civil aviation aircraft order when it signed contracts for 120 Airbus A350s, 11 A380s, and 12 Boeing 777-300ERs, worth an estimated US$34.9 billion in list prices. The agreement with Airbus comprises firm orders for 50 A350-900s and 20 A350-1000s, plus 50 options for the A350-900s. The first A350 will be delivered to Emirates in 2014. The company also firmed up orders on the eight A380s for which it had signed letters of intent earlier in 2008, and placed firm orders for an additional three of the double-decker aircraft, bringing its total firm order for the A380s to 58. With the new order for 12 777-300ERs, valued at US$3.2 billion, by mid-2008 Emirates had 57 Boeing 777s pending delivery and remained set to become the

A380 AIRCRAFT AND UAE AIRLINES

One of the biggest stories in the aviation world during 2007–2008 was the introduction of the first Airbus 380 super-jumbo aircraft. Both Emirates and Etihad have placed orders for the unique aircraft that offers both comfort and fuel efficiencies for long-haul flights.

Emirates, which had placed the largest order for the 380, made its first commercial flight with it on 1 August 2008 when it flew from Dubai to New York's John F. Kennedy International Airport. The huge aircraft, carrying 489 passengers in varying degrees of luxury, landed smoothly and on time after a thirteen and a half hour flight from the UAE.

The impressive plane is fitted out with lie-flat beds, flat-screen televisions and spacious, windowed bathrooms in first and business class.

With a list price of US$327 million, the A380 has a number of key advantages, from its fuel-efficient engines to its load capacity, which will reduce the number of aircraft required to fly certain routes. It uses up to 20 per cent less fuel per seat than a Boeing 747, and when fully loaded and flying long distances it is reported to be more fuel efficient, per passenger, than a small family car.

Emirates, presently the world's seventh largest airline in terms of international passengers, is the biggest buyer of A380s, with 58 on order. In addition to New York, it plans to deploy the plane on London, Sydney and Auckland routes. Both Emirates and Etihad expect the new planes will strengthen the UAE's position as an aviation hub. Etihad has four A380s on order and, like all other purchasers of the European-made plane, it is in a delivery queue that has been affected by a number of delays.

There is no doubt that the A380 is a bold step forward in aviation history and the UAE's major airlines are proud to be playing a significant role in the process.

There is no doubt that the A380 is a bold step forward in aviation history and the UAE's major airlines are proud to be playing a significant role in the process.

Emirates airline profits were a record Dh5 billion (US$1.36 billion) for the financial year ending March 2008, up from Dh3.1 billion (US$844 million) a year earlier.

world's largest 777 operator in the next few years. The second A380 aircraft for Emirates longhaul fleet was delivered in late October 2008.

Etihad Airways

Etihad, the national airline of the UAE, made its first flight on 5 November 2003 and is now recognised as one of the fastest-growing national airlines in the history of aviation. Like Emirates, Etihad operates one of the youngest and most environmentally efficient fleets in the world. This reached 45 aircraft by the end of 2008 and there are plans to boost this figure in the near future.

Etihad began life with the largest-ever start-up fleet order, announced at the 2004 Farnborough Air Show, for 29 Airbus and Boeing aircraft with a total value of US$8 billion. In July 2008, Etihad placed an order for up to 205 wide-body and narrow-body planes worth approximately US$43 billion, one of the largest in commercial aviation history. This breaks down to 100 firm orders, 55 options and 50 purchase rights in a combination of Boeing and Airbus aircraft.

Etihad Airways continued to show impressive growth in 2008 with passenger figures for the first nine months indicating a 35 per cent rise on the same period in 2007. During the period 1 January to 30 September 2008 the airline carried 4.4 million passengers across its network of (at that time) 48 destinations, compared to 3.3 million for the same period in the previous year. Seat occupancy averaged 75 per cent. Etihad was clearly on course to exceed its 2008 target of six million passengers.

In July 2008, Etihad announced a record-breaking order at Farnborough Airshow for up to 205 aircraft, including firm orders for 100 aircraft.

Etihad's services to Asia and Australia turned in particularly strong performances with overall seat factors averaging 82 per cent across the region. Passenger loads in the economy cabin averaged 84 per cent, led by Manila (94 per cent), Jakarta (90 per cent), Sydney (87 per cent) and Bangkok (83 per cent). Within Europe, flights to Dublin, Brussels, Manchester and Paris all achieved average seat factors of more than 80 per cent in economy. Middle East routes that performed well during the first nine months of the year included Amman and Damascus and both achieved overall average seat factors of 78 per cent. Cairo remains the airline's most popular African route, with an overall seat factor of 80 per cent.

Etihad launched six new destinations in 2008, to Beijing, the Indian cities of Kozhikode (Calicut) and Chennai (Madras), Minsk in Belorussia, Almaty in Kazakhstan and to Moscow. Plans for early 2009 include adding routes to Melbourne and Lagos.

The airline was particularly delighted to have been voted the 'Middle East's Leading Airline' at the 2008 Middle East World Travel Awards. In addition Etihad scooped the 'Middle East's Leading First Class', along with the 'Middle East's Leading Airline Website' awards (www.etihadairways.com).

Etihad in five years has flown nearly 14 million passengers on more than 87,000 flights to 48 destinations across the Middle East, Africa, Australia, Asia, Europe, and North America.

Other Airlines

Air Arabia's financial results for the period ending 30 June 2008, demonstrated a net profit for the first half of 2008 of Dh160 million, an increase of 39 per cent compared to Dh115 million for the first six months of 2007. Listed as a public joint stock company on the Dubai Financial Market, Air Arabia is the Middle East and North Africa's leading low-cost carrier (LCC). It commenced operations in October 2003 and operates a fleet of new Airbus A320 aircraft, serving a wide range of destinations across the Middle East, North Africa, Europe, CIS, South and Central Asia. Its main base is Sharjah International Airport and its vision is to be one of the world's leading budget airlines. It recently announced plans to launch a hub in Morocco with a dedicated fleet of A320s.

Passenger traffic on Air Arabia reached 1.6 million passengers during the first half of 2008, a 33 per cent increase compared to 1.2 million passengers during the same period in 2007. Air Arabia has won a number of prestigious aviation awards, including the 2008 World Airline Award for 'Best Low-Cost Airline in the Middle East' for

www.uaeinteract.com/air

the second consecutive year, the prestigious gold award in the best airline category at the MENA Travel Awards 2008 and the award for Operational Excellence 2005–2007 by Airbus, one of the world's leading aircraft manufacturers.

RAK Airways, under the title 'I Fly You', operates flights to Calicut (Kozhikode), Dhaka, Chittagong, Colombo, Beirut, and Sofia. The airline was established in February 2006 and began operations in November 2007. In 2008 the new airline signed a Dh1.65 billion deal with Boeing for the purchase of four new-generation 737-800NG aircraft, making it the first airline in the UAE to buy the Boeing 737-800NG – a short-to-medium-range jet. It will take delivery of the first two aircraft in 2011 and the two others in 2012. Until the deliveries of these aircraft, RAK Airways will continue to operate with its leased planes, adopting a 'hub and spoke' network strategy by attracting passengers from other countries to Ra's al-Khaimah and then flying them to other destinations.

Royal Jet, the international luxury executive flight services company headquartered in Abu Dhabi, launched a new pricing structure in 2008, based on where the guests commence their flight instead of where the privately booked aircraft originates its journey. In other words, if clients are travelling from Jeddah to Beirut, they are only charged for that part of the journey, and not for the Abu Dhabi to Jeddah leg that is necessary to position the aircraft. Royal Jet was recently voted the 'World's Leading Private Jet Charter' and 'Business Jet Provider of the Year'.

FlyDubai, due to be launched in mid-2009, is one of the most recent new additions to the UAE's aviation business scene. The company appointed Gaith Al Gaith, a former Emirates Airline executive, as chief executive officer of FlyDubai in March 2008. FlyDubai plans to start operations with 12 destinations but eventually aims to build a network of 70 destinations. The airline ordered 50 Boeing 737-800 aircraft and signed a lease agreement for four similar planes.

ALUMINIUM

Dubai Aluminium Company Limited (Dubal), the world's seventh largest producer of high quality primary aluminium, achieved a major production milestone, having produced its ten millionth cumulative tonne of hot metal in mid-July 2008. The company, which celebrates its thirtieth anniversary in 2009, began operating with three pot lines offering an initial production capacity of 135,000 metric tonnes per year at its inception in 1979. Dubal produced approximately 890,000 tonnes of molten aluminium in 2007, representing a 12.6 per cent increase on the 2006 figures. The company is planning to produce 970,000 tonnes in 2009. Dubal's ambitious vision is to become the world's fifth largest producer of primary aluminium by 2015, by producing 2.5 million tonnes of the metal per year.

Abu Dhabi-based Emirates Aluminium's (Emal) extensive production facility in Taweelah is being built in two phases and is set to become the world's fifth largest aluminium producer. Phase one, scheduled for completion by 2010, will have a production output of approximately 700,000 tonnes. At full capacity, it will boast an output of 1.4 million tonnes of primary aluminium. The company awarded a Dh36 million contract to Italian manufacturer, Società per Impianti Generali (SPIG) for the supply of cooling towers at Emal's power plant. These innovative structures will reduce the temperature of the water used during the energy production process and ensure that water is returned to the sea within a one degree celsius temperature range (within Abu Dhabi Environmental Agency guidelines which allow up to a five degree celsius increase).

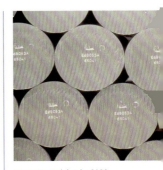

It is estimated that by 2020 the GCC aluminium industry will provide 20 per cent of global aluminium production.

STEEL

The UAE steel industry has been through very buoyant times with strong market fundamentals supported by large-scale developments occurring throughout the UAE, all of which require steel in their construction. Market forces have been impacting on the price of steel with the 2008 average price over Dh4000 per ton compared with around Dh2500 in 2007. Indeed, figures from Dubai Chamber of Commerce and Industry (DCCI) indicated that the price of steel had increased by as much as 14 times in five years. Massive structures such as Burj Dubai, the world's tallest building, consume huge quantities of steel rebar. Thirty-nine thousand metric tons of steel rebar were used to construct the building, enough to extend a quarter of the way around the earth if laid end to end.

The UAE produced 1.7 million tonnes in 2007 and this output is expected to more than double by 2012. Major players in the UAE steel industry are Emirates Steel Industries, Al Nasser Industrial Enterprises, Alam Steel Industry LLC and Qatar Steel Company. In March 2008 the UAE Government exempted reinforced steel (together with cement)

Steel prices surged to Dh6000 a tonne in July 2008. A slide that began in August turned into an avalanche with falling to Dh1800 in November.

Steel reinforcing bars doubled in price from January to July 2008, then halved, ending the year in the same range as at the beginning of the year.

from custom duties. However, steel prices fluctuated throughout the year, affected almost as much by global prices as local conditions. The upward spiral in steel prices, surging by 91 per cent from January to the end of July 2008, halted in August 2008 when prices on the Abu Dhabi steel market began to decline.

Emirates Steel Industries plant at ICAD-1 in Abu Dhabi is in a rapid expansionary phase, underlined by the signing of a Dh1 billion contract with Italy's Danieli Corporation. Once completed, the larger plant will have a total production capacity of 3 million tonnes p.a. as against its previous production capacity of 2 million tonnes p.a. Emirates Steel Industries (ESI), formerly Emirates Iron and Steel Factory (EISF) is wholly owned by the Abu Dhabi government. The factory is the largest steel plant in the UAE, utilising the latest rolling mill technology to produce reinforcing bars for the construction industry.

Given the continued surge in building activity in the UAE, it is not surprising that analysts have predicted a dramatic growth in the country's steel industry with some experts stating that it is expected to grow by more than 200 per cent between 2008 and 2012.

FILM INDUSTRY

A somewhat surprising development in the UAE's industrial sector has been the emergence of serious plans and projects in the movie-making business. Dubai has led the way in this with the establishment of Dubai Studio City, a member of Tecom Investments, as a one-stop-shop for film-making in Dubai. It invested Dh110 million to create 18 boutique studios that were opened in 2008 as part of Dubai Studio City's phase one development. All the studios were taken up by regional and international broadcasters. Spread over an area of over 2 million square metres, Dubai Studio City will have 14 sound stages, a 325,000 square metre back lot for outdoor shoots, commercial offices, pre-built studios, a business centre and post-production studios. The media cluster's mission is to provide world-class infrastructure and services to boost the growth of the film, TV, radio production, post-production and broadcast industries in the region, helping to shape UAE nationals and expatriates into award-winning film-makers.

Indian star Aishwarya Rai with Jamal Sharif of Dubai Studio City celebrating the premiere of Rai's new movie 'Provoked' in Dubai.

Meanwhile, Abu Dhabi has its own major plans for a film industry based within its borders. In 2008 Abu Dhabi Media Company (ADMC) established a film financing subsidiary with plans to spend more than

Sheikh Hamdan bin Mohammed Al Maktoum, Chairman of Dubai Executive Council, examines the model of Universal Studios theme park, which is being built in Dubai.

US$1 billion (Dh3.67 billion) developing, financing and producing as many as 40 feature films over the next five years. The new company, called 'imagenation abu dhabi', is forming joint ventures with Hollywood and other international producers to create globally distributed movies and digital content, while also working with Middle Eastern filmmakers to produce Arabic language and dual-language films with crossover appeal. The idea behind imagenation is to create a relationship with the filmmaking community so that skills can be developed in Abu Dhabi to grow an industry (see chapter on Media & Culture).

ADMC was also behind the multi-billion dollar deal signed in 2007 with Warner Brothers and Aldar Properties to build a theme park, hotel complex and chain of movie theatres. That deal also created two film funds – one dedicated to Arabic-language films, and another for the development of video games.

INDUSTRIAL ZONES

The policy of clustering businesses and industries in order to achieve economies of scale and to exploit synergies for the mutual benefit of enterprises operating with these specialised zones has been hugely successful in the UAE. The clustering has taken three main forms, i.e. free zones where businesses united by common interest factors may enjoy 100 per cent foreign ownership, special tax and

www.uaeinteract.com/economicdevelopment

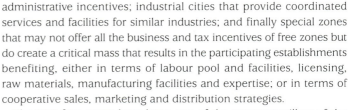

administrative incentives; industrial cities that provide coordinated services and facilities for similar industries; and finally special zones that may not offer all the business and tax incentives of free zones but do create a critical mass that results in the participating establishments benefiting, either in terms of labour pool and facilities, licensing, raw materials, manufacturing facilities and expertise; or in terms of cooperative sales, marketing and distribution strategies.

> The UAE's free zones have been one of the strongest pillars of the country's economic performance, attracting significant amounts of foreign investment, creating thousands of jobs, and facilitating technology transfer into the country.

The UAE free zones have been one of the strongest pillars of the country's economic performance, attracting significant amounts of foreign investment, creating thousands of jobs, and facilitating technology transfer into the country. The combined output of the country's free zones accounts for more than half of its non-oil exports and underpins the UAE's ranking as the third most important re-export centre in the world.

The UAE's cluster projects have been reviewed in some detail in previous editions of this *Yearbook*. In the current edition, we focus on some of the main developments in this field over the past 12 months.

Abu Dhabi's Industrial Cities

Abu Dhabi Higher Corporation for Specialised Economic Zones (ZonesCorp), the Abu Dhabi government authority that establishes and manages industrial cities for cluster industries, has already developed three industrial cities in Mussafah. These projects, known by their acronym ICAD, are referred to as ICAD-1, ICAD-2 and ICAD-3. ICAD-4 is now under development. The industrial zones are being established under the Plan Abu Dhabi 2030. ICAD-I and ICAD-2 were developed from the existing industrial units in Mussafah and then brought under the management of ZonesCorp, while ICAD-3, which contains the Polymers Park plastic processing zone, is a new city.

ICAD-3, the new industrial city in Abu Dhabi, will feature Polymers Park, a dedicated plastic processing zone.

Most of the proposed specialised cluster industry areas in the ICADs are free of both tax and customs duties. ZonesCorp is also planning to build residential units for more than 800,000 workers employed in the industrial cities and surrounding areas, with completion due in 2012.

Western Region Free Zone

Abu Dhabi Customs is commencing work on a Dh500 million free zone at the Western (Al Gharbia) Region's border exit of Al Ghweifat. The free zone is expected to lead to an increase in the number of individuals and companies transiting through the outlet and will offer a host of goods free of any custom tariffs.

Future Energy Free Zone

Masdar City is establishing a new free zone for the renewable energy industry. The US$22 billion project will provide an attractive base for 1500 firms involved in innovation, research and development. The zero carbon footprint city will contain light industries operating within a number of sub-sectors of renewable energy, including advanced energy, sustainable transportation, and green efficiencies. This will create innovation hubs, fostering development of new technologies and solutions. In addition a commercialisation unit is being deployed for the application and rapid deployment of these solutions. The free zone will also host world-class laboratories conducting research and development in the renewable sector.

The city will help to establish Abu Dhabi as a global centre for 'future energy' activities, providing a platform for collaboration in creating new energy solutions (see Alternative Energy below)

EnPark

In August 2008, Dubai's Energy and Environment Park (Enpark) announced a Sustainable Development Policy, with plans to implement eco-friendly initiatives. The policy focuses especially on energy and water conservation. Adopting an inclusive approach to its development, Enpark plans to work closely with all authorities to enlist their participation in the project. As a commercial venture, Enpark is aiming to prove that conducting business in a sustainable manner will generate long-term benefits for the company as well as the entire community at large.

Jafza

Jebel Ali Free Zone (Jafza) is one of the largest and fastest growing free zones in the world and Dubai's biggest exporting zone. In 2007 Dh96.1 billion worth of total exports and re-exports moved through Dubai's free zones compared to Dh82.6 billion in 2006. Meanwhile, Jafza companies contributed 77.60 per cent of Dubai's non-oil foreign trade figures in 2007, reaching Dh74.6 billion. The strategic location of the Jebel Ali Port, construction of Al Maktoum International Airport and development of Dubai World Central complex are providing a further boost to Jafza's development.

Jafza offers business and tax incentives to corporations and serves Dubai Port, which ranks ninth in the world in terms of container

Jebel Ali Free Zone is one of the largest and fastest growing free zones in the world.

traffic. The free zone also provides warehousing and distribution facilities to international and local corporations.

Jafza International

Jafza International, the global free zone management and consultancy arm of Economic Zones World (EZW), opened its North American office in Charleston, South Carolina in 2008, marking the company's entry into the US market. The opening of the headquarters was the first step in Jafza International's plan to launch its landmark US$600 million modern logistics and business park in Orangeburg. This involves transforming 1300 acres of land into a modern logistics and distribution park that will include light manufacturing, warehousing and distribution facilities. The ambitious project will generate 8000 to 10,000 jobs in the next decade and become one of the biggest logistics hubs in the US. Jafza International's ultimate aim is to establish a global platform of logistics and business parks.

Dafz

By mid-August 2008 Dubai Airport Free Zone (Dafz) had attracted more than 1425 companies and it was continuing to attract new ventures. The location of the free zone, within the boundaries of Dubai International Airport, is a key benefit to international companies that need to remain closely connected with international markets.

Dafz is also playing a valuable role for many overseas corporations in their international tax planning strategy, sharing the tax exemption enjoyed by companies already established in the zone, while having the freedom offered by 100 per cent foreign ownership.

Health Industry

The UAE has invested heavily in providing medical and health services for its citizens and has nurtured the growth of related industries in the country, from pharmaceuticals to medical equipment, overall wellness resorts and private hospitals. The scale of these developments, a number of which are described in the section on Health, has created a critical mass that is encouraging others to establish related enterprises in the UAE.

In August 2008 Tatweer announced an investment of Dh3.68 billion in a New Wellness Resort to be based in phase two of Dubai Healthcare City (DHCC), also a member of Tatweer. The move brought Tatweer's investments in DHCC to a total of Dh12.5 billion. DHCC has also attracted over Dh15 billion of additional investments from its partners. Situated alongside the Dubai Creek, within DHCC's Wellness Cluster, the resort will serve as a premier location for preventative and integrative medicine, and for promoting health-enhancing lifestyles in the region.

DuBiotech

The UAE's well-established pharmaceutical business, led by companies such as Julphar, Neopharma, Globalpharma, Medpharma and Gulf Injects, has been joined by ground-breaking biotechnology companies that are being encouraged to cluster in the Dubai Biotechnology and Research Park (DuBiotech), a member of Tecom Investments.

The science and business park for life sciences industry, launched in 2005, had 42 companies in mid-2008 with many more in the pipeline. The innovative zone is keen to promote clinical research, clinical trials, and work on genetic development. But activities within the zone are not restricted to medical sciences since they encompass the whole biotechnology industry, including environment and agriculture. The zone has attracted major international companies such as Amgen, Genzyme and Pfizer.

In operation for just over three years, the biotech hub has launched a number of significant initiatives such as its subsidiary, BioTiqania and the Gulf Anti-doping and Monitoring Enterprise (Game). The free zone views its role as an incubator for scientific research and development. BioTiqania is a training institute for scientific and industrial disciplines. Game is a pioneering laboratory dedicated to conducting anti-doping measures for professional and amateur athletes in the UAE.

In 2007 NeoBiocon Ltd, an international joint venture between an Indian biotechnology giant Biocon Ltd and the Abu Dhabi-based pharmaceutical manufacturer NeoPharma, established its regional headquarters at DuBiotech. Bridging research, education and industry through national and international collaboration, the research park is working closely with the UAE Ministry of Health, the Dubai Health Authority, and other regulatory bodies to further develop the life sciences industry in the country.

DuBiotech's Dh250 million research laboratory was due to come into operation in December 2008.

Bridging research, education and industry through national and international collaboration, the research park is working closely with the UAE's regulatory bodies to further develop the life sciences industry in the country.

www.uaeinteract.com/economicdevelopment

Dubai Techno Park

Asia Gulf Horizons Fund Technology Centre was established at Dubai Techno Park, the Dubai government's technology initiative. Dubai Techno Park is managed by DP World whilst the fund is managed by Korea Technology Investment Corporation (KTIC), a veteran private equity management company based in Seoul, South Korea. It is expected that locating the Dh1.1 trillion (US$300 million) fund in Dubai Techno Park will result in approximately ten to 15 Asian and European technology companies establishing research, development and commercial operations in Dubai in the next two years. These companies will focus on environmental and telecommunications technology, energy, water and infrastructure, and are considered essential to Dubai's long-term technology development plan.

Ra's al-Khaimah Free Zone

Ras Al Khaimah Free Zone continued its growth as more companies discover the attractions of locating within this northern emirate. Eight hundred and forty-seven new firms were registered at the zone during the first half of 2008, bringing the total number of companies operating from the zone to 4773 companies with a total investment of Dh10 billion.

Sharjah Free Zones

Free zones in Sharjah are a leading source of revenue for the emirate. By mid-2008 Sharjah free zones had 4716 companies and the government was planning new free zones designed to attract foreign investment. Existing Sharjah free zone enterprises included 440 aviation companies, 2434 trading companies, 1429 service companies and 413 industrial companies.

Ajman Free Zone

The emirate of Ajman has continued to develop its new free zone project, complementing the emirate's existing free zone (AFZ), which has attracted numerous foreign companies and has the highest number of ready-made garments factories in the world. The zone's 19 factories export to GCC countries, the US, Europe, Canada and elsewhere.

Fujairah Free Zone

Fujairah's location on the east coast of the UAE, bordered by the open waters of the Gulf of Oman and the Indian Ocean, and adjacent to one of the world's busiest shipping routes has been a positive factor in the rapid development of Fujairah Free Zone. The zone operates a user-friendly website at www.fujairahfreezone.com and in answer to the frequently asked question of how to establish a base of operations at the zone, the administration promises to issue licences within 48 hours of final agreement on the terms and conditions of the contract and the fulfilling of the first year's financial commitments (premises rent, licensing fees, Fujairah Chamber of Commerce registration).

Investors leasing trading offices or other pre-built units can take over the premises with immediate effect upon the issuance of a licence. In addition, investors signing contracts for constructing their own customised building may utilise free zone facilities to prepare their manufacturing units during the period of constructing their units. Over 600 companies are registered with the free zone, operating within the fields of assembly, consulting, distribution, financial, general manufacturing, commercial, contracting, general trading and logistics.

PETROCHEMICALS & FERTILISERS

The UAE's oil and gas industry has spawned a major associated petrochemicals industry that produces a variety of materials including plastics, melamine, fertilisers and urea. Abu Dhabi has several major petrochemical and fertiliser industrial complexes: the Ruwais Fertiliser Industries Company (Fertil), the Abu Dhabi Polymers Company (Borouge), and Abu Dhabi Fertiliser Industries Company (Adfert). It is also pioneering environmental initiatives in relation to this and other potentially polluting industries.

The UAE's oil and gas industry has spawned a major associated petrochemicals industry that produces a variety of materials, including plastics, melamine, fertilisers and urea.

Borouge

Borouge's current production capacity in the UAE is 600,000 tonnes of Borstar polyethylene per year. With the ongoing Borouge 2 project expansion, this will increase to 2 million tonnes per year by the middle of 2010 and will add polypropylene to the product mix. The Borouge 2 facility comprises a 1.5 million tonne ethane cracker, the world's largest olefins conversion unit (with a capacity of 750,000 tonnes), two Borstar polypropylene plants with a total capacity of 800,000 tonnes and a 540,000 tonne Borstar polyethylene plant. A feasibility phase for Borouge 3 was scheduled for completion by the end of 2008.

Borouge recently took steps to move the main base of its operations from Port Zayed to Khalifa Port. In June 2008 it signed an MoU with

Abu Dhabi Ports Company (ADPC) to enable a smooth transfer of its port operations. Borouge requires the provision of expanded port services to handle an increase in production, expected to reach 4.5 million tonnes upon the completion of Borouge 3 in 2014.

Borouge also recently awarded a service contract to Agility Pjsc to build the Borouge Compound Manufacturing Unit (CMU) and Shanghai Logistics Hub in Shanghai, China, and to provide local logistics services for Borouge's customers in Asia for a duration of ten years with effect from its operational start-up date in 2010. Agility is undertaking the design, development and subsequent operation of the logistics hub, to ensure sufficient infrastructure, storage facilities, packaging and distribution services to accommodate Borouge's products that are dispatched to China from Abu Dhabi. Agility will handle and distribute a total volume of approximately 600,000 tonnes of polyolefins out of the Shanghai logistics hub annually.

PHARMACEUTICALS

At the present time there are approximately ten pharmaceutical and related products manufacturing companies in the UAE. The leader is Gulf Pharmaceutical Industries, known as Julphar, which is based in Ra's al-Khaimah.

Julphar opened two new plants in April 2008 to produce antibiotics as part of the company's ambitious expansion plan. Julphar 8 and 9,

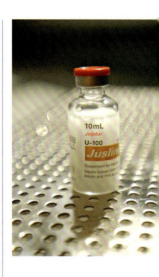 **117**

which cost Dh30 million, are initially producing over 50 kinds of antibiotics with a total capacity of 30 million syringes a year. The two facilities produce injection ready units of penicillin and cephalosporin. Meanwhile, work was under way on building seven new state-of-the-art manufacturing plants in Ra's al-Khaimah at a total cost of Dh800 million. The company also announced that it would be opening a chain of retail pharmacy outlets across the MENA region.

Until recently Julphar was the only notable UAE-based manufacturer, but it has been joined in the last few years by relative newcomers, including Neopharma in Abu Dhabi, Globalpharma and Gulf Injects in Dubai and Medpharma in Sharjah. The biotechnology field is also bringing new pharmaceutical companies to the United Arab Emirates, principally to DuBiotech, the specially created free zone in Dubai that is mentioned above.

CERAMICS

RAK Ceramics presently accounts for 5 per cent of the total world production of ceramic tiles and it owns a 50 per cent stake in a 15 million pieces per year ceramic tableware company. The company's UAE factories are located 20 kilometres south of Ra's al-Khaimah City, along the highway to Dubai. While it runs the global business from its UAE base, it has also established an extensive international network of factories.

In March 2008 RAK Ceramics announced a net profit of Dh169.7 million for the year 2007, registering a 10 per cent increase from Dh153.7 million in 2006. The annual revenue of the company touched Dh2.27 billion, posting a 35 per cent increase from Dh1.68 billion in 2006. Global production reached 98 million square metres of tiles and 3.3 million pieces of sanitary ware in 2007.

RAK Ceramics is involved in a total of 32 joint ventures and projects, encompassing 12 operating joint ventures, 11 ceramic distribution companies and another nine new joint ventures. These include RAK Paints LLC, RAK Warehouse Leasing LLC, and a 70 per cent stake in Acacia Hotels LLC, which is opening a number of new four-star hotels in the region.

RAK Ceramics presently accounts for 5 per cent of the total world production of ceramic tiles and it owns a 50 per cent stake in a 15 million pieces per year ceramic tableware company

GOLD & JEWELLERY

Dubai is a long-established market for gold bullion and wholesale and retail jewellery. The trade is fuelled by strong demand from the Arab

www.uaeinteract.com/gold

The UAE is a long-established market for wholesale and retail jewellery.

world and India, the world's top gold market. Dubai, also known as 'City of Gold', has the highest concentration of jewellery shops in the world, and the industry witnessed trade worth US$35 billion in 2007, accounting for 20 per cent of the global jewellery trade of US$173 billion in that year. The Gold and Diamond Park and the new gold souk in Dubai Mall are providing strong support for this business sector in the UAE. Dubai Mall houses the world's largest indoor Gold Souk, a precinct with over 220 gold and jewellery retailers. This fascinating venue recreates the traditional charm of an Arabian souk reflecting the rich regional heritage of the gold trade.

In 2007, Dubai's gold imports reached 559 tonnes while exports amounted to 287 tonnes. Sale of gold within the country has increased year-on-year despite rising prices with retail sales worth almost Dh500 million during the 2008, 65-day Dubai Summer Surprises (DSS). The local industry is supported by Dubai Gold and Jewellery Group, a trade association with more than 700 members who represent all sectors of the business, including bullion, manufacturing, wholesale and retail.

UAE gold sales increased by 56 per cent in the third quarter of the year to reach Dh4.3 billion (US$1.17 billion) compared to Dh2.8 billion in the same period of the previous year.

Turmoil in global financial circles did, however, have an impact on gold sales in 2008 with second-quarter gold imports falling 2.1 per cent to 143 tonnes, compared with 2007, and exports falling 15.8 per cent to 64 tonnes. Total gold imports for the first half of 2008 were down 4.7 per cent, at 265 tonnes. Total exports during the same period rose 26.1 per cent to 179 tonnes. Spot gold powered to a record of US$1030.80 an ounce on 17 March 2008 due to record-high crude oil prices, fears of inflation and expectations of more rate cuts in the United States, making the metal more attractive as an alternative investment. Gold is seen as a safe-haven metal and as a hedge against inflation.

In early October 2008 Dubai Gold and Commodities Exchange (DGCX) announced that gold futures had risen by 37 per cent year-to-date (January–September), reaching 695,000 contracts, whilst the average daily volume for gold futures stood at 3200 contracts in September, up 51 per cent on September 2007.

MARITIME INDUSTRIES

Abu Dhabi Ship Building (ADSB)

ADSB is a UAE public joint stock company listed on the ADX. With an order book in excess of Dh2.5 billion (US$681 million), 10 per cent of the company is owned by the Abu Dhabi government, 40 per

Dubai, which has been dubbed 'City of Gold', has the highest concentration of jewellery shops in the world.

Bus manufacturing plant in the UAE.

In November 2008 ADSB was awarded a multi-million dollar contract to build four landing craft for the Bahrain Naval Forces in the face of stiff competition from international boatyards. This is the second Bahraini order for the company, which has the only dedicated naval shipbuilding and repair facility in the Arabian Gulf.

cent by Mubadala. and 50 per cent by more than 6000 UAE national shareholders. The company, in business since 1996, is the largest major shipbuilder in the region. ADSB completed more than 200 repairs and retrofits from its yard in Abu Dhabi in 2007 and is the only naval shipyard in the Middle East, providing both build and support services for all Gulf Cooperation Council (GCC) naval vessels.

Following its establishment, ADSB quickly evolved from retrofitting vessels into building new craft from steel and aluminium, and most recently carbon fibre composites. It is currently building six 72-metre corvettes for the UAE Navy in a contract worth more than Dh3.67 billion (US$1 billion).

It was also recently awarded a contract by the UAE Coast Guard to build 12 patrol boats branded as the 'Al-Saber' class. The 34-metre boats, constructed of composite materials, have a 'mother-daughter' design. The 'mother' vessel has a stern ramp that accommodates a smaller, high-speed 'daughter' boat, which can be launched at sea to enable fast interception. The patrol boats will be laminated in ADSB's new state-of the-art composite workshop at the company's Musaffah shipyard.

Meanwhile, UAE GHQ awarded ADSB a contract for the operational refits of the UAE Navy's two 65-metre Murray Jib Class Corvettes. The value of the contract is estimated at between Dh150 million and Dh200 million. And in September 2008 ADSB and Rolls-Royce Marine Middle East announced another agreement to set up a Waterjet Centre of Excellence in Abu Dhabi to provide support services to its customers in the Arabian Gulf region.

ADSB announced in August 2008 that it had established a joint venture with BVT Surface Fleet (itself a joint venture between BAE Systems and VT Group), one of the world's largest marine defence contractors to provide services and support to navies in the Gulf. The new entity was expected to win a long-term contract to service a large number of vessels under the purview of the UAE Navy, Coast Guard, Marine Police and other organisations.

The new venture is expected to be larger than ADSB, which in 2007 earned Dh448 million (US$122 million) in revenues and Dh26 million in net profit. The joint venture is the second for ADSB, which is also the local partner in Abu Dhabi Systems Integration – a military systems support provider – with Selex Sistemi Integrati, part of Finmeccanica, the Italian defence and aerospace conglomerate.

Dubai Maritime City

Boat manufacturing in the UAE.

Construction work on Dubai Maritime City began in January 2008. The first step was to dredge for the 'fill' to create the 2.3 million square metre peninsula that will house Dubai Maritime City (DMC). Rocks from the mainland were transported by barges and deposited in the sea off Dubai Ports Authority's (DPA) Port Rashid Terminal and Dubai Drydocks, where the new maritime facility is being built.

DMC is an integrated state-of-the-art development that will provide every element of infrastructure required by key marine and maritime related industries from six diverse sectors – marine services, marine management, product marketing, marine research and education, recreation, ship design and manufacturing – and will offer world-class facilities and services to maritime businesses in the region and worldwide.

Dubai Maritime City Authority (DMCA), governing body of the maritime centre and member of the Dubai World Group, has recently announced that registration and licensing of all maritime businesses in Dubai, which was previously the responsibility of Dubai's Department

of Economic Development (DED), will now be handled by DMCA as part of initiatives to provide a centralised point of access for all maritime-related activities in the emirate.

Under the new setup, DMCA will facilitate various maritime-related transactions including trade name, issuance of licence, renewal of licence, amendment of licence and cancellation of licence, in accordance with the Dubai Maritime City Law No 11 of 2007, which mandates DMCA to enhance Dubai's position in the maritime industry.

In June 2008 DMC launched its Maritime Centre, comprising a group of five high-rise towers called the Creek Towers and Plaza, a landmark tower located at the head of the man-made peninsula and seven plots reserved for potential developers planning to construct their own towers. The Centre will also feature a five-star business hotel and premium service apartments, and will be the first exclusive maritime cluster in the world.

OIL & GAS

The UAE has the sixth largest proven oil reserves and the fifth largest proven natural gas reserves in the world. It is also the world's third largest exporter of crude oil. By 2030 it is predicted that the world will require 118 million barrels per day of oil, 42 per cent more than it was consuming in 2005. Whilst the UAE is in a strong position with natural resources of oil and gas capable of lasting, at present production levels, for more than 100 years, it is clear that the country is not isolated from the world community and that, as supplies elsewhere dwindle, there will be increased pressure on the UAE and fellow members of OPEC to meet rising demand for oil and gas. The success or failure of government strategies in the field of energy management will thus have implications far beyond national borders. Given the fact that we are also entering a period of accelerating climate change linked to carbon emissions, the UAE has a significant role to play in seeking ways to mitigate the impact of fossil fuels on our planet.

Recognising these evolving conditions, and cognisant of its own national and global responsibilities, the UAE has been active in three main fields, i.e. firstly increasing its production capacity and efficiency for both oil and gas so as to be in a position to meet demand; secondly utilising state-of-the-art technologies and implementing strong policies in its hydrocarbon industries so that the environmental impact of

The UAE has the sixth largest proven oil reserves and the fifth largest proven natural gas reserves in the world. It is also the world's third largest exporter of crude oil.

OIL PRODUCTION (thousand barrels)

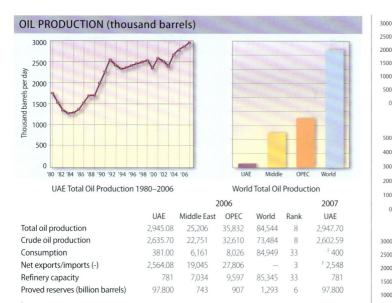

UAE Total Oil Production 1980–2006

World Total Oil Production

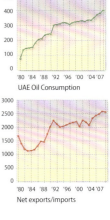

UAE Crude Oil Production

UAE Oil Consumption

Net exports/imports

	UAE	Middle East	OPEC	World	Rank	UAE
		2006				2007
Total oil production	2,945.08	25,206	35,832	84,544	8	2,947.70
Crude oil production	2,635.70	22,751	32,610	73,484	8	2,602.59
Consumption	381.00	6,161	8,026	84,949	33	F 400
Net exports/imports (-)	2,564.08	19,045	27,806	--	3	F 2,548
Refinery capacity	781	7,034	9,597	85,345	33	781
Proved reserves (billion barrels)	97.800	743	907	1,293	6	97.800

F = Forecast value
Source: Energy Information Administration (US)

these activities is minimised; and thirdly playing an active role in developing technologies for future energy solutions. These three main areas of activity are also in harmony with the UAE's efforts to promote sustainable development by stimulating economic growth, nurturing social development, and promoting environmental protection.

The Emirates exported around 2.6 million barrels of crude oil per day (bpd) in 2007 and had a production capacity of around 2.7 million bpd with work well under way to raise that figure to 3.3 million bpd by 2010 and possibly to over 5 million bpd by 2014. The country's proven crude oil reserves stand at 97.8 billion barrels, or slightly less than 8 per cent of the world's total reserves. Abu Dhabi holds 94 per cent of this amount, or about 92.2 billion barrels. Dubai contains an estimated 4 billion barrels, followed by Sharjah and Ra's al-Khaimah, with 1.5 billion and 100 million barrels of oil, respectively.

Recent and planned investments in Abu Dhabi's oil industry have been focused on maximising potential of its oil fields whilst minimising environmental impacts. The impressive list of large-scale hydrocarbon projects being implemented to raise the UAE's output capacity has

The UAE exported around 2.6 million barrels of crude oil per day (bpd) in 2007 and had a production capacity of around 2.7 million bpd, with work well under way to raise that figure to 3.3 million bpd by 2010.

www.uaeinteract.com/oilgas

The impressive list of large-scale hydrocarbon projects being implemented to raise the UAE's output capacity has consolidated its position as one of the top crude producers in the world.

consolidated its position as one of the top crude producers in the world. Development of the offshore Upper Zakum field by the Zakum Development Company, (Zadco), at a cost of Dh5.5 billion, is planned to increase its capacity to 750,000 bpd. A similar amount is being spent by the Abu Dhabi Marine Operating Company (Adma-Opco) for the expansion of the giant Umm Shaif offshore field, and Dh7.3 billion was spent on the Nasr field development.

The Abu Dhabi Company for Onshore Oil Operations (Adco) has so far invested almost Dh5.5 billion into phase one of its development programme, bringing three new fields into production in north-eastern Abu Dhabi (Al Dabbiya, Rumaitha and Shanayel) at an initial rate of around 100,000 bpd and expanding the capacity of Bu Hasa and Bab field by 180,000 bpd and 100,000 bpd respectively. A further Dh5.1 billion is being channelled into the development of the onshore Sahil, Asab and Shah fields.

Also onshore, US major Occidental were awarded a concession in late 2008 to develop the Jarn Yaphour and Ramhan fields, near the city of Abu Dhabi, which are expected to add an initial 20,000 bpd to production capacity. Around Dh1.835 billion will be spent on the fields' development.

ExxonMobil, the world's largest private oil company, is undertaking the development of Upper Zakum under a contract awarded to it by the Supreme Petroleum Council in 2006. The agreement allowed it to acquire 28 per cent in Zadco, while the Japan Oil Development Company kept its 12 per cent and Abu Dhabi National Oil Company (Adnoc) maintained overall control with its 60 per cent holding. Upper Zakum, the third largest offshore oilfield in the Gulf and one of the biggest in the world, is believed to contain in excess of 50 billion barrels of reserves in place, with estimated recoverable resources of around 16 to 20 billion barrels, using extensive water injection.

Meanwhile, Umm Shaif, about 150 kilometres north-west of Abu Dhabi City, has 268 oil wells producing 200,000 bpd. Under the above mentioned development contract, Umm Shaif's long-term sustainable capacity will be raised to 300,000 bpd.

Adma-Opco's largest oilfield, Lower Zakum, has raised its capacity to 300,000 bpd, while, with the completion of Adco's projects, its capacity rose from 1.2 million to 1.4 million bpd, with further development to 1.8 million bpd under way. Additional expansion in output was expected from Adma-Opco and other offshore oilfields.

Dubai's offshore oil production, once over 200,000 bpd, has fallen significantly in recent years, although it also continues to produce gas from offshore and condensate from onshore.

Whilst in the 1980s the oil sector accounted for around half of Dubai's GDP, and the emirate's light and sweet crude was the benchmark for all of the Middle East's production, the industry now accounts for only 3 per cent of Dubai's GDP. But Dubai has certainly not turned away from the energy sector, seeing itself as a natural location for trading in oil and gas as well as a huge consumer of both forms of energy.

Most of the major energy sector companies have regional offices in Dubai. The decision by Halliburton, the US oil industry services company, that it would locate its regional headquarters in Dubai, reaffirmed the city's status as a business hub for the energy sector.

The oil sector accounts for only 3 per cent of Dubai's GDP.

Upstream majors such as BP and Shell are also well represented in the emirate. BP controls its regional downstream activities of refining and distribution from Dubai while its production activities remain centred in Abu Dhabi.

Shell directs its regional upstream activities from Dubai, using the emirate's links with south-east Asia to control the company's assets in Pakistan and elsewhere. Meanwhile, PSI Energy Holding, formerly based in Bahrain, announced its decision to move most of its corporate operations to Dubai in an effort to better access projects in the region. The emirate is thus leading a new impetus towards regional energy trading, both physically and on paper markets. Both the Dubai Mercantile Exchange and the Dubai Multi Commodities Centre have established trading in energy futures for fuel oil and Omani crude oil.

Sharjah is the third UAE hydrocarbon producer. In July 2008 it announced a 20-year farm-out agreement between the Sharjah government and BP Sharjah Ltd with RAK Petroleum PCL. The deal created a new, 34 square kilometre, East Sajaa concession in which RAK Petroleum will drill for gas on the basis that any discoveries are to be processed through the existing Sajaa plant operated by BP Sharjah Ltd. RAK Petroleum holds a 55 per cent stake and operation control in the new concession, with the Sharjah government and BP Sharjah Ltd holding 27 per cent and 18 per cent respectively.

BP Sharjah Ltd will continue to operate the principal Sajaa Gas Concession, in which the Sharjah government holds 60 per cent stake and BP Sharjah Ltd holds 40 per cent stake, and which includes the Saja'a, Moveyeid and Kahaif fields.

OIL REFINING

Takreer's new oil refinery in Ruwais, which is scheduled for completion in 2013, will raise Abu Dhabi's total refining capacity from the current 485,000 bpd to 885,000 bpd.

In February 2008 the Abu Dhabi oil refining company, Takreer, revealed new plans to build a 417,000 bpd refinery in Ruwais, expected to go into operation by 2013. When completed, this will raise Abu Dhabi's total refining capacity from the current 485,000 bpd to 885,000 bpd. The move follows a steady increase in fuel demand in the country with a 4.6 per cent hike in usage, to more than 223,000 bpd in 2007. With the rate of consumption continuing to rise (by at least 5 per cent in 2008) there is a strong demand for refined products, primarily diesel (95,600 bpd in 2007) followed by gasoline (83,000 bpd). These are supplied by refineries in Abu Dhabi and in other emirates, with excess being exported.

Ruwais refinery, nearly 250 kilometres east of Abu Dhabi, currently produces approximately 400,000 bpd while Umm al Nar's capacity is estimated at nearly 85,000 bpd. The UAE's total refining capacity stood at 778,000 bpd at the start of 2007 but expansion projects and new refineries, including one being built in Fujairah by the International Petroleum Company (IPIC) with a capacity of 500,000 bpd, are expected to raise production to over 1.5 million bpd by 2012.

Clearly, the new refinery at Ruwais will play a very significant role in strengthening the UAE's refining capacity. Progress has been steady with Takreer signing an agreement on technology and engineering services with a subsidiary of Honeywell International, UOP, at the end of September 2008. At the same time an announcement was made concerning the new refinery's proposed output, which will include propylene, unleaded gasoline, naphtha, liquefied petroleum gas (LPG), aviation turbine fuel, kerosene, gas-oil, bunker fuel and other hydrocarbon derivatives. It is expected to be complete in 2014 and will utilise a wide range of UOP technologies for the production of clean, low sulphur distillate and gasoline.

In December 2007, independent oil trader Vitol recommissioned and restarted part of the 82,000 barrels per day refinery in Fujairah that had been mothballed for about four years. The small refinery is being used primarily to support Vitol's fuel oil business both regionally and for export to Asia.

DOLPHIN GAS PROJECT

In May 2008 the Dolphin Gas Project was formally inaugurated in a ceremony in Qatar attended by HH Sheikh Tamim bin Hamad Al Thani, Crown Prince of Qatar, HH Sheikh Mohammed bin Zayed Al Nahyan, Crown Prince of Abu Dhabi and Deputy Supreme Commander of the UAE Armed Forces, HH Sheikh Hamdan bin Zayed Al Nahyan, UAE Deputy Prime Minister and Chairman of Dolphin Energy Limited, and HH Sheikh Mansour bin Zayed Al Nahyan, UAE Minister of Presidential Affairs and Chairman of the International Petroleum Investment Company, IPIC. Senior Qatari, UAE and Omani government officials, Dolphin's board of directors and senior management, along with other guests also attended the formal inauguration ceremony.

The Dolphin Gas Project was formally inaugurated in May 2008.

The Dolphin Gas Processing Plant is the largest single-build gas plant in the world and is central to Dolphin's operations. The ceremony marked the successful completion of the Dolphin Gas Project – the largest gas initiative ever undertaken in the Gulf region. The seven-year construction programme saw the creation of a full energy value chain – from gas wells offshore Qatar, onshore processing plant, gas export pipeline to the UAE and substantial gas supplies to customers across the seven emirates. Transportation of the dry gas by sub-sea

export pipeline from Qatar to the UAE began in July 2007 and Dolphin supplies up to 2 billion standard cubic feet of refined natural gas, every day, to utilities, industries and consumers throughout the UAE. Major customers for Dolphin gas from Qatar are Adwea (Abu Dhabi Water and Electricity Authority), Uwec (Union Water and Electricity Company), Dusup (Dubai Supply Authority) and, from October 2008, OOC (Oman Oil Company). Each has signed a gas supply agreement with Dolphin Energy for 25 years.

Dolphin Energy is 51 per cent owned by Mubadala, on behalf of the Abu Dhabi government, and 24.5 per cent each by Total of France and Occidental Petroleum of the USA.

The Dolphin export pipeline has been constructed for maximum physical throughput of some 90.6 million cubic metres, nearly 60 per cent more than was being transmitted under initial development and production-sharing agreements. Dolphin has initiated discussions with the Qatari authorities on the possibility of further gas supply in the future. Meanwhile, the company's officials have estimated the total cost of the project at US$5 billion, including the US$1.6 billion gas processing facilities at Ra's Laffan, which serves the giant offshore North Field, the world's largest single reservoir of non-associated gas, with deposits of more than 900 trillion cubic feet.

Dolphin Energy's prime activity is in transporting gas from its source to the end users through major pipelines. It is in this context that a new pipeline from Taweelah to Fujairah (TFP), announced in July 2008, fits into the company's overall strategy. The Dh1.5 billion project involves a 48-inch diameter pipe being laid over more than 240 kilometres of desert and mountainside – one of the longest and most substantial overland pipelines in the UAE. The TFP will link Dolphin Energy's gas receiving facilities at Taweelah, on the coast of Abu Dhabi, with the Adwea power and water desalination plants at Qidfa, in Fujairah.

Dolphin Energy commenced supplying gas to Oman on 2 November 2008, completing the strategic Qatar–UAE–Oman natural gas grid first proposed in 1999.

GAS PRODUCTION

The UAE is pumping billions of dollars into projects to boost its hydrocarbon production, establish more gas-related industries and increase oil extraction from its fields by gas injection. With its proven gas wealth exceeding 6 trillion cubic metres the UAE is the fifth largest gas power in the world and is one of the top LNG producers. Its sprawling LNG complex on Das Island produces in excess of 8 million tonnes per year. Increasing quantities of gas are being used to enhance oil recovery by injection into underground reservoirs.

The two Abu Dhabi companies directly involved in natural gas industry are Abu Dhabi Gas Industries Company Ltd (Gasco), onshore, and Abu Dhabi Gas Liquefaction Company Ltd (Adgas), offshore. Gasco was founded in 1978 to process the associated gas of Abu Dhabi's onshore gas and then pump it to Ruwais gas liquefaction plant where it is fractionated and exported. Adnoc utilises part of the Gasco-produced gas locally.

Gasco's recent projects, costing more than Dh14.68 (US$4 billion), are briefly discussed below.

The onshore gas development phase III (OGD-III) project is designed to process 1306 million standard cubic feet per day (mmscf/d) of condensate rich gas (from the Thamama "F" reservoir) at Habshan and to produce 11,800 tonnes per day (tpd) of NGL (including 3400 tpd ethane) and 130,000 bpd condensate. Residue gas will be re-injected back into the reservoir for pressure maintenance purposes (gas re-cycling).

The Ruwais third NGL Train is designed to process the additional 24,400 tpd of NGL produced from OGD-III, AGD-II (Asab gas development – phase II) and other projects and to produce about 6400 tpd of raw ethane for transfer to the petrochemical plant at Ruwais (Borouge), 6000 tpd each of propane and butane and 5800 tpd of pentane plus products. The project comprises a new NGL fractionation train and new storage tanks for propane, butane and pentane plus.

AGD-II is designed to recover 400 tpd of NGL from the sour condensate-rich gas from the existing Asab gas plant. As with OGD-III, residue gas will be re-injected back into the reservoir for pressure maintenance purposes. Main facilities include two trains for gas treatment and two for NGL recovery together with a new NGL pipeline from Asab to Habshan and other required facilities.

The Habshan gas complex expansion (HGCE) involves installation of enhanced gas processing facilities at Habshan to process additional associated gas produced by Adco through their crude oil expansion projects at Bab and Bu Hasa and to introduce operational flexibility between Bu Hasa and Habshan. The project also includes installation of an acid gas enrichment unit (AGEU) for processing acid gas from OGD-III facilities as well as installation of two additional sulphur recovery units (SRU).

Adnoc announced in December 2008 that it will implement all its future projects according to the framework of the Kyoto Agreement's Clean Development Mechanism (CDM) related to the reduction of carbon emissions.

The offshore associated gas project (OAG) envisages transporting the excess offshore associated gas from Das Island through a 200 kilometre-long, 30-inch diameter offshore/onshore pipeline and to process it at Habshan, thereby establishing a strategic link between the offshore and onshore facilities. The project is being implemented through three separate EPC packages: one for the Das Island facilities, one for the offshore pipeline, and one for the Habshan facilities and onshore pipeline.

In addition to the above major developments, Gasco is preparing a master plan for the company and is involved with the Bu Hasa upgrade project, the Asab and Bab integrated control systems, the Bu Hasa–Habshan gas pipeline, gas supply to Al Ain Air College, replacement of NGL pipelines, a new lean gas station at Bu Hasa and development of non-process buildings at Habshan. Looking ahead, a re-structuring of Abu Dhabi's onshore gas operations is being planned, with Dolphin Energy also due to play a major role.

Adgas, Gasco's fellow company involved with Abu Dhabi's gas resources, is the Gulf pioneer in the field of gas liquefaction. Its plant on Das Island is unique worldwide in its ability to process both associated gas, which is a by-product of oil extraction operations, and natural gas extracted as a free product from gas reservoirs. Adgas plant's feed-gas, both associated and non-associated gas, comes from Abu Dhabi's offshore fields. The company's plant comprises three process trains with an average annual production of 8 million tonnes of liquefied natural gas, liquefied petroleum gas, pentane and liquid sulphur.

In early 2007 Adgas awarded Technip a lump-sum turnkey contract worth approximately Dh2.238 billion for gas compression plants and associated facilities to be located at Das Island. The plant's facilities, which include compressor and booster stations, fuel gas treatment and gas dehydration units, will treat 211 mmscf/d of associated gases produced by offshore fields in Abu Dhabi.

Meanwhile, Abu Dhabi is considering using its abundant sour gas stocks to meet fast-growing domestic gas demand from power stations, homes and industries. With this in mind Adnoc signed an interim agreement in July 2008 with ConocoPhillips of the USA, for development of a major project to tap into the sour gas resources at the Shah field. The project, involving several gas-gathering systems, construction of processing trains to process 1 billion cfd of gas at

Shah, is expected to deliver a minimum of 570 mmcf/d of network gas, in addition to new gas and liquid pipelines and the construction of sulphur exporting facilities at Ruwais.

National Gas Shipping Company

Since 1994 The National Gas Shipping Company Ltd. (NGSCO) has provided uninterrupted transportation of LNG produced by Adgas from Das Island to Tokyo Electric Power Company (Tepco) in Japan. NGSCO operates a fleet of eight modern LNG vessels and also provides transportation for LPG and sulphur to various destinations across the world, extending its expertise to the Adgas supply chain.

Taking over full operation of its fleet of eight Moss Rosenberg liquid natural gas carriers on 13 December 2007 and making safe delivery of its one thousandth cargo on its own vessels at the Japanese terminal of Higashi in Tokyo Bay on 13 April 2008, NGSCO is regarded as one of the world's leading companies in LNG transportation.

Dana Gas

Dana Gas, the first regional private-sector natural gas company in the Middle East, was established with over 300 founder shareholders from across the GCC region, and some 425,000 investors from over 100 nationalities. Headquartered in Sharjah, the company is listed on ADX and has assets and projects in gas exploration and production,

processing, transportation and marketing in several countries. Dana is active in the natural gas business throughout the Middle East–North Africa (MENA) region across the entire natural gas value-chain, including upstream exploration and production, through the midstream transmission and distribution of gas, including LNG trading, and downstream into gas-related industries and petrochemicals. It has gas projects in Kurdistan and has also implemented a drilling campaign of 19 new wells in Egypt.

The company also formed a new joint venture with Emarat to build, own and operate a 48-inch common-user gas pipeline with capacity of 1 billion cfd, to serve customers in the UAE. It also completed an acquisition to lead a consortium for development of the Gulf of Suez gas liquids plant in partnership with the state-owned Egyptian Natural Gas Holding Company (Egas) with processing capacity of 150 mmscf/d of natural gas and production of approximately 120,000 t/y of propane and butane in liquid form.

RAK Petroleum

RAK Petroleum is part-owner and operator of five concessions in the Sultanate of Oman, one in Ra's al-Khaimah and one in Sharjah. Having acquired 754 kilometres of 2D seismic in 2007, the company committed itself to drill three exploration wells in 2008 and 2009. Exploration and field development expenditure in 2008 was in the region of Dh330 million.

Production from RAK Petroleum's offshore gas / condensate field, Bukha, is projected at around 20 mmscf/d of gas in 2008 (gross) with associated liquids production of 1500 bpd. Development of the nearby West Bukha field was progressing with first production expected in late 2008, increasing production by a further 35 mmscf/d of gas (gross) with associated liquids production in excess of 10,000 bpd. Both fields are located in Oman Block 8.

The Bukha field supplies about 10 per cent of the emirate's gas demand. This has now been boosted with production from Umm al-Qaiwain's Atlantis offshore field (see below), with the gas processed by RakGas, which is yielding over 90 mmscf/d, or 30 per cent of the emirate's gas demand.

Umm al-Qaiwain Gas Production

Umm al-Qaiwain commenced production of up to 92 mmscf/d of wet gas on 2 May 2008. The gas is being transported through a sub-sea pipeline for processing at the Rakgas plant in Ra's al-Khaimah. Development and operation of the new offshore gas field is being carried out by Field Atlantis (UAQ) Ltd, a subsidiary of Sinochem Corporation. The field is located 20 kilometres off the coast of Umm al-Qaiwain and the unmanned platform is set in 33 metres of water. The Khor Khwair gas plant, which receives the wet gas, extracts condensate and sulphur before the gas is introduced into the local gas grid. The UAQ field is the first offshore gas field development in the emirate and its timely gas production is contributing significantly to the energy needs in the northern emirates.

Fujairah's Oil & Gas

The rapidly expanding east coast port of Fujairah is the second largest bunkering port in the world (handling about 1 million tonnes of fuel from neighbouring countries per month). Arrival of natural gas, via the Dolphin Energy gas pipeline from Qatar, has boosted local industry, in particular power generation and water desalination. Exports of gas have also increased. Meanwhile, the Abu Dhabi government has made a strategic investment by strengthening its ability to supply crude oil to tankers outside the Arabian Gulf, at Fujairah. In August 2008 Abu Dhabi-owned International Petroleum Investment Company (IPIC) began construction of a 500,000 bpd refinery and associated storage tanks close to Fujairah Port, part of the Abu Dhabi Crude Oil Pipeline Project (ADCOP), which will see the construction of a 360 kilometre pipeline, capable of handling 1.5 million bpd from Habshan in Abu Dhabi to Fujairah. It is due to be completed in 2010.

ALTERNATIVE ENERGY INDUSTRY

Abu Dhabi's bold moves into the field of alternative energy and sustainable development have earned it worldwide respect and admiration. The visit to the UAE by the US President George W. Bush in early 2008 was accompanied by a special briefing on the Masdar Initiative which involves much more than building Abu Dhabi's innovative 'zero carbon' city. As we have already seen in the section on industrial zones, it is, in fact, a multi-billion dollar commitment to invest in alternative and renewable energy sources; sustainable development; education; manufacturing and carbon management.

The Abu Dhabi government and Masdar regard their initiative in both commercial and socio-environmental terms. Just as the UAE has

Abu Dhabi's bold moves into the field of alternative energy and sustainable development have earned it worldwide respect and admiration.

www.uaeinteract.com/oilgas

developed a successful economy supported by oil and natural gas, so will alternative energy become a cornerstone of the country's future economic stability.

The President was presented with a comprehensive display outlining the six business units of the initiative, including plans for Masdar City, and the Masdar Institute of Science and Technology (MIST), the region's first graduate-level academic institution focused on energy and sustainability, which is being developed in cooperation with the Massachusetts Institute of Technology (MIT).

Masdar, which means 'the source' in Arabic, has four principal objectives: firstly, to help drive the economic diversification of Abu Dhabi; secondly, to maintain and expand Abu Dhabi's position in evolving global energy markets; thirdly, to help Abu Dhabi become a developer of technology and last, but by no means least, to make a meaningful contribution to sustainable human development.

Masdar is owned by the Abu Dhabi Future Energy Company (Adfec), a wholly owned company of the government of Abu Dhabi through the Mubadala Development Company. Following President Bush's visit, Masdar hosted the inaugural World Future Energy Summit (WFES) bringing together the world's leading innovators, educators, scientists, venture capitalists and experts in the field of alternative and renewable energies. The successful summit was the largest ever meeting of the 'future energy' movement and a premier event for world leaders to preview new solutions and technologies and to seek partners.

In addition to some high profile presentations made by the CEO of Masdar to world leaders in 2008, including special presentations to British leaders at Buckingham Palace in London and to the US Congress Select Committee on Energy Independence and Global Warming in Washington, D.C., Masdar has been quick to put real flesh on the framework it is creating for sustainable technology development in the UAE and around the world.

During his speech to the US Congressional Committee, Masdar's CEO, Dr Sultan Al Jaber, stated, 'For the first time in history, more than half of the world's population now lives in cities, with their traditional energy inefficiencies, waste and pollution. We must fundamentally re-think how cities can conserve energy and other resources. We must heavily employ new technologies and even create new urban models, as we are doing in Masdar City'.

In November 2008, Masdar and the UK Government signed a collaboration agreement on the development of renewable energy and clean technology solutions. The contracting parties will leverage each other's expertise and influence to help accelerate adoption of technologies in order to make renewable energy scalable and affordable to the global community.

Masdar's approach to achieving its admirable goals is to create constructive partnerships with world-class companies specialising in technologies that are helping to solve our planet's energy and climate challenges. There is also a sense of urgency and priority to Masdar's efforts. 'Today, governments and businesses worldwide are facing a common problem of strain on natural resources and environment', Dr Al Jaber told attendees at a seminar at Buckingham Palace:

Energy security, climate change and sustainable development require engaging, aligning and collectively committing to investing in and shaping a better and more secure future. Through Masdar, we want to play a major role in developing solutions that answer present challenges – challenges which are made all the more important due to the limited time we have to solve them' he stated. 'We are not simply a renewable energy initiative, our aspirations are far higher. We truly believe that we can make a difference.

In August 2008, less than three months after announcing a strategic investment into thin-film photovoltaics, Masdar broke ground on its first photovoltaic production plant in Ichtershausen, Germany. The plant will use advanced production technologies to bring PV closer to grid parity. The US$230 million (EUR 150 million) German plant marked the first phase of Masdar's US$2 billion (EUR 1.3 billion) investment in thin-film PV manufacturing, one of the largest investments ever made in solar. To be opened in Q3 2009, the plant has a targeted annual production capacity of 70 MW, and will create more than 180 green jobs. It will produce the world's largest (5.7 square metre) and most powerful PV modules. The German plant will act as a blueprint for technology and knowledge transfer to a 140 MW Abu Dhabi plant, which will begin initial production by Q3 2010. Output from both facilities has been committed to major PV system installers in Europe, and for Masdar's own energy generation requirements. Abu Dhabi's geography and its vision to become a world leader in renewable energy, makes thin-film PV a natural area of focus for Masdar.

In September 2008 Masdar announced that it had made a EUR120 million investment in wind energy company, WinWinD Oy, a Finnish wind turbine manufacturer. WinWinD is active in design, development and assembly of technologically advanced one-megawatt and three-megawatt wind turbines. The investment helped Masdar to move

In July 2008 Masdar joined forces with Gulf Petrochemical Industries Company (GPIC) to monetise the emission reduction associated with carbon dioxide capture and recycling at GPIC's fertiliser facility in Bahrain. The new venture fits into the Kyoto Protocol's Clean Development Mechanism (CDM) and will capture carbon dioxide from flue gas and then recycle the captured gas as feedstock in the production of urea and methanol.

rapidly into the worldwide wind market enabling it to diversify its renewable energy asset portfolio. Masdar intends to develop a full range of sustainable energy capabilities, including solar power, wind turbines and geothermal energy projects, as well as building a hydrogen-generated power plant.

In mid-October 2008 Masdar announced that it had acquired a 20 per cent interest in the London Array wind farm project, destined to become the world's largest offshore wind farm. Other partners are E.ON and Dong Energy. UK's Prime Minister Gordon Brown welcomed the decision. 'I very much welcome Masdar's decision to invest in renewable energy in the UK. This is an excellent example of the partnership that we need between oil producing and oil consuming countries to develop new energy sources and technologies, diversifying their economies and reducing our dependence on carbon. The scale and vision of the London Array is groundbreaking, and places the UK at the forefront of offshore wind development,' he said.

TOURISM

The UAE has much to offer as a tourist destination.

A report by BMI in September 2008 stated that the growth rate in visitors to the UAE in 2007 was a relatively strong 7.5 per cent year-on-year, equating to some 8.5 million arrivals. Europe accounted for the largest group of tourists visiting Dubai in 2007 (32 per cent of the total), followed by Asia (23 per cent). The study predicted a possible steadying of demand from the United States and key European economies that together accounted for 40 per cent of total arrivals to the UAE in 2007. 6.95 million guests stayed in Dubai hotels, an increase of 8 per cent year-on-year. Guest nights were up a buoyant 16.7 per cent to 20.5 million nights. Dubai hotels also recorded an impressive average occupancy rate (beds) of 81.4 per cent in 2007. At the end of 2007, Dubai had 319 operating hotels, up nearly 6 per cent year-on-year, while the number of hotel rooms increased by a similar rate, bringing the total room capacity to around 32,600.

Abu Dhabi National Hotels (ADNH) reported net profit of Dh477 million in preliminary financial results for 2007, representing a substantial increase of 63 per cent compared with the previous year. Total revenue increased to Dh1.3 billion from Dh1.2 billion in 2006. Abu Dhabi has been investing heavily in development of its tourism

The UAE, which has been described as the 'rising star' in the world of tourism, is expected to become a major tourist destination over the next five years.

facilities with many new projects coming on-stream in 2008. These and other ongoing projects are expected to result in very strong growth of this sector of the emirate's economy.

The last year has seen dynamic acceleration in the UAE's drive towards creating a world-class tourism destination. Whilst the statistics tell part of the story, one needs to look beyond the numbers to understand the whole picture. The background to attractive and successful developments such as Emirates Palace Hotel, the Burj al-Arab, Emirates Mall or the Atlantis Resort on Jumeirah Palm is full of imaginative planning, forward thinking and, above all, professional organisation. The significant investments being made throughout the sector, whether in hotel construction or resort development and promotion of leisure activities, require considerable focus and highly professional organisation and this has been facilitated by restructuring of existing bodies or creation of new ones with clear responsibilities to work in particular areas of tourism development. In Abu Dhabi it is the responsibility of the new Abu Dhabi Tourism Authority (ADTA)

An acrylic tunnel leads visitors to the centre of the aquarium at Dubai Mall.

The award-winning Emirates Palace Hotel in Abu Dhabi.

to promote the emirate as a tourist destination, whilst creating the tourism infrastructure within Abu Dhabi falls to the Tourism Development Investment Company (TDIC), an ADTA subsidiary, that is involved, among other things, with extensive cultural developments on Saadiyat Island (see section on Urban Development). Meanwhile, the national airline, Etihad, works in tandem with these and other bodies to enhance tourism to Abu Dhabi in particular and the UAE in general.

A key ingredient of the UAE's tourism development campaign is the creation of theme parks. There are over 30 such entertainment resorts and theme parks being developed with a projected total investment of Dh228 billion (US$62 billion). Prominent among them are Warner Brothers Theme Park, Ferrari World Abu Dhabi and the Abu Dhabi Water Park. Meanwhile, 'Dubailand', a multi-billion dollar enclave of theme parks, four and a half times the size of Manhattan, has been described as 'the Middle East's answer to Disneyworld'. Overall, the massive projects at Dubailand are expected to boost the contribution of the tourism sector to the emirate's gross domestic product from its current 19 per cent to 35 per cent by 2015!

In addition, Ra's al-Khaimah is developing WOW RAK that will include two adjacent theme parks – Ice Land Water Park and Planet Earth Theme Park – complete with a 12,000 square metre shopping mall and entertainment plaza and a resort.

www.uaeinteract.com/economicdevelopment

Visitors can interact with dolphins at the Atlantis resort.

The UAE's first dolphinarium opened in Dubai in May 2008. The 1250-seat indoor arena at the Dubai Dolphinarium in Creek Park stages three live shows a day. Visitors are encouraged to learn about marine life in classrooms after the performances. The Dh33 million (US$9 million) dolphinarium also has a multimedia science library and an aqua-themed gym and fitness centre. The dolphins have all been born in captivity, many from parents that were also born in captivity. A more extensive dolphinarium known as Dolphin Bay opened in November 2008 as part of the Atlantis hotel development on Palm Jumeirah. This had its own first captive born baby dolphin in September 2008 and the resort operates a programme enabling visitors to engage in close contact with dolphins.

AGRICULTURE

Agriculture in the UAE has been going through very challenging times with the growing acceptance that whilst the country has proven its expertise in cultivating a wide range of crops in an exceedingly arid climate, cost-benefit analysis of these activities calls into question the sustainability of certain areas of the agri-sector.

New strategies are necessary if agriculture in the UAE is to remain a viable business.

The UAE's only natural source of irrigation water is in underground aquifers that are 'tapped into' by over 30,000 wells. Pumping groundwater from the wells that tap into the vast subterranean aquifers deep beneath Arabia's desert sands has had a natural toll on the water table and salinity levels. As fresh water has been depleted, saline water has replaced it in many areas, to the great detriment of soil fertility. With the water table in steady decline and incursions of saline water on the increase there has been a realisation that new strategies are necessary if agriculture in the UAE is to remain a viable business.

There have been a number of approaches to this issue, including the introduction of high-tech solutions such as water filtration and recycling in livestock rearing units; intensive cultivation in controlled environments and drip irrigation systems that optimise use of water. These efforts have been met with some notable successes and there are several positive indications that food production in the UAE can be continued on a sustainable basis, albeit on a reduced scale in some areas.

The key limiting factor to raising the UAE's agricultural production, the shortage of naturally occurring freshwater suitable for agricultural use, has been counteracted to some extent by the use of both desalinated and recycled water. But the costs of doing this are becoming prohibitively high and there has been a growing awareness that agriculture accounts for 80 per cent of freshwater use but only contributes 1.7 per cent to GDP. It is a situation that will not be allowed to continue indefinitely and a great deal of work is taking place to redress this imbalance by making local agriculture more efficient in terms of water conservation and focusing on crops that create high value products with minimum water consumption.

Despite these efforts to improve the UAE's agricultural methods, today's farms seem unlikely to provide the desired levels of self-sufficiency in food production that were achieved in the past.

The area under organic cultivation in the UAE will be increased to 3000 acres as the demand for natural food products is on the rise.

A farm in Liwa contrasts with the surrounding desert.

Biotechnology has a role to play in UAE agriculture.

Meanwhile, the need for food production in the UAE has never been greater. With population rapidly increasing the demand curve is on an upward trajectory that local agriculture is simply unable to meet. The traditional solution has been importation of food from overseas suppliers. More recently a refinement of this approach has been direct investment in certain overseas areas where agricultural potential may not have been fully realised. The UAE has started to identify such areas with a view to investment in agricultural development and helping to serve the UAE's own food needs. Recent acquisitions have included 100,000 acres of land in Pakistan and 70,000 acres of farmland in Sudan.

Despite the natural tendency to assume otherwise, not all farming in the UAE is aimed at meeting local demand. A number of UAE farms are using hydroponic methods to grow crops such as strawberries, lettuce, peppers, tomatoes and roses in specially formulated nutrient solutions. One such farming company, Mirak, with 200 acres of farms under hydroponic production at Dhaid, Al Hayer, Sweihan and Al Ain, grows more than 3500 tonnes of produce annually, exporting more than 65 per cent of this to world markets such as Japan, Singapore and Europe. Mirak's successful operations are expected to increase to five times their current size, boosting its trade volumes to more than Dh100 million a year.

Whilst traditional farming practices in the UAE may be proving somewhat impractical in terms of meeting the needs of the Emirates' growing population, this does not mean that there is no future for such methods in the country's agricultural regime. Organic farming methods, many of which have their grounding in traditional farming methods, are gaining momentum and earning the appreciation of local consumers. The first internationally certified organic farm in the UAE was awarded its credentials in late 2007. Spread over five hectares, Abu Dhabi Organic Farm grows tomatoes, mushrooms, cabbage, carrots, cucumbers and herbs as well as strawberries and mangoes, all under organic conditions. The Food and Agriculture Organisation of the United Nations supervised the certification process undertaken by a European certification centre.

Biotechnology has a role to play in UAE agriculture in a number of different areas including possible resuscitation of depleted soils. Farmers are learning to embrace scientific advances to solve seemingly intractable problems of local agriculture.

INFRASTRUCTURE

The UAE continues to spend billions of dollars on infrastructure projects and is the biggest projects market in the region.

Through visionary leadership and the philosophy of excellence ingrained in all infrastructural developments, the intention is to lead the region and the world in shaping sustainable cities.

INFRASTRUCTURE

THE UAE CONTINUES TO SPEND BILLIONS OF DOLLARS on infrastructure and is the biggest projects market in the region, accounting for 37 per cent of total project value within the construction, oil and gas, petrochemicals, power and water and waste sectors. The last 12 months have seen huge investment poured into real estate, tourism and leisure, with developments such as Masdar City and Saadiyat Island highlighting Abu Dhabi's status as an emerging market.

But the UAE's future isn't just about diversifying into travel and tourism: building better cities, thereby providing a better life for the people of the UAE, is a key focus of government strategy. Through visionary leadership and the philosophy of excellence ingrained in all infrastructural developments, the intention is to lead the region and the world in shaping sustainable cities.

Entire conurbations, complete with the requisite infrastructure, are being built to meet the unprecedented demand for housing generated by a rapidly rising population and liberalised real estate laws. As we have seen in the previous chapter, industry and trade is also being fostered with the construction of free zones, dedicated industrial areas and commercial clusters.

These developments are particularly evident in the larger emirates of Abu Dhabi and Dubai. However, governments in the northern emirates are rapidly following suit, providing major incentives for developers of residential and commercial property.

In addition, UAE President Sheikh Khalifa bin Zayed Al Nahyan has allocated Dh16 billion (US$4.4 billion) for infrastructure projects in the northern emirates The allocation will be used to fund the construction of road networks, new housing communities, drainage networks and other projects, providing integrated solutions to some infrastructure deficits in these areas.

Building better cities, thereby providing a better life for the people of the UAE, is a key focus of government strategy.

www.uaeinteract.com/infrastructure

URBAN DEVELOPMENT

ABU DHABI

Capital city of the emirate and the federation, Abu Dhabi is at the centre of the unprecedented prosperity and growth sweeping across the region. Driven by a boom in real estate and tourism sectors, the total value of announced projects in Abu Dhabi is close to the Dh1,835 billion (US$500 billion) mark, and industrial and commercial activity is thriving. In response, therefore, to the need to effectively manage burgeoning development, the visionary urban structure framework 'Plan Abu Dhabi 2030' was formulated in 2007 with the assistance of eminent urban planners. This is designed to help Abu Dhabi filter and respond to current and future development needs, establish a planning culture and introduce strong guidelines for sustainable development. Implementation and development of the framework was entrusted to the recently formed Abu Dhabi Urban Planning Council (www.upc.gov.ae).

Central to the plan is the creation of a sustainable city built around vibrant neighbourhoods. This necessitates concentrating growth, introducing transportation choice, creating mixed-use, pedestrian-friendly streets, implementing more sustainable, cost-effective infrastructure, and protecting and enhancing the natural environment.

Abu Dhabi's espousal of best practice in urban planning has earned it accolades, with a survey of 130 cities worldwide by one of the world's largest property advisory firms singling it out as the ultimate 'power city' of the next millennium. Identifying Abu Dhabi as one of the world's fastest growing 'urban stars' destined to be on the 'radar screen of the real estate industry' for the next decade, the report also predicted that Abu Dhabi would be a 'city of substance' by 2010, a 'regional hub' by 2015 and a 'world winning city' by 2020, a decade ahead of the Plan 2030 deadline.

The report pointed out that Plan 2030 was unique to the region and created a 'structured and clearly articulated framework for the city's long-term growth'. It added that the city epitomised a fresh spirit of city building, which is almost 'unmatched anywhere else in the world' and an expansion programme 'that puts culture and community ahead of pure commercialisation.' The research also identified the challenges ahead for the city and emirate.

Core Districts

To achieve its aim of sustainable development, Plan 2030 proposes a radical transformation of the capital city, based on the development of core districts. Sowwah Island along with the adjacent fringes of Mina Zayed and Al Reem Island will form Abu Dhabi's new Central Business District. This will encompass 105 hectares of commercial, residential and retail infrastructure supported by an extensive network of 13 bridges, public transport links and pedestrian facilities, all connecting with the already existing city centre.

Sowwah will feature the distinctive new headquarters of the Abu Dhabi Securities Exchange and it will also be home to the first Cleveland Clinic in the Middle East. Residential neighbourhoods will surround the Central Business District, decreasing in density from an impressive skyline of high-rise residential towers towards the centre to low-rise traditionally planned Emirati communities on the outskirts.

Clustered around the city's newest landmark, the Grand Mosque District lies mid-way between the Central Business District and Capital City, an important secondary downtown. The Officer's Club and Zayed Sports City are already located here, and further development allows for more residential and commercial units, including mid-rise residential developments, with pockets designated as Emirati housing. However, building heights are being carefully regulated to ensure that views of the minarets of the Grand Mosque remain the most prominent feature of the area.

The Capital City District is destined to be a key seat of local and federal government, containing departmental offices and embassies as well as cultural institutions and commemorative spaces of national importance.

This new downtown development covering 49 million square metres will provide over 150,000 jobs and housing for more than 350,000 people and include a university quarter and a regional sports hub. An integrated, high-capacity transit network will serve the local population and link the Capital City District to the surrounding region.

The development of an area of Saadiyat Island into Abu Dhabi's Cultural District is an exciting step for the city, creating for the first time a dedicated home for cultural and arts activities in the capital. The district will include five landmark museums or performance spaces, all designed by world-renowned architects, including Guggenheim Abu Dhabi, the Abu Dhabi Louvre, and the Sheikh Zayed National

The Abu Dhabi Urban Planning Council defines the shape of the emirate, ensuring factors such as sustainability, infrastructure capacity, community planning and quality of life are taken into consideration in all developments.

The Arzanah project surrounding Zayed Sports City is just one of the many innovative developments that have contributed to Abu Dhabi's designation as one of the world's fastest growing 'urban stars'.

Museum, with additional pavilion spaces throughout for temporary exhibitions. The Cultural District will also be home to a New York University (NYU) campus, the first comprehensive liberal arts campus to be operated abroad by a major US university.

Designed for easy, shaded pedestrian access, Saadiyat Island is just seven minutes from downtown Abu Dhabi via the ten-lane Saadiyat Bridge, which is nearing completion, and 20 minutes from Abu Dhabi International Airport via the Saadiyat Link highway from Shahama, which is currently under construction.

As well as ensuring that residential and commercial sectors are given space to expand, Plan Abu Dhabi 2030 sets aside areas for the growth of the city's current international airport and port, both of which are essential for tourism and industry. Abu Dhabi International Airport and its industrial zone will form part of the city's new transport system as a major portal for those entering the city, with connection to the proposed metro and high-speed rail systems. The current port (Mina Zayed) will be phased out by 2010, whilst work has commenced on Khalifa Port, a purpose-built container port half-way between Abu Dhabi and Dubai. The latter will be surrounded by an industrial zone and a free zone that will allow businesses to locate production centres close to suppliers.

A key principle of Plan Abu Dhabi 2030 is to respect, be scaled to, and be shaped by the natural environment, in particular the sensitive coastal and desert ecosystems.

Development Themes

Several key 'development themes' or frameworks have helped to shape Plan 2030. Keeping economic sustainability in mind, the goal is to bring complementary land uses and developments together in one place, while also discouraging uncontrolled growth beyond the defined city limits.

Growth away from the two city centres is restricted and protected environmental areas surrounding the city prevent unwanted urban sprawl. Within these limits, areas at the south of Hudairiyat and Abu Dhabi Island have been designated for major development opportunities to complement the two city cores. Outside the main residential and commercial zones, industrial areas in Mussafah and Mafraq will be further developed and linked by an effective freight transport network. In addition, high-tech industries will be developed in the industrial zone surrounding Abu Dhabi International Airport, and heavy industries will be housed in the industrial zone linked to Khalifa Port.

www.uaeinteract.com/urban

An example of a 'Fareej' – the smallest unit of an Emirati community as conceived under the Abu Dhabi Urban Structure Framework Plan – shows a group of homes clustered around a central courtyard. This pattern is based on the traditional organisation of Emirati settlements and reflects the very high importance of family relationships.

Fareejs grouped together in 'Local Clusters' around a central park complex, with a kindergarten, outdoor play area and local mosque.

Local clusters are grouped into 'Neighbourhoods', supporting two primary schools, a Friday mosque, a park, and a women's centre, as well as local shops and higher density housing.

The thrust of the plan is to ensure that Abu Dhabi's future shape reflects its heritage and retains its unique identity, allowing it to become a contemporary expression of an Arab city. An important part of this is the creation of communities that reflect local Emirati customs and ways of life. Plan Abu Dhabi 2030 contains descriptions of 'building blocks' – smaller-scale elements that make up the city, designed around the specific needs of Emiratis. These include the 'fareej'– modelled on a set of villas around a central courtyard, reflecting an extended Emirati family structure – as well as island and desert eco-villages. The villages are based on traditional Emirati ways of life, and the aim is to ensure these environments are provided across the emirate in a way that reflects local customs. Sustainability initiatives such as solar and wind power will also make these communities more self-reliant in the future.

A key principle of Plan Abu Dhabi 2030 is to respect, be scaled to, and be shaped by the natural environment, in particular the sensitive coastal and desert ecosystems. The plan protects Abu Dhabi's ecological wealth through a National Park system, with development restricted around these areas. Furthermore, by creating a protected 'sand belt' around the city and 'desert fingers' reaching from the desert to the shore, the plan contains urban growth and prevents unplanned sprawl, a key factor in protecting the environment.

In addition, environmental policies ensure that sustainability is the major consideration in the Abu Dhabi Urban Planning Council's decisions on all new development and infrastructure.

The plan stresses the need to design public spaces in a way that encourages Abu Dhabi's residents to feel ownership of, and to identify themselves with, the city. New landscaped parks are to be introduced, building on existing assets such as Lulu Island and the Corniche. Other public spaces, including recreational parks and nature reserves, informed by environmental policies, are to be introduced into new developments and retroactively fitted into older city blocks.

Alongside the provision of new public spaces, the plan emphasises attractive, high-quality street design and the creation of cycle and pedestrian-friendly routes around the city – encouraging residents to enjoy travelling through their city and to identify more closely with the capital city's distinct character.

Recognising that an effective and integrated transport network is crucial to a growing, modern city, Plan Abu Dhabi 2030 sets out a schedule for developing a world-class transport system. The transportation framework puts pedestrians as a priority. Streets will be designed with continuous sidewalks and shading will be provided through landscaping or shading structures.

Sustainable Buildings Programme

Within the context of Plan 2030, Estidama ('sustainability' in Arabic) is an integrated programme that will oversee a set of discretionary guidelines and mandatory regulations for sustainable (green) design, operation and maintenance of all types of buildings and communities within the Emirate of Abu Dhabi. The programme, which includes the formation of a specialised government body, has been initiated by UPC and a group of government agencies and developers (EAD, ADM, Masdar, Aldar and Sorouh).

Estidama has three key components: the Estidama New Building Guidelines launched in May 2008, the Estidama Community Guidelines, and the forthcoming Estidama Building Guidelines. The first phase, the Estidama New Building (ENB) Guidelines, have been formulated to provide all concerned parties and stakeholders (decision makers, developers, the public, consultants, etc.) with outline information for an integrated holistic approach to sustainable building design. ENB Guidelines identify ten major sustainability elements that need to be addressed through a variety of design criteria. These are: water; energy use; indoor environmental quality; ecology; management; transport; pollution; materials; waste management; and land use.

Abu Dhabi Corniche.

Developers as well as consultants and selected government entities have also been invited to evaluate the updated interim community guidelines as part of an ongoing pilot programme. The test phase will apply to selected community projects in the Emirate of Abu Dhabi that are being reviewed by the UPC. The IECG will be revised and final Estidama guidelines are scheduled for publication in early 2009.

The Estidama management team is also working on publishing the third key component of the programme, the Estidama Existing Building Guidelines. It will also use a pearl rating system similar to, but not confined to, the system that was launched in May 2008 alongside the New Building Guidelines.

www.uaeinteract.com/urban

Saadiyat Island, which is being developed by TDIC, has a budget of more than Dh80.7 billion (US$22 billion).

In a series of measures announced in December, Abu Dhabi went on the offensive in terms of boosting investor confidence, ensuring that an already steady real estate sector is further strengthened and underlined its plans to stay on course to meet the broader goals of the UAE's 2012 plan.

Significant Projects

A great deal of money has already been invested in infrastructure in Abu Dhabi, particularly in projects to regenerate the centre of the city, Aldar Properties flagship extensive Central Market development being a prime example. However, much more investment is being pledged to realise the potential of the master plan and at least Dh734 billion (US$200 billion) will be pumped into various projects in the coming five years, with government investment constituting only 40 per cent of the total spending, in line with its policy to move from infrastructure provider to regulator.

The sheer scale of these combined projects is remarkable. Land reclamation features prominently in many of the coastal developments. But this is on a much smaller scale than in Dubai because Abu Dhabi is making ample use of some of the natural islands adjacent to the capital for development purposes.

Sorouh Real Estate's master plan for Lulu Island, reclaimed land in front of the Corniche, features high-end, low-rise development with large open spaces and easy access to a wide range of services, facilities and community leisure activities. Transport options will include a bridge, underground tunnel, monorail and water taxis.

Mubadala are working with MGM Mirage to develop the MGM Grand Abu Dhabi, the centrepiece of the Mina Zayed development and a key part of Abu Dhabi's tourism strategy. The project will include a 10,000-seat indoor arena with a 3000-seat outdoor amphitheatre, part of a 150-acre urban waterfront high-end retail, dining and entertainment venue. The existing dhows and fish market will be retained and accommodated on adjacent land. The design and planning stages of the project are already under way. Construction will commence in 2009, with phase one opening in 2012 (log on to www.mubadala.ae and www.mgmmirage.com).

Meanwhile, Mubadala's property and hospitality division is filling in land around Sowwah Island, which, as outlined above, is set to become the capital's new financial centre with ready access to the mainland and surrounding islands of Abu Dhabi.

Saadiyat Island, probably the region's most exciting offshore development, has a budget of more than Dh80.7 billion (US$22 billion). The project will be developed in three phases, finishing in 2018. As well as the prestigious Cultural District described above, the island development includes 19 kilometres of beachfront, 29 hotels, three marinas, 8000 residential villas and more than 38,000 apartments, three harbours, a park, golf course and sailing club.

Tourism Development & Investment Company (TDIC) has already launched a limited phase one release of its impressive Saadiyat Beach Residences in Saadiyat Beach District, one of seven distinct neighbourhoods that will skirt the championship Saadiyat Beach Golf Course. TDIC is on track with its construction schedule, which will see the St Regis resort open in early 2010 and the first phase of Saadiyat Beach villas being handed over to owners towards the end of that year.

Saadiyat Island has been named by international tourism scouts as one of the world's top ten emerging 'trendy' destinations and the island recently topped a poll of 167,000 travel professionals worldwide, including more than 110,000 travel agents, to earn the fourteenth World Travel Awards' mantle of 'The World's Leading Tourism Development Project.'

Other signature projects in the TDIC property portfolio include the landmark 35-storey downtown Grand Corniche Hotel and Residences; the Lagoon Club, a five-star beach resort convention centre and office/residential complex; Emirates Pearl Hotel and serviced apartments; Angsana Eastern Mangrove Resorts and Spa, a delightful eco-retreat; Park Rotana mixed-use development; the five-star Abu Dhabi Creek Business Resorts; and Abu Dhabi Golf Hotel Residences and Spa. TDIC also set an environmental example by ensuring that the

Land reclamation features prominently in many coastal developments. But Abu Dhabi is also making ample use of some of the natural islands adjacent to the capital for development purposes.

TDIC manages an extensive property portfolio with many prestigious projects under development throughout the emirate.

Five new draft laws will control all details of real estate ownership and organisation in Abu Dhabi, resulting in an integrated system of real estate legislation.

design of its new office headquarters in Abu Dhabi is being built to the highest standards in sustainable development.

Aldar Properties is currently involved in at least Dh264.24 billion (US$72 billion) worth of development projects in Abu Dhabi. These include the Dh47.71 billion (US$13 billion) Al Raha Beach project on the mainland coast, a huge, 11-kilometres-long, mixed-use waterfront development that will eventually house 120,000 people. Al Raha Beach, which is on track for completion in 2014, comprises 11 precincts and has a total development area of 12 million square metres. Serviced water taxis or the LRT (light rail transportation) will provide access to the wider community.

Nearby is the Yas Island development, a massive Dh143.13 billion (US$39 billion) mixed-use project. The island will have a total developed area about one-third the size of Abu Dhabi Island, with Aldar's three theme parks, Ferrari World Abu Dhabi, Warner Bros Theme Park and Water Park, providing a focal point for marinas, hotels, entertainment facilities and residences. Aldar is on schedule to finish phase one infrastructure work on the entertainment destination, with the remaining scheduled for completion well before the race track plays host to the 2009 Formula One Etihad Airways Abu Dhabi Grand Prix. Other Aldar projects include Motor World, a haven for motoring enthusiasts on a 3.5 million square metre site close to Abu Dhabi airport.

Two distinctive commercial and residential towers, to be completed in the last quarter of 2010, will be key features of the Dh8 billion (US$2.18 billion) Capital Centre development surrounding Abu Dhabi National Exhibition Centre. The business and residential micro-city will include the state-of-the art exhibition centre, a 2.4 kilometre marina development, and a gravity defying, iconic feature tower known as Capital Gate.

Capitala, the Abu Dhabi-based real estate developer formed through a joint venture between Mubadala and the Singapore-based CapitaLand, is developing a substantial and innovative mixed-use project as one of the key elements of the 1.4 million square metre Arzanah scheme, the high-profile residential development taking shape in the Grand Mosque District. Arzanah surrounds Zayed Sports City and features a waterfront and canal weaving throughout luxurious high-rise apartment towers and family villas, communal gardens, and extensive walking and cycling trails. Contracts have been awarded for the five-tower Rihan Heights, the first phase of the project, which is scheduled for completion by 2012.

Reem Island is being developed by Sorouh Real Estate and a number of other property developers. Residential, commercial and recreational centres will be accompanied by gardens, museums, an aquarium and amusement parks for children. The Reem master plan started with a maximum residential population of 344,000, but this is to be reduced to 250,000.

Surouh is developing the Gate District on Reem, a cluster of eight towers located at the entrance to Shams Abu Dhabi. Other Surouh projects in Abu Dhabi include Alghadeer, an integrated multidimensional mixed-use development in Saih As Sidairah between Abu Dhabi and Dubai, which is expected to house around 18,000 people; Surouh's Sky Tower is destined to be the highest skyscraper in Abu Dhabi and Surouh is also responsible for the Dh729 million Golf Gardens luxury residential development adjoining Abu Dhabi Golf Club. In addition, Surouh is building Saraya Abu Dhabi, a Dh3.5 billion mixed-use development in Abu Dhabi City.

Hydra Properties has completed the foundation work for its six-building Hydra Avenue Towers in Al Reem's City of Light ahead of schedule and the Towers project is listed for completion by 2011. Hydra Properties are also developing Hydra Village at Al Reef City, an eco-project of 2500 villas, which is scheduled for handover to end-customers in 2010.

A Dh80.74 billion (US$22 billion) budget has been allocated for Abu Dhabi Future Energy Company's ambitious 6-square-kilometre Masdar City project. Masdar and WWF have entered into a Sustainability Action Plan for what has been billed as the world's greenest city. The aim is to exceed the ten sustainability principles of 'One Planet Living', a global initiative launched by the WWF (Worldwide Fund for Nature) and environmental consultancy BioRegional. These targets are to be achieved by the time Masdar City is completed and fully functioning in 2015.

With a budget of Dh23.85 billion (US$6.5 billion), Sheikh Mohammed bin Zayed City will comprise 374 residential and commercial buildings as well as the associated infrastructure and entertainment facilities. The development is on the Abu Dhabi–Al Ain highway.

Bani Yas Investment & Development (BID) Company, established in 2005 as a majority owned subsidiary of Baniyas Sports Club, has

Demand for residential units in Abu Dhabi will outstrip supply until the end of 2011 as the population grows and household size shrinks in the emirate.

Abu Dhabi's Masdar City has been billed as the world's greenest city.

The objective of the UAE's urban planning is to provide the infrastructure that will attract tourism, trade and industry.

launched a multi-use real estate project in Abu Dhabi's Bani Yas City budgeted at Dh2.2 billion (US$600 million). The 108-hectare Bawabat Al Sharq project will provide the community with modern residential, medical, educational, commercial and entertainment facilities in addition to a brand new headquarters and sports facilities for the club, which includes a FIFA-standard football stadium with a seating capacity for over 20,000 spectators. The design and major plans have been in the works since early 2007, and phase one of the project is due to be completed during the first quarter of 2010.

Urban planning for Al Ain seeks to preserve its image as a traditional garden city.

Abu Dhabi Urban Planning Council (UPC), in partnership with the Emirates Foundation and in accordance with the principles of Plan Abu Dhabi 2030, has launched an extensive revitalisation scheme for the communities of Shahama and Bahia in Abu Dhabi, located along the Abu Dhabi–Dubai highway. The area planning is addressing issues ranging from housing and community amenities, through to transportation, hospitals, schools, shops, landscaping, and infrastructure. This and related projects involve consultation between planners and members of the community to research community needs.

UPC's objective is to set up an advanced digital network concept to be called 'city e-motion' that will provide a platform of contacts among generations from all over the emirate and create an interactive relationship between UPC and Abu Dhabi citizens, carrying on the tradition of consultation and consensus inherent in historical government.

Eastern and Western Regions

The UPC has also focused attention on the rest of the emirate outside Abu Dhabi City and environs: city planners are drawing up an ambitious new blueprint for developing Al Ain and the Western Region (recently renamed Al Gharbia). The prospect of large-scale development in Al Ain coincides with the city's bid to be selected as a World Heritage Site by Unesco.

The challenge in Al Ain is to redevelop a city of 300,000 residents with a density as low as one household per hectare. Planners will also seek to protect the traditional image of Al Ain as a green haven for the rest of the emirate and as an authentic Arab city.

Designs for a Dh3.67 billion (US$1 billion) unique concept, Al Ain Wildlife Park and Resort, echoes these aspirations. Occupying 900 hectares at the foothills of Jebel Hafit, this is a mixed-use development

www.uaeinteract.com/urban

Large-scale redevelopment
is under way in Al Ain.

firmly rooted in the heritage and culture of Al Ain. The first phase is due for completion by the end of 2010.

Aldar Properties has also revised their extensive mixed-use Noor Al Ain project in the heart of Al Ain to meet the new guidelines developed by UPC.

Al Gharbia covers a staggering 60,000 square kilometres, 83 per cent of Abu Dhabi emirate and 71 per cent of the total landmass of the UAE, but it only contains 8 per cent of the population. Construction, public administration, agriculture, and oil and gas are the main high-level economic activities in this region. An estimated Dh98 billion has already been pledged for infrastructure, tourism, and economic development projects to enable economic growth and raise the standard of living for Al Gharbia's residents. Tourism, especially eco-tourism centred on the area's unique coastline and offshore islands, is a key feature of the radical regeneration programme orchestrated by the Western Region Development Council (WRDC), the central coordinating body for development in the region.

The first phase of TDIC's Discovery Islands destination opened in October 2008. This will be spread over eight adjacent islands and an onshore gate near Jebel Dhanna, approximately 250 kilometres from Abu Dhabi City. The new 64-room Desert Islands Resort and Spa is on Sir Bani Yas Island, the former private eco-retreat of the UAE's late President HH Sheikh Zayed bin Sultan Al Nahyan. The island is noted for its spectacular wildlife park, unspoilt beaches, dramatic desert terrain, significant archaeological sites and extensive mangrove reserves. Desert Islands is expected to generate Dh88.82 million (US$326 million) in tourism revenues when fully operational by 2020 and create a total of 6500 jobs.

Liwa's tourism potential
is being boosted by the
opening of a number of
top-class resorts.

Al Gharbia's tourism potential will be given a further boost with the planned September 2009 opening of the deluxe Qasr Al Sarab retreat in the Liwa desert in the Empty Quarter (Rub al-Khali). Construction work on the TDIC luxury resort is progressing well. Two new hotels are also planned for the city of Madinat Zayed in the centre of the emirate.

DUBAI

Efforts are also being made in the other constituent emirates of the UAE to ensure that development is planning-led, as opposed to demand-led, which is the case in many of the world's major cities.

As already emphasised, the objective is to provide the infrastructure that will attract tourism, trade and industry, including valuable service industries, at the same time creating living sustainable communities.

Dubai Strategic Plan 2015 (DSP) recognises that urban planning is a prerequisite to optimise land use in order to meet the needs of sustainable development while preserving natural resources. To implement the strategy, Dubai's Urban Planning Committee, which includes key stakeholders such as Dubai Municipality, the Road and Transport Authority (RTA), Dubai Electricity and Water Authority (Dewa), Dubai Land Department, and The Executive Office, as well as developers like Dubai Holdings, Emaar and Nakheel, drew up the Dubai Urban Development Framework (DUDF), an integrated master plan that will offer a comprehensive roadmap for Dubai's future up to 2020 and beyond, hopefully solving the main concerns of today's urban life. Key elements of the framework will include integrated land use and mobility, housing provision, economic and demographic growth, urban character and design, heritage management, integrated community facilities provision, civic harmony and sustainability strategy.

Dubai Municipality was re-organised in January 2008 in line with the requirements of the DSP and the Municipality's Strategic Plan 2007–2011, to ensure a smooth and effective implementation of the plans and programmes envisioned in the DSP.

More than 33 per cent of Dubai's budget expenditure in 2009 will be earmarked for infrastructure projects.

Green Building Code

From 2009, all proposed building plans in Dubai must comply with a new Green Building Code being introduced by Dubai Municipality. The Emirates Green Building Council (EGBC) has already launched a building sustainability assessment system for the UAE based on the US Green Building Council's (US GBC) Leadership in Energy and Environmental Design (LEED) rating system, with modifications made to account for local environmental conditions.

The main modifications include an increased emphasis on water conservation. The potential total possible points have also been raised from 69 to 72. Feedback from a pilot programme run by the EGBC will be used to update the rating system.

From 2009, all proposed building plans in Dubai must comply with a new Green Building Code being introduced by Dubai Municipality.

Burj Dubai, destined to be the world's tallest skyscraper, overlooks the Old Town quarter of Downtown Dubai.

Outstanding Projects

Dubai has gained a reputation for executing innovative infrastructural projects, The Palm trilogy and The World being two of the most famous in this category. The property developer Nakheel, a division of Dubai World, has been responsible for most of these offshore extravaganzas. Construction began in 2001 on Palm Jumeirah. Today, more than 2000 homes are occupied and work is continuing on the trunk section. New developments include the construction of a palatial pier to house QE2, which travelled to Dubai from Southampton in November 2008. The plan is to turn the liner into a luxury floating hotel to complement the spectacular Atlantis Hotel, which opened in 2008, the forthcoming Cirque du Soleil and a series of other impressive projects.

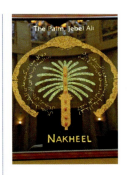

Nakheel commenced construction in 2002 on the Palm Jebel Ali, which is twice the size of Palm Jumeirah and is expected to accommodate 1.7 million people by 2020. Palm Deira was announced in 2004 and, at five times the size of Palm Jebel Ali, will be the largest man-made island in the world. Infrastructure development for Palm Deira is on schedule.

Nakheel has also completed land reclamation on The World project, the cluster of 300 man-made exclusive islands that were built in the shape of the world map about 4 kilometres off the coast of Dubai. Over 50 per cent have been sold.

Nakheel is again expanding Dubai's coastline with the launch of a massive real estate development, The Universe, a cluster of large coral-shaped islands on 3000 hectares of land, which will spread from Palm Jumeirah to Palm Deira and will take 15 to 20 years to develop.

Nakheel is also responsible for the redevelopment of Dubai's Port Rashid and has commenced reclamation on Dubai Promenade, a waterfront community that will create a peninsula along the Dubai shoreline adjacent to Dubai International Marine Club (DIMC). This will be anchored by a five-star, wheel-shaped hotel.

In addition, Nakheel is involved in the regeneration of Jebel Ali Village, which was originally built in 1977 to provide accommodation for expatriates working on construction of the Jebel Ali Port. The project will be completed by 2013.

Nearby, the Waterfront development will transform 1.4 billion square feet of desert and sea into an international community for an estimated population of 1.5 million people.

Nakheel announced in December 2008 that it was delaying long-term infrastructure work on some of its projects, including parts of Jumeirah Garden City, the Trump International Hotel, the Tower on Palm Jumeirah, and the planned kilometre-high tower. Some projects at the Waterfront have also been affected and reclamation work on Palm Deira and construction on Palm Jebel is expected to slow down. Limitless too, revealed that it is reviewing its construction schedule for the Arabian Canal.

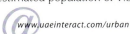

Grading work on the third phase of Dubai World Central (DWC), the massive, 140-square kilometre multi-phase development under construction near Jebel Ali, has been completed. Phase one grading included Dubai Logistics City (DLC), whilst phase two grading was spread across areas earmarked for Al Maktoum International Airport and parts of DWC Residential City, DLC's headquarters and office park.

Real estate developer Limitless is carrying out excavation work on the Dh40.37 billion (US$11 billion), 75-kilometre-long 150-metre-wide Arabian Canal that will encircle Dubai World Central, bisect Dubai Industrial City and practically link Palm Jebel Ali and Palm Jumeirah.

During 2008, Industrial City (DI), the third largest non-real estate project in Dubai, successfully completed a comprehensive wildlife relocation programme, transferring over 900 animals, including gazelles and reptiles, from the project site of the largest industrial destination in Dubai to Al Marmoom Conservation Reserve. The extensive operation took place ahead of the commencement of construction work across DI's six industrial zones.

Property developer Emaar's Burj Dubai is a Dh3.67 billion (US$1 billion) tower that is destined to be the world's tallest skyscraper. The tower had reached a new record height of 688 meters (2257.2 feet) by mid-2008, surpassing North Dakota, USA's KVLY-TV mast (628.8 metres; 2063 feet) in April 2008. The ultimate height is being kept secret. When completed, Burj Dubai will meet all four criteria listed by the Council on Tall Buildings and Urban Habitat, which classifies the world's tallest structures. However, by then it may have competition from Nakheel's newly launched Harbour and Tower, which the company is claiming will be the tallest in the world.

Burj Dubai anchors Emaar's Dh73 billion (US$20 billion) Downtown Burj Dubai featuring the Old Town quarter and Souk al-Bahar, a new leisure and retail destination set within the context of a traditional Arabian souk, phase one of which was opened in 2008. The Palace Hotel, The Armani Hotel and the massive shopping and entertainment complex Dubai Mall, which also opened in 2008, with its adjoining five-star hotel, The Address, are also integral parts of the Burj Dubai environs.

The third tallest building in the world may also be sited in Dubai. Anara Tower, being developed by Tameer next to the American University of Dubai on Sheikh Zayed Road, will be 650 metres high (or even slightly higher according to the developers).

Real estate developer Limitless is carrying out excavation work on the 75-kilometre-long, 150-metre-wide Arabian Canal that will link Palm Jebel Ali and Palm Jumeirah.

The Meydan project is under construction near Nad Al Sheba. This includes a massive racecourse, a hotel, golf courses, shopping and entertainment centres, modern stables, Godolphin racing gallery and a 4-kilometre canal running from Dubai Creek to the racecourse. This project is scheduled for opening in 2010 to host the Dubai World Cup.

Dubai Properties has ambitious plans to build an entire city in the desert at a cost of over Dh220.2 billion (US$60 billion). Mohammed bin Rashid Gardens will extend over 74.322 million square metres and incorporate educational, financial and commercial facilities, civic buildings and tourist landmarks connected by a series of landscaped parklands. Four centres, or 'houses', The House of Humanity, The House of Commerce, The House of Wisdom and The House of Nature, will host world-class facilities in their respective fields.

Dubailand

As we have seen, leisure and entertainment facilities are a very important aspect of the UAE's tourism strategy and Dubailand, a massive Dh235 billion (US$64 billion), 279 million square metres complex, will be a major player in this sector. Dubailand will eventually contain 45 major projects and more than 200 sub-projects, encompassing theme parks, sports complexes, themed well-being retreats, cultural, ecological and historical projects, hotels and residential accommodation and, of course, shopping and entertainment.

Dubailand, destined to be the region's premier leisure and entertainment facility, will contain 45 major projects and more than 200 sub-projects, encompassing theme parks, sporting, commercial and residential facilities.

The development is being built in four phases, with the entire project scheduled for completion by 2020. However, the development of roads and infrastructure will continue until 2010 and finishing touches are already being applied to some areas. To date, Dubailand comprises 24 projects being developed by third party developers, plus Tatweer-owned attractions such as Global Village, Universal Studios, Dreamworks, Six Flags, Marvel, Freej and Legoland.

Ground was broken in August 2008 for the 650,000 square metre Universal Studios. Construction will take place in three phases, commencing with the theme park, retail area, and four hotels in 2008. When completed in December 2010, Universal Studios Dubailand will join the family of world-renowned theme parks in Hollywood, Florida, Japan and Singapore.

DreamWorks Animation signed up in January 2008 to a multi-billion dollar strategic alliance with Tatweer to develop a range of

Activity and theme parks feature prominently in the UAE's tourism strategy.

tourism and leisure projects, the highlight of which will be the 464,515 square metre DreamWorks Animation-branded park.

In April 2008, real estate concern Al Ahli announced a deal with Marvel Entertainment to bring Marvel's full library of superheroes to Dubai for a Dh3.67 billion (US$1 billion) theme park. Al Ahli also unveiled another long-term partnership with Nickelodeon. Dreamworks, Marvel and Nickelodeon are scheduled to open in 2012.

In June 2008, Paramount signed a licensing deal worth Dh 9.175 billion (US$2.5 billion) with Ruwaad Holdings for a series of parks and rides and a conceptual master plan has also been developed for Six Flags Dubailand, a 464,515 square metre multi-billion dirham theme park. The first phase of the project is expected to be ready in 2011.

Another massive theme park, this time based on the popular locally based cartoon 'Freej', is to become the centrepiece of Dubailand. Freej, renamed 'Hayyak', or 'Come In', features four cartoon characters, a group of Emirati grandmothers whose misadventures have proven to be a hit. It will be the only development that focuses solely on Arab culture and will include a recreation of old Dubai anchored by a Middle Eastern garden. Hayyak will open in 2013.

In May 2008 Dubailand's Sports City released its first commercial property, The Gateway, iconic twin towers located at the entrance. Sports City's Tiger Woods Golf Course opened in September 2008, the Manchester United Academy in October 2008 and the Formula One theme park in Motor City is scheduled to open in 2009.

Phase one of the gigantic Mall of Arabia in Dubailand's City of Arabia, measuring 464,515 square metres gross leasable area (GLA), is well under way. Phase two will have a further 557,418 (6 million square feet) of GLA.

Integral infrastructure works have been completed on the 1.858 million square metres City of Arabia site and superstructure work has commenced on the project's main components. City of Arabia will have a phased opening commencing at the end of 2010.

All phases of Dubailand's Remraam community have commenced on schedule. With over 100 apartment buildings, a dedicated shopping mall and extensive community facilities to build, the Remraam community is adjacent to the 10-kilometre Bawadi Boulevard and Arabian Ranches.

PROJECTS IN OTHER EMIRATES

The northern emirates are also undergoing a major transformation to one degree or another, depending on their size and inclination.

Sharjah City and emirate, the third largest of the seven emirates, is tapping in to the worldwide property boom with Al Hanoo Holding's largest project, Al Nujoom Islands, the star attraction. This Dh18 billion (US$4.90 billion) project is being developed on a 3-kilometre stretch of the Arabian Gulf coast in the Hamriya area of Sharjah. Phase one construction and phase two of infrastructure was initiated in 2008. Among other developments, Sharjah City Centre shopping complex is undergoing a major expansion, renovation and redevelopment programme. Set for completion in December 2008, the mall will be home to an additional 22 new shops, including internationally renowned anchor stores.

The launch of freehold developments in tiny Ajman has brought a flurry of activity to this historically underdeveloped emirate.

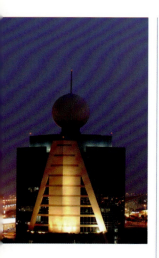

Al Zorah, a self-contained master-planned city with free zone and freehold status, intends to keep its ecological footprint to a minimum.

Spearheaded by Ajman Development and Investment Authority, efforts are being made to ensure that urban planning is undertaken in a sustainable manner so that Ajman can develop its own unique identity. Ajman government is also setting up a tourism authority to market the emirate. Four new hotels will be built by 2010, the museum is undergoing an expansion programme and there are three shopping malls under construction. Plans are in place for a heritage centre and two old-style souks.

Aqaar, a private development company that was formed in 2006 in association with Ajman Development and Investment Authority, is responsible for the Dh2.7 billion (US$735.7 million) Ajman 1, a 72,000 square metre complex consisting of 16 towers, a hotel, a convention centre and leisure and retail amenities. Phase one should be completed by early 2010. The emirate also recently unveiled the redevelopment of its marina in conjunction with Tanmiyat, a Saudi company. The project will include 500 berths for yachts, restaurants, shops and housing for thousands of people.

However, this is dwarfed by a Dh220 billion (US$63 billion) project being developed by Al Zorah Development, a joint venture between the government and the Beirut-based Solidere International. The project, which has free zone and freehold status, will cover 12 square kilometres of coastline and include a self-contained master-planned city with a built-up area of 22 million square metres. Al Zorah intends to keep its ecological footprint to a minimum with environmentally friendly design and energy-efficient infrastructure.

Unfortunately, development in the northern emirates has been compromised by a shortage of electricity and water, leading to the suspension of projects such as Al Salaam City, a Dh31.19 billion (US$8.5 billion) mixed-use project in Umm al-Qaiwain by Tameer Holding. While planning for new power and desalination plants is under way, it will be some time before these are finished, and some delays in completion of a number of the larger projects can be expected.

The government of the northernmost emirate, Ra's al-Khaimah, is actively pursuing a programme of economic renewal as is evidenced by the groundbreaking of several major projects in real estate, tourism and industry. Again, freehold rights and the granting of free zone privileges have been a hugely stimulating factor in the mushrooming of projects in this emirate.

RAK Investment Authority (RAKIA) has launched the Gateway City, a Dh3.7 billion (US1 billion) development venture. Located on Emirates Road, the project offers 5.57 million square metres of land for real estate developers to build residential and commercial properties offering freehold ownership: 60 per cent of the project area will be dedicated to services and parkland. The project will be constructed in at least five phases, the first three of which are scheduled for completion by the end of 2009.

Ra's al-Khaimah-based property developer Rakeen, master planner and the real estate development arm of the Ra's al-Khaimah government, unveiled a new shopping complex and office tower in early 2008, key components of the 'Bab Al Bahr' development. Bab Al Bahr is the inaugural project of the Dh 6.6 billion (US$1.8 billion) Al Marjan Island mixed-use project being developed on 2.7 million square metres of a recently reclaimed island that extends for 4 kilometres into the Arabian Gulf. Aside from a wide range of residential and commercial options, Bab Al Bahr also features a world-class resort hotel, as well as leisure and entertainment facilities.

Ra's al-Khaimah's Bab Al Bahr development is the inaugural project on Al Marjan, a recently reclaimed island that extends for 4 kilometres into the Arabian Gulf.

Reclamation work has commenced on Dana Island, another major mixed-use Rakeen project that was launched in 2008. Rakeen is also involved in a host of other upscale projects in Ra's al-Khaimah, such as the RAK Financial City, RAK Convention Centre, Azure Hotel, Jebel Al Jais mountain resort and the Banyan Tree resort.

RAK Properties developments in Ra's al-Khaimah include Julfar Towers and Mina Al Arab, a Dh10 billion mixed-use waterfront resort community. Another significant development is Noor City, a Dh3.67 billion (US$1 billion) island near the Kuwaiti Street Corniche that will feature three resorts, cafes and boutiques, and will accommodate more than 150,000 people.

Saraya Islands, based on a 7-kilometre-long natural island that runs parallel to the coast of Ra's al-Khaimah, is emerging as a mixed-use resort destination. The first phase of the project is expected to be operational in 2011.

Two new industrial zones will also be created: Al Ghail will specialise in a mix of light and medium industry, with heavy industry destined for Saqr Port where quarries and cement factories are already located. To balance economy with environment, a large wildlife reserve is planned for the island of Hulayla, south of the port. The RAK government has also pledged to continue to address its electricity shortage problems, and plans to build a power plant near the industrial zones.

www.uaeinteract.com/urban

In the stunningly beautiful Emirate of Fujairah, the real estate emphasis is naturally on improving tourism infrastructure, with several new five-star hotels having opened their doors to the public in recent years, and many more under construction

Abu Dhabi-based Mina Al Fajer Real Estate LLC is developing a Dh600 million mountain-sea resort property near Dibba that will be completed before the end of 2009, giving Fujairah the first of what is expected to be a growing number of world-class, exclusive real estate projects.

Abu Dhabi-based Escan Pjsc's developments in Fujairah include Al Fanar Towers, a 30-floor residential tower, a 25-floor commercial tower, and a 300-room hotel in the centre of Fujairah City, as well as developments in the extremely scenic Wadi Al Wurrayah Valley, north of Fujairah.

Several new hotels are also under construction in the northern Al Aqqah area, close to Dibba, where the Al Aqqah Meridien, a Rotana hotel and a JAL hotel have already paved the way for what is intended to become the focus of the emirate's tourist industry, while the offshore Dana (Pearl) development will provide resort-style living, surrounded by the waters of the Gulf of Oman.

The picturesque Emirate of Fujairah is developing a growing number of world-class, exclusive real estate projects.

ROAD & RAIL

TRANSPORT ABU DHABI

In recognition of the central role that transport occupies in supporting and sustaining growth, Abu Dhabi Department of Transport (DoT) was established in 2006 to ensure fully coordinated planning in all aspects of transport policy and development in Abu Dhabi emirate. Previously, Abu Dhabi's transport responsibilities were handled by a variety of entities across both the local and federal governments.

DoT has formulated a five-year strategic plan for 2008–2012, in accordance with Abu Dhabi Policy Agenda 2008–2012 and Plan Abu Dhabi 2030. Strategies for motor transport, maritime, civil aviation and public transport are being integrated to deliver an effective transport system that contributes to the economic growth, quality of life and environmental sustainability of the Emirate of Abu Dhabi.

A Surface Transport Master Plan (STMP) for Abu Dhabi was commissioned by DoT in February 2008 to translate the conceptual transport strategy into a detailed master plan and implementation programme. The objective of the year-long process is to evaluate and draw up a comprehensive set of plans that will reflect leading international best practice, and will deliver a world-class sustainable transport system.

The STMP as a whole has been designed as a consultative process in order to ensure that stakeholders and the general public have the opportunity to contribute to the master plan and a dedicated website at www.transportabudhabi.ae encourages feedback from the public.

As far as public transport is concerned, a metro system, high-speed rail throughout Abu Dhabi and linking to other emirates, buses, trams and water taxis are all under consideration and it is highly likely that mass transit will feature prominently when the STMP is released in February 2009. Much discussion has already taken place on the need to introduce the high-speed rail system by the year 2015.

Plan Abu Dhabi 2030 called for at least two high-capacity metro lines, with one originating from Saadiyat Island and Al Mina, turning left (east) at Central Station and following Airport Road to the Grand Mosque district, Capital district, and Raha Beach. The other line would

Plan Abu Dhabi 2030 sets out a schedule for developing a world-class transport system that includes a hierarchy of streets distributing local traffic while connecting key points within the city; a light-rail metro network for everyday and commuter travel; a frequent and reliable local tram/bus service; a high-speed rail line to connect Abu Dhabi with the rest of the UAE; and large parking surfaces to be moved underground.

Light-rail projects under way in the UAE will help to relieve traffic congestion.

cross the downtown area from north-east to north-west, connecting Al Reem and Al Sowwah to Central Station and the Marina Mall development.

The document also called for 'a fine-grained network of surface light rail, streetcars and buses' to make sure there would never be more than a five-minute walk required by those using public transport.

Work is already taking place on some new public transport systems: Aldar Properties has begun laying the groundwork for seven of 16 stations earmarked for a tramline at the Al Raha Beach development and the DoT are reserving space for a tram loop and a metro on Yas Island, the future home of the Formula One motor-racing Grand Prix.

DoT is also focusing on upgrading existing public transport. The first steps toward an integrated system took place in 2008, when buses began operating on four routes in Abu Dhabi. The government plans to have 21 routes operating by 2009 and to have 1360 new buses on Abu Dhabi roads by 2010, assisted by sophisticated passenger information systems and journey planners. DoT has also awarded the contract for 550 air-conditioned bus shelters to enhance the experience for travellers..

Road projects worth Dh20 billion (US$5.44 billion) are under way in Abu Dhabi, including the network of highways that will be required to service the massive new real estate, tourism and industrial developments taking place in the city.

The new road projects are focused on facilitating traffic flow on main arteries into and out of the capital, such as Al Salam Street and Airport Road. The largest single project in terms of cost will transform Al Salam Street: a Dh 3 billion (US$817 million), 3 kilometre-long tunnel which will eventually run under the city is being dug out on the eastern coastal flank of the capital. The project also involves a 500 metre flyover linking the city to nearby Reem Island. Once the tunnel is complete in 2011, motorists coming from Dubai and other emirates can take the expanded surface road into the tunnel, which will run underground from the capital's north-eastern entrance, just under Al Salam Street, straight to Port (Mina) Zayed and other coastal areas in the north-eastern part of the city. The contract also includes the construction of additional local roads from Al Salam Street to neighbouring areas as well as the construction of other tunnels linking Corniche Street with Al Salam Street.

Abu Dhabi's second massive road project is under way along Corniche Street. The first phase, which has already been completed, included the construction of the new Corniche East Street, the expansion of the old road, and the construction of three tunnels to facilitate traffic movement at main junctions. The project's second phase on the western part of Corniche Street has commenced.

Aldar and TDIC, along with DoT and UPC, have formed a consortium to construct the Dh1.83 billion (US$500 million), ten-lane Shahama–Saadiyat highway and incorporated bridges, which is scheduled for completion in summer 2009. The motorway and bridges will link the Central Business District, Saadiyat Island, Yas Island, Al Raha and the airport, relieving congestion in the Salam Street corridor. The design makes provision for future mass transit options in the central median.

The bridge linking Saadiyat Island with Abu Dhabi Island is well under way. Set to become one of the world's great non-suspension bridges, the concrete span carrying five lanes of traffic in each direction as well as two future passenger rail system tracks will connect Saadiyat Island with the Mina Zayed main port area, creating a five-minute drive access between the two.

Work is also under way on the Dh901 million (US$245 million), 40-metre-high Sheikh Zayed Bridge, the third strategic crossing for the island of Abu Dhabi after Al Maqta and Al Musaffah bridges, which will also relieve congestion.

The new bridge linking Saadiyat Island with Abu Dhabi Island, which is nearing completion, will be one of the world's great non-suspension bridges.

www.uaeinteract.com/roads

Abu Dhabi has completed a fully serviced 51-kilometre-long network of internal roads at Khalifa City (A) at a total cost of Dh185 million. The project, which commenced in 2006, will cater for the expansion of Khalifa City (A).

Improvements are also being made to a 327-kilometre, eight-lane motorway, the longest in the country, linking the eastern parts of Abu Dhabi emirate to the Saudi border. This will be completed by 2011 and will link Mafraq with Ghweifat, in the west, to assist with the Al Gharbia regeneration scheme,

DUBAI

Dubai has the highest rate of car ownership of any city in the world, with one car for every 1.84 residents, giving an average vehicle occupancy rate of 1.7.

Dubai has the highest rate of car ownership of any city in the world, with one car for every 1.84 residents, giving an average vehicle occupancy rate of 1.7. It is not surprising, therefore, that reliance on private transport is clogging the motorways of the emirate. However Dubai's Road Transport Authority (RTA) has initiated a transport master plan, based on the Dubai Strategy Plan, which will see the emirate spend about Dh80 billion (US$21.7 billion) by 2020 on expansion of the road network and development of a mass transport system, including Dubai Metro, buses and marine transport. The challenge is to cope with the expected increase in population from the current 1.4 million to 5.2 million by 2020.

Out of the Dh80.74 billion budget, Dh44.04 billion will be spent on road development comprising some 500 kilometres of new roads and 90 interchanges; Dh24.22 billion is being spent on four lines of the Dubai Metro; about Dh9.19 billion will be spent on a tram network, Dh2.2 billion on the public transport bus system, and Dh1.83 billion is being spent on development of a marine transport system.

More than Dh5 billion worth of RTA roads and bridges projects were either completed or nearing completion by the end 2008. These include the Arabian Ranches Interchange, phases three (A and B) of Ra's Al Khor project, the upper deck of the Finance Centre Road, Dubai Bypass Road, Al Nahda Bridge and Wafi Centre It also includes Phase one and two of widening of Al Ittihad project, Jumeirah Lakes Interchange, and landscaping of Zaabeel, Jumeirah and other areas.

One of the biggest projects being carried out by the RTA is the Dh1.7 billion Parallel Roads Project (parallel to Sheikh Zayed Road), extending 108 kilometres from Sheikh Rashid Road in the north.

The scheme also includes road improvements in the Business Bay Crossing and Burj Dubai areas, as well as construction of 30 bridges, two underpasses and 10 kilometres of surface roads.

Efforts to relieve traffic congestion in Dubai include investing Dh3 billion (US$ 817 million) to build the world's longest arched bridge over Dubai Creek. The 15-metre-high bridge, which will be completed in four years, will have 12 lanes with Dubai Metro's Green Line running through its centre.

RTA has already increased the number of lanes across Dubai Creek from 19 in 2006 to 48 in 2008. The new Al Garhoud bridge, which is now named after Sheikh Rashid bin Saeed Al Maktoum, was officially opened early in 2008 following completion of construction of its 14 lanes in both directions.

Public Transport

The RTA is also pursuing a range of measures to optimise car use, encourage use of public transport and integration of mass transit modes, not only to relieve congestion but also for environmental reasons. RTA research has revealed that public transport is used for only 5 per cent of trips. The authority's challenge is to increase this to between 30 and 35 per cent by 2020. Innovative policies include incentivising car pooling, introducing deluxe coach services and upgrading and extending the bus services, building air-conditioned bus shelters, providing buses for women, improving the taxi service and increasing use of marine transport. RTA is using the latest technology to publicise these venture – see its car pooling website www.sharekni.ae and entries on Youtube and Facebook.

A work team has also been formed to explore the substitution of existing taxis and public buses with new environment-friendly vehicles using hybrid engines and replacing the existing engines of the abra ferry boats with CNG-operated engines.

RTA commissioned 70 double-decker buses to run on the Dubai-Sharjah route in 2008 and will introduce 100 additional double-deckers on Dubai's internal roads in 2009. A deluxe coach service between Dubai and Abu Dhabi commenced in 2008 and the Dubai–Al Ain route will follow suit.

RTA's plans include construction of a Dh400 million Public Bus Depot. In March 2009 RTA will take delivery of the last of the 620

The Dh15.5 billion (US$4.2 billion) Dubai Metro project is the most ambitious part of the RTA's integrated mass transport system.

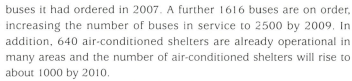

A technical and engineering taskforce has been set up by the UAE Ministry of Public Works to oversee implementation of the Dubai–Fujairah highway.

buses it had ordered in 2007. A further 1616 buses are on order, increasing the number of buses in service to 2500 by 2009. In addition, 640 air-conditioned shelters are already operational in many areas and the number of air-conditioned shelters will rise to about 1000 by 2010.

The Dh15.5 billion (US$4.2 billion) Dubai Metro project is the most ambitious part of the RTA's integrated mass transport system. The 52-kilometre Red Line viaduct, which stretches the length of Sheikh Zayed Road between Al Rashidiya and Jebel Ali, was completed in August 2008 after round-the-clock work for three years. Laying out of track and fitting out of stations is under way to meet the 9 September 2009 deadline. The Red Line will carry an estimated 27,000 passengers per hour in each direction on 42 trains, stopping at Burj Dubai, Internet City and Jebel Ali among other stations.

Work started on the 22-kilometre Green Line, which will link Al Qusais to Dubai Healthcare City, in 2006 and is scheduled for completion in March 2010. RTA are also planning a 49-kilometre Purple Line running the length of Al Khail Road to connect Dubai International Airport with Al Maktoum Airport in Jebel Ali and a 50-kilometre Blue Line, which will link Dubai International Airport to Jebel Ali Airport, passing through Emirates Road.

In addition, at least eight to ten new monorails are being planned in various part of Dubai, including the three Palm projects, Dubai World Central Jebel Ali, Dubai Waterfront, International City.

NORTHERN EMIRATES

Transport initiatives between and in the other emirates that constitute the federation are also proceeding apace. Much work has already been completed to improve road connections between Dubai and neighbouring Sharjah. A technical and engineering taskforce has also been set up by the UAE Ministry of Public Works to oversee implementation of the Dubai–Fujairah highway. The Dh1.2 billion road, part of a series of strategic projects to improve the federal road network, will reduce the distance between the two cities by 60 kilometres. The 45.4-kilometre-long dual carriage highway is scheduled for completion by 2010. The UAE government also plans to establish a rail-link stretching from Fujairah to Abu Dhabi.

In the meantime, Dubai RTA is introducing state-of-the-art inter-

city buses to link Dubai with Sharjah, Ajman, Umm al-Qaiwain, Ra's al-Khaimah and Fujairah. Other key cities and towns, such as Al-Ain, Dhaid, Masafi and Jebel Ali, will also be covered by this service .

Internally, massive mixed-use developments in some of the northern emirates necessitate a restructuring and upgrading of road systems. For example, in Ra's al-Khaimah the new Al Jais Mountain Road, already under construction, will allow access from Emirates Road to the summit of Al Jais on the Oman border where a new resort is planned. It is estimated that the road will reach the 1900-metre summit in two years.

AIRPORTS

IATA has estimated that the Middle East and North Africa (MENA) region will experience the largest growth in aviation in the world between 2008 and 2011, almost 40 per cent more than the global average. The Gulf countries are expected to spend in the region of US$43 billion during this period, with airport projects in the UAE alone costing close on US$30 billion.

This is hardly surprising: economically, the area is booming with trade, travel and tourism being key factors in development; geographically, the country's reach is considerable, sweeping through Africa and the Middle East and linking these regions to Europe, Asia, Australia and the Americas.

Over Dh77.5 billion (US$28.4 billion) is being spent to develop seven airports in the UAE. The projects include Dh26 billion (US$7.08 billion) on Abu Dhabi International Airport; Dh16.5 billion (US$4.5 billion) on Dubai International Airport; Dh36.7 billion (US$10 billion) for the development of Al Maktoum International Airport at Jebel Ali, part of the Dh121.1 billion (US$33 billion) Dubai World Central complex; Dh227.64 million (US$62 million) on Sharjah Airport; Dh2.9 billion (US$800 million) on Ajman International Airport; Dh183.6 million (US$50 million) on Fujairah Airport; and Dh1 billion (US$272 million) on Ra's al-Khaimah Airport.

The pattern of regional airport expansion is being fuelled by strong economic growth and the rapid development of state-owned airlines, including relative newcomers such as Abu Dhabi's Etihad Airways.

Over Dh77.5 billion (US$28.4 billion) is being spent to develop seven airports in the UAE.

A 140-million-year-old dinosaur on display at Abu Dhabi International Airport.

ABU DHABI AIRPORTS

Abu Dhabi Airport Company (ADAC), a public joint-stock company wholly owned by Abu Dhabi government, has set in motion a large-scale development programme to transform Abu Dhabi International Airport (ADIA).

Abu Dhabi's rising popularity as a business centre, tourist destination and aviation hub has meant that passenger volumes have been increasing steadily at the airport, especially since the launch of Abu Dhabi-based national airline, Etihad Airways. This has had such an impact that figures released in a comprehensive, independent analysis of global airport passenger traffic for 2007 placed Abu Dhabi as one of the joint leaders in a top-ten of the world's top performing intercontinental hubs, in terms of relative growth.

A record 6.9 million passengers passed through ADIA in 2007, a 31 per cent increase over 2006. Forecasts for 2008 estimate that 7.6 million passengers will use the airport and figures to date indicate that the facility is on target to achieve this: ADIA registered 6.67 million passengers in the first nine months of 2008, up by 32.9 per cent on the corresponding period in 2007. The trailing 12 month figures (September 2007 to September 2008) fared even better, demonstrating a solid 34.6 per cent growth with over 8.5 million passengers handled through the airport during that period. Cargo handled in the first nine months of the year also enjoyed steady growth, being up 14.8 per cent, with aircraft movements showing a healthy 15.5 per cent increase.

A new Terminal 3, costing Dh1 billion, was opened in phases throughout 2008. When fully operational, the new terminal will accommodate 5 million passengers, bringing the total passenger capacity between Terminals 1, 1A and 2 to over 12 million.

Terminal 3, including immigration areas, baggage handling and the airport's new retail environment, is for the exclusive use of Eithad Airways and is an interim facility with eight gates capable of handling the new generation of wide-bodied aircraft, two being Airbus A380 compatible. Supporting these developments, a new 4100 metre second runway and a new Air Traffic Control Complex (ATCC) will become operational in 2009, along with a new cargo terminal due for completion in 2010.

The new terminal will meet Etihad's needs until the first phase of a huge Midfield Terminal Complex (MTC) is completed in 2012. Construction work has already commenced on this new x-shaped facility, which will boost the airport's overall capacity to around 20 million passengers a year, with room for further phased expansion to 40 million by 2016. The project also includes new cargo facilities, an airport free zone, and retail and maintenance facilities.

More than 50 hectares have been reserved for building the three new cargo terminals, two for Etihad Airways, and one for the use of other airlines, with an ultimate combined capacity of around 2.5 million tonnes per year, up from 150,000 tonnes per year at present.

Abu Dhabi Duty Free (ADDF), which was established in 1984, is targeting a 25 per cent increase in turnover in 2008, up from US$102.6 million in 2007, which was 36.29 per cent higher than 2006. Sales in 2007 were buoyed by robust growth across the core categories of beauty and fragrance, liquor and tobacco, confectionery and gold, the best performing being electronics at 52.22 per cent increase. ADDF services extend across the emirate with operations at Abu Dhabi International Airport, Al Ain International Airport, which serves Abu Dhabi's Eastern Region, and the Ghweifat land-border outlet between the UAE and Kingdom of Saudi Arabia.

A huge new Midfield Terminal Complex, which will eventually increase capacity to 40 million passengers a year, is under construction at Abu Dhabi Airport.

www.uaeinteract.com/transport

Al Ain International Airport serves Abu Dhabi's Eastern Region. This is not only a vibrant international airport with full facilities and an ideal base for low-cost and low-fare carriers, it is also a sought-after cargo hub facility.

ADIA was recently presented with the Airports Council International (ACI) 'Service Quality Assured' certification. Its service quality management system was credited with having met industry best practices and ADIA was praised for its commitment to continual improvement in the area of delivering quality of services to passengers.

Security is also constantly under review at ADIA: a face recognition electronic system based on a highly advanced biometric technology is being implemented, initially at Abu Dhabi airport and, subsequently, at all ports of entry in the UAE. The system complements iris-recognition technology, in use at all land, sea and airports.

New Airports

ADAC is adding a third airport to its portfolio with the announcement in July 2008 that it would establish the Middle East's first dedicated executive airport at Al Bateen just 10 kilometres from Abu Dhabi city centre. The Bateen facility will be developed as an exclusive corporate jet facility and ADAC will invest more than Dh200 million in additional services at the airport, formerly the capital's airport but which has been a military airbase since the early 1980s. The intention is to develop a 'one-stop shop' business jet facility, offering VVIP and VIP passenger terminals, airport services, maintenance, repair and overhaul, fuel, handling and all other fixed-base operational services.

This airport will become the focus for one of the fastest-growing areas of air travel. There are more than 380 corporate jets based in the Middle East, a figure that is forecast to grow to 900 by 2014 and this latest move by ADAC will further its goal to promote the UAE capital as the region's business aviation leader.

ADAC is also developing and operating airports at island resorts such as Sir Bani Yas and Dalma, so that they can be easily accessed via air taxis or air-shuttle services operating from both Bateen and Abu Dhabi International Airport. The intention is to extend the air-shuttle service to the rest of the extensive Al Gharbia region, which is being rapidly revitalised, and discussions are taking place between ADAC, the Department of Transport and Abu Dhabi Aviation to evaluate the prospects for an airport in the area's isolated hinterland, as well as on other islands,

Dubai Airport's impressive new Terminal 3 commenced operations in October 2008.

AIRPORTS IN DUBAI

Dubai International Airport (DIA) was the world's fastest growing airport in 2007 in terms of international passenger throughput, with a growth of 19.31 per cent or 34.34 million passengers. DIA handled a record 18.46 million passengers in the first half of 2008, registering a growth of 13.8 per cent over the first six months of 2007. The airport handled an average of 3 million passengers per month throughout this period, making it the busiest in the airport's history. Some 40 million passengers are expected to use the airport in 2008.

Cargo also showed robust growth at Dubai International with Dubai Cargo Village handling 831,978 tonnes of freight in the first half of 2008, up 10.70 per cent over the same period in 2007.

The airport handled a total of 135,144 aircraft movements (both inbound and outbound) between January and June 2008, as against 127,568 in the first half of 2007. On average, there are 715 aircraft movements per day at Dubai International.

A phased transition of operations to DIA's impressive new Terminal 3, a multi-level underground structure with a 40 million passenger capacity, commenced on 14 October 2008. This was preceded by operational trials using members of the public to ensure that systems were working to the highest standards of efficiency.

The Dh16.6 billion (US$4.5 billion) facility will cater to the rapid expansion of Emirates fleet, especially the superjumbo Airbus A380s:

www.uaeinteract.com/transport

two airside facilities will have 25 gates specifically designed for twin deck embarking and disembarking. Seven of these were operational at the end of 2008 and the second airside facility will be ready in 2009. Terminal 3 will increase the airport's capacity to 65 million passengers annually, thereby easing the flow at the existing terminals.

Dubai Duty Free (DDF) also announced record-breaking results for 2007, with sales reaching Dh3.175 billion (US$880 million), a 24 per cent increase over the previous year. Sales also surged by 31 per cent to Dh1.9 billion in the first half of 2008. This is set to increase since the opening of Concourse 2 and Terminal 3 has added 10,000 square metres to DDF's retail area.

For the ninth consecutive year, DDF walked away with the award for 'Middle East Travel Retailer of the Year' at the annual DFNI Awards ceremony, formerly known as the Raven Fox Awards. The DFNI award followed closely on the heels of the 'Business Traveller Middle East Award' for Best Duty Free, which was presented during the Arabian Travel Market in May. DDF also won 'Best Duty Free' at the Naseba MENA Airport Awards 2008.

Dubai International Airport itself is no stranger to awards having recently won 'Best Airport in the Middle East', at the Business Traveller Awards, along with the 'Fastest Growing Airport' at Naseba MENA Airports Awards.

But Dubai is not content with expanding Dubai International Airport, it is also building a new airport on the outskirts of the city. Al Maktoum International, when it is fully operational, is expected to handle 120 million passengers a year. The entire project will cost Dh128.4 billion (US$35 billion), with Dh36.7 billion (US$10 billion) earmarked for the airport alone.

A dedicated Executive Flight Centre for general aviation, mainly business jets and VIP flight operations, has seen double-digit growth at Dubai International Airport for several years and a new facility is also planned for Jebel Ali: the Dubai World Central (DWC) Executive Flight Centre will be able to accommodate 100,000 aircraft movements per year.

NORTHERN AIRPORTS

Sharjah International Airport (SIA) celebrated its seventy-fifth anniversary in 2008: the facility was founded in 1932 when Imperial

Airways, the forerunner of British Airways, constructed an airfield at Sharjah as a stopover en route to India and Australia. When the modern Sharjah International airport opened on 1 January 1977, it was the first category II airport in the Arabian Gulf and had an annual capacity of 2 million passengers.

SIA, too, has recorded steady growth in passenger traffic and the launching of the very successful Air Arabia has played a major role in the overall activity at the airport. In 2007, passenger throughput was 4,324,313, there were 51,314 aircraft movements and 570,363 tonnes of cargo was shifted through the airport. In the first nine months of 2008, Shanjah Airport recorded an impressive 24.78 per cent increase in passenger traffic.

Ongoing developments are expected to boost the capacity of SIA to handle more than 8 million passengers a year. Expansion plans include new gates, departure and arrivals lobbies and airside facilities for regular passengers, VIPs, and cargo. The cost of the project, which is nearing completion, is approximately Dh500 million (US$136.23 million).

Ajman announced in December 2007 that it is building a new airport at a cost of Dh12 billion (US$3.26 billion) in the Manama area of the emirate, close to the western flank of the Hajar Mountains. Spread over an area of 6 million square metres, the Ajman airport project will be completed in two phases, the first comprising the main arrival and departure terminal buildings, runway, cargo complex, aviation school, aircraft maintenance workshop, free zone and commercial area.

Scheduled for completion in 2011, it is estimated that Ajman airport will handle more than 1 million passengers in the first three years of operation and at least 400,000 tonnes of cargo. Driven largely by low cost carriers and cargo operations in the initial phase, the new airport expects to achieve significant international passenger traffic within five years.

Ra's al-Khaimah International Airport is striving to create a name in the aviation industry. Currently 16 airlines use the facility, including the recently established Ra's al-Khaimah Airways. The airport is implementing a four-year plan to construct new arrival and departure lounges, a free zone, automated cargo warehouses, parking lots, offices, and restaurants. Plans are also in place to construct a new five-star airport hotel and build a new runway.

Ajman is building a new airport in the Manama area of the emirate, close to the western flank of the Hajar Mountains.

www.uaeinteract.com/transport

Fujairah is planning to phase out its existing international airport on the edge of Fujairah City, to permit the area to be utilised for urban expansion. A completely new airport is planned near Siji, on the western side of the Hajar Mountains and close to the new Fujairah–Dubai highway. From Siji, using the new road, it will be only a 25-minute drive to Fujairah.

PORTS

The United Arab Emirates has over 20 ports, ranging from state-of-the-art oil terminals, world-class industrial ports and container-handling facilities to smaller dhow and wooden-boat wharfs. All UAE ports experienced record performances in 2008 as the region's economic boom meant that imports of the necessary materials, foodstuffs and luxury goods flooded into the country. As a result, UAE port operators are focusing on finishing expansion plans as well as upgrading equipment and facilities in an attempt to keep ahead of the frantic pace of growth.

All UAE ports experienced record performances in 2008 as the region's economic boom meant that imports of the necessary materials, foodstuffs and luxury goods flooded into the country.

ABU DHABI

Abu Dhabi Terminals (ADT) is in charge of operations at Mina Zayed, Abu Dhabi's main commercial port. However, day-to-day management is carried out by DP World–UAE under the terms of an agreement concluded in 2006.

Much of the success of Abu Dhabi's ambitious plans for the future that have been outlined in previous sections will be determined by the efficiency of the ports since 80 per cent of goods arriving into Abu Dhabi emirate do so by sea. For example, commodity imports surged 69 per cent at Mina Zayed from January to July and in the first seven months of 2008, steel and iron imports to Abu Dhabi rose by 76 per cent to 1.2 million metric tonnes, while imports of plywood for construction went up by 351 per cent to 43,500 metric tonnes. The number of container moves at Mina Zayed reached 200,000 in the same period.

By 2011 Mina Zayed's central role is set to change when Khalifa Port and Industrial Zone (KPIZ) will take over as the emirate's primary port. The Dh37 billion (US$10 billion) greenfield port project is being constructed 4.6 kilometres offshore of Taweelah on 3.4 square kilometres of reclaimed land, roughly halfway between the two cities of Abu Dhabi and Dubai. The adjacent industrial, logistics, commercial, educational and residential zones are spread over 137 square kilometres. The world-scale industrial and container port will have the capacity to handle 2 million TEUs (twenty-foot equivalent units) in its first phase. By 2028, it is estimated that the port will handle 37 million tonnes of cargo and 5 million containers each year

The decision to build offshore was taken following a two-year environmental study conducted by Abu Dhabi Ports Company (ADPC), probably the most extensive modelling study ever done in this region. The design ensures that coral communities will be unaffected by shipping traffic further offshore. A Wetlands National Park is planned just south of the Khalifa Port. Another protected area will be created among the mangroves and tidal flatlands just north of the new port, along the Dubai border.

DP World–UAE will also manage Khalifa Port and DP World's sister company Economic Zones World (EZW), one of the largest developers and operators of free zones in the world, has been contracted to operate an initial 25 square kilometre trade and logistics free zone within the larger industrial zone.

A massive new port, Khalifa Port and Industrial Zone, is being constructed 4.6 kilometres off Taweelah on 3.4 square kilometres of reclaimed land.

DUBAI

In addition to Mina Zayed, DP World-UAE manages ports at Dubai's Jebel Ali, the largest port in the Middle East, Port Rashid, also in Dubai and Fujairah on the east coast. In 2007, the company recorded 19 per cent growth in throughput with the handling of 11 million TEUs at its marine terminals during 2007, as compared to 2006.

A substantial increase in throughput was recorded at Jebel Ali and Port Rashid, showing a growth of 20 per cent compared with 2006, to reach 10.7 million TEUs. Jebel Ali port operations alone grew by more than 25 per cent, with the port handling over 9.9 million TEUs, compared with the volume handled throughout 2006. Container volumes at Jebel Ali increased by 22 per cent in the first half of 2008.

DP World is scaling down operations at Port Rashid and shifting all cargo operations to the Jebel Ali Port as the Port Rashid area is being redeveloped for urban real estate and other maritime activities such as cruise tourism.

> Jebel Ali will have an additional 2500 metres of quay length with a draft of 17 metres. This will enable the port to cater for the new generation of massive ships.

The opening of the first phase of a new container terminal (T2) at Jebel Ali in August 2007, which added 2 million tonnes, contributed to a substantial increase in handling capacity. By the time the Dh5.5 billion (US$1.5 billion) T2 becomes fully operational in February 2009, an additional 3 million tonnes will have been added, raising capacity to 15 million tonnes. Terminal 2, like Terminal 1, will be used for both import and export cargo and transshipment business.

Jebel Ali will have an additional 2500 metres of quay length with a draft of 17 metres. This will enable the port to cater for the new generation of massive ships (12,000 + TEUs). The port has already played host to one of the world's largest ships when it welcomed the 367-metre *Grete Mersk*, which has a capacity of 8200 TEUs, in August 2008.

Jebel Ali has been voted 'Best Seaport in the Middle East' for 13 consecutive years and DP World–UAE was recently awarded a 'Recognised for Excellence' five-star rating by EFQM, the European Foundation for Quality Management, a prominent international body that assesses the performance of companies and their commitment to quality standards.

DP World now ranks fourth in the world in managing and operating marine terminals with an expanding network of operations in the Indian subcontinent, Far East, the Americas, Australia and also in the UAE. The UAE's ports account for around 25 per cent of the total handled TEUs in DP World's terminals worldwide, which was 43.3 million TEUs in 2007.

SHARJAH'S PORTS

Container volume at Sharjah's ports, Sharjah Container Terminal (Port Khalid) (SCT) on the Gulf coast and Khor Fakkan, Sharjah's east coast facility, grew by 8 per cent in 2007. The combined throughput was 2.17 million TEUs. The two terminals achieved about 2 million TEUs in 2006. Both ports are operated by Gulftainer.

Construction commenced in early 2007 on a major expansion at SCT to keep pace with demand. The overall draft has been increased by 1 metre to 12.5 metres, enabling the port to handle bigger ships. The quay wall has been buttressed, additional storage areas allocated and two new large gantry cranes, post-panamax cranes, also became operational in September. The improvements should increase the capacity of the port by 20 per cent.

Khor Fakkan Container Terminal (KCT) has shown a 20 per cent increase in volumes during the first half of 2008 compared with the same period in 2007. To accommodate growth, Gulftainer has also increased capacity at this terminal. It had already increased its docking capacity with the addition of 400 metres of quay in 2006 and is now engaged in a second phase of expansion. The project will increase KCT's existing 1460 metres of quay by 440 metres. and the new quay will be protected by an 800 metre breakwater. Much of the dredging required to provide 16.5 metres of water depth alongside the quay wall has already been completed and the infilling for the berth's foundation is under way.

Upon completion of the new berth, six new ship-to-shore super post-panamax gantries will be installed, taking the number of such cranes at the port to 20. The terminal will also benefit from new rubber-tyred gantries and road trains. All this development work is essential if Sharjah is to avoid the costly delays and congestion affecting many other regions.

PORTS IN OTHER EMIRATES

Traffic at Ajman Port, which only commenced container operations in April 1999, was expected to rise in 2008 with the expansion of business in the area and the fact that the port provides cost-effective services and facilities to the adjacent free zone and the wider business community. Facilities include eight wharfs and a covered storage area totalling 43,200 square metres. The Port Authority also has two dry docks for ship repairs and maintenance.

The Ahmed Bin Rashid Port and Free Zone is located about 30 miles north-east of Dubai in the Emirate of Umm al-Qaiwain. The free zone complex comprises four wharves totalling 845 metres of quay wall within a secured area of 400,000 square metres, which is capable of handling ocean-going vessels, and 118,000 square metres of land reserved for light industrial development. The entrance channel has a minimum depth of 10 metres and a width of 100 metres, and connects with a swinging basin of 500 metres.

Saqr Port, Ra's al-Khaimah's window on the world, has experienced a robust 107 per cent increase in cargo handling over the past four years and an annual growth of more than 30 per cent, reflecting the fast-paced development activities taking place in the emirate. During that period, the port has undertaken an ambitious expansion

Dubai was the first city in the Middle East to launch the IATA e-freight initiative and the fourteenth e-freight location worldwide to deliver cargo paper-free.

Fujairah port authorities have raised Dh900 million to finance the building of additional container terminals at the port. A new oil pipeline between Abu Dhabi and Fujairah and the construction of an oil refinery nearby will also make Fujairah Port an important player in oil exporting.

programme involving an investment of Dh221 million to improve the efficient handling of containers, bulk and general cargo.

A new container terminal with a capacity of 350,000 TEUs, which was developed by the Kuwait-based KGL Ports International (KGLPI), was recently added. Four new berths, a high-tech container scanning system and other upgraded infrastructure have been commissioned and new offices for the RAK Customs and Ports Department were opened. The four new berths have a total length of 795 metres and will substantially increase the cargo handling capacity of the port. Saqr Port Authority operates the remaining eight berths.

Fujairah Port is strategically located on UAE's east coast, approximately 70 nautical miles from the Straits of Hormuz, an attractive location for a range of users of the multi-purpose port and the significant number of vessels calling at the Fujairah anchorage for bunker supplies and services. Since commencing operations in 1983, Fujairah Port has embarked on a continuing process of enhancement of its facilities and functions. Improvements in recent years include the dredging of the entrance and the inner basin to 15 metres, the completion of an additional 600 metres of main quay (giving 1.4 kilometres of continuous quay), an additional 720 metres of tanker berth quays along the northern breakwater additional paved area, (storage for up to 30,000 TEUs), and the provision of a bulk loader to cater for the emirate's aggregate export market.

The offshore tanker anchorage, supervised by Fujairah's Port Authority, has been a major component of the port's success and Fujairah is now the second-largest oil bunkering port in the world.

The port handles all types of business including bulk cargo, general cargo, oil and other commodities, as well as providing marine services. Currently, the port is not using its container loading facilities and DP World, which currently leases the quay and cranes, has expressed a wish to unload larger vessels and handle more containers.

The Port of Fujairah has raised Dh900 million to expand existing operations and invest in new facilities to alleviate existing capacity shortages at the terminal and cater for anticipated growth over the next 25 years.

ELECTRICITY & WATER

An adequate supply of electricity and water is an absolute prerequisite to fuel the massive economic and infrastructure developments outlined in the previous sections. It is no surprise, therefore, that considerable effort is being expended to meet burgeoning demand, which some analysts have calculated could be growing at a rate of 15 to 20 per cent per annum.

The Federal Electricity and Water Authority (Fewa) is the body responsible for overseeing federal utilities, whilst authorities in individual emirates, including Abu Dhabi Water and Electricity Authority (Adwea), Dubai Water and Electricity Authority (Dewa) and Sharjah Water and Electricity Authority (Sewa), oversee power and water generation in their individual emirates.

As government moves from provider to regulator, privatisation has featured prominently in utility provision. Part-privatisation has been a long-established policy in Abu Dhabi, and a new federal law governing utility privatisation under Fewa was introduced in 2008. Other emirates are also actively pursuing this business model.

WATER RESOURCES

Despite the scarcity of natural water resources, residents of the UAE are among the highest per capita water users in the world, consuming an average of 550 litres per day. The UAE relies on renewable and

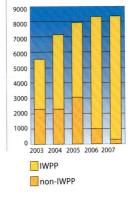

IWPP
non-IWPP

Abu Dhabi IWPP and non-IWPP electricity in gross megawatt.

www.uaeinteract.com/elec_h$_2$o

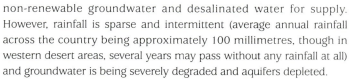

non-renewable groundwater and desalinated water for supply. However, rainfall is sparse and intermittent (average annual rainfall across the country being approximately 100 millimetres, though in western desert areas, several years may pass without any rainfall at all) and groundwater is being severely degraded and aquifers depleted.

Irrigation for agriculture, forestry and amenity plantation accounts for a massive 82 per cent of total groundwater use and it is generally recognised that this position is untenable. If water continues to be abstracted at the current rate, fresh and brackish groundwater resources will probably be depleted in 50 years. One of the worst affected areas is Al Khazna, an agriculture area 40 kilometres from Al Ain, where the water table has dropped 80 metres in 25 years. Near the coast, depleted aquifers have been contaminated by seawater. Higher soil and water salinity is also a problem.

The UAE plans to build 68 rechargeable dams in the coming five years to augment the 114 dams in existence, all but two of which are rechargeable. Higher than average rainfall in 2008 has helped to fill dams. However, desalination now supplies almost all of the water used for human consumption and for industry. Five of the world's top ten desalination plants are located in the UAE. Most desalination plants are cogeneration projects using excess heat from power production.

The UAE's investment in power and water projects increased by 20 per cent from Dh42.64 billion (US$11.62 billion) in 2007 to Dh 51.34 billion (US$14 billion) in 2008, 50 per cent of which was earmarked for processing wastewater while water generation and transportation accounted for 36 per cent and 13 per cent, respectively.

Adwea is spending Dh 4.77 billion (US$1.3 billion) for the expansion of five existing desalination plants; one is scheduled for completion in 2008, another will come on-stream in 2009 and the remaining three will be in operation by 2010.

Under Adwea's five-year strategy, the agency will increase its water production from the current 626 million gallons per day (MIGD) to 969 MIGD by 2013. However, demand for water in Abu Dhabi is expected to grow by anything up to 43 per cent in the next five years, depending on whether developers meet their schedules.

Dewa is spending Dh1.23 billion (US$335 million) on water projects, 80 per cent of which is dedicated for water generation and transportation and 20 per cent for processing.

Sharjah and Ajman's spending currently stands at Dh4.28 billion (US$1.166 billion) and Dh1.31 billion (US$357 million), respectively, while Fujairah's projects are put at Dh3.14 billion (US$856 million).

Regulating Usage

The government recognises that the issue is not just one of supply, demand management is equally vital for sustainable development and long-term water security. Increasing public participation in water resources management programmes is just one of the priorities of the recently adopted Water Master Plan for Abu Dhabi emirate, which was developed by the Environment Agency –Abu Dhabi (EAD). The aim is to reduce the usage of water to 350 litres per capita per day over the next five years.

Steps are being taken too by EAD to tackle water resource management issues, including monitoring and management of groundwater resources, wastewater treatment management, water quality monitoring, and general water wastage in distribution systems.

EAD is also responsible for a technologically advanced soil resources mapping project that is greatly facilitating the exploration, licensing and regulation of well drilling, and the finding of a gigantic aquifer in the Western (Al Gharbia) Region of Abu Dhabi was a significant success for the project. Recent legislation is also curbing the drilling of unlicensed wells.

In addition, a satellite imagery project run by the Centre for Remote Sensing, Boston University, USA, in cooperation with Sewa, was crucial in preparing a long-term strategic plan for the rational use of groundwater resources in Sharjah and other northern emirates.

EAD has set a target for farms to cut water consumption from 23,500 to 18,000 cubic metres per hectare and for forestry to reduce its usage from 3500 to 2500 cubic metres per hectare by 2012. Some savings may be achieved by advanced irrigation techniques and adherence to the master plan will prohibit new forestry plantations.

The use of treated water for irrigating landscaped gardens is also being encouraged to save desalinated water and it is estimated that within two years all treated sewage water will be used for irrigation. The ultimate aim of the strategy is to meet the needs of the industrial and agricultural sectors with treated wastewater and to use desalinated water only for domestic purpose.

One of the priorities of the recently adopted Water Master Plan for Abu Dhabi emirate, which was developed by the Environment Agency–Abu Dhabi (EAD), is to reduce the water usage to 350 litres per capita per day over the next five years.

www.uaeinteract.com/elec_h₂o

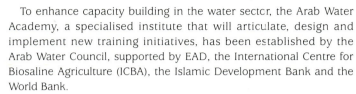

Abu Dhabi Sewerage Services Company is implementing Step, the Strategic Tunnel Enhancement Programme, to cater for increased demands on the emirate's sewerage system.

To enhance capacity building in the water sector, the Arab Water Academy, a specialised institute that will articulate, design and implement new training initiatives, has been established by the Arab Water Council, supported by EAD, the International Centre for Biosaline Agriculture (ICBA), the Islamic Development Bank and the World Bank.

To further enhance integrated water management, in 2008 the UAE Environment and Water Minister signed a Memorandum of Understanding (MoU) with the United Nations University International Network on Water, Environment and Health, on cooperation in the fields of research, capacity building and sustainable management of water resources in the UAE.

Public awareness of conservation issues is also a major component of Dewa's efforts to curb demand escalation. Recognising that the residential sector consumed 60 per cent of water and 30 per cent of power supplied in 2007, Dewa launched a campaign under the slogan 'Now that you know, don't let it go.'

Focusing on the behaviour of consumers, the campaign seeks to educate the public and provide tips to save water and electricity. Under their new conservation programme entitled the 'Best Consumer Award', Dewa is also offering residents the chance to win cash prizes by reducing the amount of electricity and water they use on a daily basis.

Pricing is also being used to curb demand: Dubai has devised a new tariff whereby the more you use the more you pay to encourage big consumers to use less water. The new price scale will only affect the top 20 per cent of consumers. Sewa has also introduced a slab system of tariff for electricity and water consumption whereby rates charged increase proportionally with consumption.

SEWERAGE

Sewage works have been stretched by the unprecedented rate of urbanisation throughout the UAE and, as already mentioned, treated sewage is a major component of water usage strategy. Over the next six years, the Abu Dhabi Sewerage Services Company (ADSSC) will implement the Strategic Tunnel Enhancement Programme (STEP) to cater to the immediate, short and long-term needs of Abu Dhabi's wastewater and drainage system. The STEP project comprises 40 kilometres of deep sewerage tunnel and two new large pumping stations. The programme will play a critical role in the implementation of Abu Dhabi's Plan 2030.

Dubai Municipality is also constructing a huge sewage water treatment plant at Jebel Ali at a cost of Dh1.56 billion (US$425 million). On completion in 2010, the new facility will replace Al Awir as the main sewage treatment plant for the city, thereby ensuring that all areas are linked to the city's main drainage network. The project covers an area of 670 hectares and is designed to have the capacity to treat 300,000 cubic metres of sewage a day.

Sharjah is allocating Dh100 million to fund the seventh phase of upgrading work on its sewage treatment plant. The project will be completed in 2011, increasing current capacity by 55 per cent.

POWER AND WATER GENERATION

Residents in the UAE draw on around 11,000 kilowatt hours per person per year. At the end of 2007, available capacity in the UAE was around 16,670 MW. Some analysts estimate that the national annual peak demand for electricity is likely to rise to more than 40,000 MW by 2020, reflecting a cumulative annual growth rate of roughly 9 per cent. However, in Abu Dhabi alone, demand will rise almost 80 per cent in the next five years to 10,600 MW, while capacity, which was 8000 MW at the end of 2007, is set to reach 12,503 MW in 2010.

Optimisation and expansion of existing facilities as well as development of greenfield sites is ongoing and billions of dirhams have been pumped into the electricity and water sector since Abu Dhabi embarked on its privatisation drive in 1998. Today, independent water and power projects (IWPPs) supply the bulk of electricity and water in Abu Dhabi, and Taweelah A-2, the UAE's first IWPP, is being used across the region as a blueprint for a successful privatisation strategy.

Taqa, the energy investment company in which the government of Abu Dhabi through Adwea owns 51 per cent, has been instrumental in providing over 85 per cent of Abu Dhabi's power and water desalination needs.

ELECTRICITY PEAK DEMAND HIGH FORECAST			
	2010	2015	2020
ABU DHABI	7,011	10,412	11,412
AL AIN	1,741	2,136	2,460
WESTERN REGION	9,822	13,947	14,340

In 2008, Taqa sold a 20-per cent interest in Shuweihat CMS International Power Company (Scipco) and a 50 per cent interest in Shuweihat O&M Limited Partnership (SOMLP) to Sumitomo Corporation for Dh638.3 million (US$173.95 million); Scipco owns the Shuweihat S1 power generation and water desalination facility near Jebel Dhanna, with a net production capacity of 1500 MW and 100 MIGD. SOMLP is the company responsible for the management,

operation and maintenance of the S1 Plant. Following this transaction, Taqa retained a 54 per cent interest in Scipco, while Adwea and International Power continued to hold 6 per cent and 20 per cent respectively.

Adwea's eighth IWPP, Shuweihat 2, costing Dh7.34 billion (US$2 billion) and producing 1500 MW and 100 MIGD was set up in 2008. Shuweihat 3, which was also announced in 2008, is due to be operational by 2012. It will have power capacity of about 1500 MW and 100 MIGD.

In Dubai, Dewa had a generating capacity at the end of 2007 of around 5500 MW, with a further 1800 MW of capacity added in 2008. So far, Dubai has been able to meet demand for electricity and water, which has been growing in the emirate at a rate of 15 per cent and 12 per cent respectively, but this is set to escalate. In total, Dubai has committed Dh72 billion (US$19.62 billion) to fund utility projects that have been implemented during 2008 or are still under construction.

Dewa is in the process of constructing three main power generation stations with a capacity of 400/132 KV, as well as electricity transference lines with a capacity of 400 KV, with the total cost of the three stations and lines amounting to Dh2.120 billion. The construction of each station will take between 22 and 26 months and they will be instrumental in supplying power to major developments such as Palm Jebel Ali and Dubailand,

Dubai is also planning to build a multi-billion dollar plant that would be capable of producing 9000 MW of electricity and 600 MIGD of desalinated water. The new complex will be located next to Dubai World Central and the Jebel Ali port and free zone where most of the emirate's power generation capacity is presently situated.

In an attempt to keep pace with Sharjah's mushrooming demand, phase one of Sewa's Hamriya power and desalination plant is currently under construction and scheduled for start-up in 2009. Initial work on the site includes a 600 MW power plant and 24 MIGD of desalination. The Sewa project will eventually supply 2000 MW of power and 168 MIGD of desalinated water.

Sewa's Khor Fakkan desalination plant, which began production in October 2008, will produce 2.5 MIGD in the initial phase but total capacity will be 5 MIGD.

To meet surging requirements in the Emirate of Ra's al-Khaimah, Adwea is providing Fewa with 10 MIGD through new pipelines from a

Phase one of Sharjah's Hamriya power and desalination plant is scheduled for start-up in 2009. The Sewa project will eventually supply 2000 MW of power and 168 MIGD of desalinated water.

plant at Qidfa, just north of Fujairah, raising its pumping capacity to 37 MIGD. Construction of the main water pipelines has recently been completed. The freshwater supplies will radically solve the problem of water shortfall in Ra's al-Khaimah. Meanwhile, Fewa is handing over the Zawra desalination plant in the Emirate of Ajman. The plant will initially produce 3 MIGD and a planned maximum capacity of 6 MIGD will be reached when the construction of a new connection pipeline is finalised.

Additionally, four electricity plants with a total capacity of 740 MW are being built by the Ra's al-Khaimah government and plans for a 2000 MW plant to meet the needs of the emirate's future expansion are being studied. The first plant at Al Hamra, with a capacity of 120 MW, cost Dh440 million (US$119.9 million) and became operational in November 2008.

An 80 MW plant at Al Ghail Industrial City and another with a capacity of 40 MW at Al Hamra will be ready for operation in June 2009. The combined cost of both plants will be Dh 32.7 million (US$120 million). The fourth plant, with a capacity of 500 MW, is due to open in September 2010.

The IWPP projects at Fujairah 1 and Fujairah 2, also at Qidfa and managed by Abu Dhabi's Adwea in association with foreign investors, significantly increase the availability of power and water. Fujairah 1 has a capacity of 880 MW and 102 MIGD, whilst Fujairah 2 will add 2000 MW of electricity and 130 MIGD.

Most of the power and desalination plants in the UAE are fuelled by gas. As we have already seen in the section on Oil & Gas, the UAE has invested heavily in projects to increase gas production over the past 20 years and the country is also importing Qatari gas through Dolphin pipelines. In addition, there are plans to obtain more than 500 million cubic feet per day from Iran through a Dana Gas pipeline.

Gas began flowing into Taweelah just outside Abu Dhabi City in 2007 at a rate of 1.6 billion cfd and supplies were expected to surge to 2 billion cfd in 2008. This includes 788 mmscf/d per day for Adwea, 730 mmscf/d for Dewa, 141 mmcsf/d for the Union Water and Electricity Company and 200 mmscf/d for Oman Oil Company.

The Fujairah plants will eventually also be supplied by gas from Qatar via the Dolphin Gas Project's receiving facility at Taweelah.

The IWPP projects at Fujairah 1 and Fujairah 2 in Qidfa significantly increase the availability of power and water.

Common GCC power

Linking the electricity
networks of the six GCC
states in a single grid
will help to ensure
security of supply,
assist in conserving
the environment and
save money in the
long-term.

Linking the electricity networks of the six GCC states in a single grid, which is currently under construction, will help to ensure security of supply, assist in conserving the environment and save money in the long-term. The total installed capacity for the GCC Interconnection Grid is predicted to be 70 gigawatts, 10 gigawatts more than the peak load currently experienced on the member countries' systems.

The UAE and neighbouring Oman have integrated their own network (South Grid) and the remaining two phases of the landmark project (interconnection of Kuwait, Saudi Arabia, Bahrain and Qatar, the North Grid, and the connecting up of North and South Grid) are scheduled for completion by 2010.

The GCC Interconnection Grid Authority, which is overseeing the project, expects it to result in a 50 per cent reduction in operational reserve and slash costs of power projects in the region in the long term. The project could pave the way for extending the grid between the GCC and other Arab nations.

CLEAN POWER

Alternative low-carbon energy sources, such as solar, wind and hydrogen power, are becoming increasingly attractive in the UAE, especially since the US$15 billion Masdar Initiative was launched in 2006, marking Abu Dhabi as the first major hydrocarbon-producing nation to embrace renewable and sustainable energy. As explained in the chapter on Economic Development, the imaginative Masdar Initiative is Abu Dhabi's multi-faceted, multi-billion dollar investment in the development and commercialisation of innovative technologies in renewable, alternative and sustainable energies together with sustainable design.

As we have already seen, Masdar will cover wide-ranging energy programmes on sustainable development and management of solar, hydrogen and wind powers, carbon emission reduction, education, industry and research and development.

In February 2008, the Masdar Initiative broke ground in Abu Dhabi on Masdar City, which will be powered entirely by renewable energy. Covering an area of 6 square kilometres, Masdar City will have its electricity generated by photovoltaic panels, some of which will be manufactured in Abu Dhabi, while cooling will be provided via concentrated solar power. Water will be provided through a solar-powered desalination plant. Landscaping within the city and crops grown outside the city will be irrigated with grey water and treated wastewater produced by the city's water treatment plant.

Masdar is collaborating with Emirates CMS Power Company to develop a UN-audited Clean Development Mechanism (CDM) project that will see the reduction of carbon dioxide emissions at Emirates CMS power generation facility at the Taweelah industrial zone in Abu Dhabi.

The UAE is also expected to agree to a proposed hydrogen plant, which will extract hydrogen and carbon dioxide from natural gas. The carbon dioxide will be trapped and injected into oilfields, pushing out the remaining oil in a process known as enhanced oil recovery. Hydrogen will be sold as a clean fuel that power plants could burn to produce electricity.

Masdar and Hydrogen Energy, a joint venture between the oil firm BP and mining company Rio Tinto, are investing in the project, which carries a US$2 billion capital cost. Masdar will present the case to government at the start of 2009, expecting a green light in the middle of the year and operation by mid-2013, a year later than Hydrogen Energy had earlier forecast.

Taqa is progressing a Dh3.67 billion coal-fired power plant in the capital to be completed in the second quarter of 2009. At the same time, construction of a Dh6 billion power station to generate electricity using hydrogen extracted from coal commenced at Ras Hasyan in August 2008. Dewa will own 51 per cent of the plant, with the remainder held by foreign investors.

For more information about the Masdar Initiative, visit www.masdaruae.com.

The prototype for a Dh18 million 'Solar Island' announced in Ra's al-Khaimah in January 2008 to produce around 250 KW of electricity will be fully operational by the beginning of 2009.

NUCLEAR ENERGY

Despite the fact that alternative energy options are being actively researched and deployed within the UAE, it is unlikely that these methods of generating electricity could supply sufficient energy to meet the predicted shortfall. Other sustainable alternatives under consideration include nuclear energy.

In 2008, the UAE set up the Emirates Nuclear Energy Corporation (Enec), with an initial capital of Dh375 million (US$102 million), to assess and develop a peaceful nuclear energy programme. In April 2008, the UAE Government unveiled its formal policy towards the development of peaceful nuclear energy following consultations with

www.uaeinteract.com/elec_h₂o

The UAE has set up the Emirates Nuclear Energy Corporation to assess and develop a peaceful nuclear energy programme.

the International Atomic Energy Agency (IAEA) and the governments of France, the US, the UK, Russia, China, Japan, Germany and South Korea. The government has stressed that it will work closely with the IAEA on the planned peaceful nuclear power programme.

In August 2008, it was announced that the UAE had contributed US$10 million towards a fuel bank proposal originally launched by the Nuclear Threat Initiative (NTI) in 2006. The NTI plan calls for a dedicated low-enriched uranium (LEU) stockpile to be owned and administered by the IAEA, the aim being to provide states with assurances of nuclear fuel supply, addressing potential disruptions of fuel shipment.

In the meantime, negotiations are taking place with interested parties to explore the feasibility of building third-generation nuclear power plants and in October 2008, Enec appointed CH2M HILL as the managing agent for the nuclear power programme.

TELECOMMUNICATIONS & POST

Telecommunications across all platforms in the UAE are fast and effective with fixed-line, internet and mobile connectivity among the best in the world.

Fostering telecommunications is a major part of UAE Government strategy, based on the awareness that connectivity is a key component of public infrastructure. Today, telecommunications across all platforms in the UAE are fast and effective with fixed-line, internet and mobile connectivity among the best in the world. This was underlined in the latest edition of the Global Information Technology Report, produced by the World Economic Forum, which lists the UAE in twenty-ninth place in its Networked Readiness Index (NRI) 2007–2008 rankings, marking it out as one of the highest rated networked economies in the world. The NRI measures economies' capacity to fully leverage ICT for increased competitiveness and development.

Recent research underlines the UAE's leadership in the Middle East when it comes to expenditure on ICT: the country is currently spending Dh41.8 billion (US$11.4 billion) on ICT, and that figure is set to rise to Dh54.3 billion (US$14.8 billion) by 2011.

Competition in the Marketplace

The UAE is presently serviced by two telecommunications operators, Etisalat and du. Etisalat, which is 60 per cent state owned, has

been investing in communications infrastructure providing fixed-line telephony, fixed and wireless secure internet access and mobile coverage to the UAE since its establishment in 1976. The company operated a monopoly until du launched mobile services in February 2007. However, Etisalat, with over 80 per cent of the market, remains the UAE's biggest telecom provider and is expanding dramatically internationally. As we saw in the chapter on Economic Development, Etisalat is now the sixteenth largest telecommunications firm in the world.

Du, offering voice, data and entertainment on mobile networks and converged broadband, TV, and landline, is concentrating primarily on building its customer base in the domestic market and is targeting a 30 per cent market share by 2010.

In January 2006 the takeover of the Tecom telecommunications company that formerly operated Dubai free zone networks and

Etisalat operated a monopoly in telecom services until du entered the marketplace in 2007.

www.uaeinteract.com/telecomms

Etisalat and du have paid Dh400 million into the Information and Communication Technology (ICT) Fund, representing 1 per cent of the companies' revenues in 2006 and 2007.

Emaar's former Sahm Telecom network gave du a good working base to develop the company. Prior to an IPO in 2006, 50 per cent of du was owned by the UAE Government, and the remaining 50 per cent split equally between Abu Dhabi's Mubadala Development Company and Emirates Communications Technology Company. Post-IPO, up to 20 per cent of du can be controlled by foreign individuals and institutions permitted to purchase du shares on the Dubai Financial Market. At this point in time, du continues to show steady growth in revenues as well as subscribers.

Exceeding market expectations, du's total number of mobile customers at 30 June 2008 crossed the 2.3 million mark, an addition of 0.5 million in the quarter. Active subscribers, as defined by the TRA, reached 1.85 million at 30 June 2008, a quarter on quarter increase of 32 per cent (1.4 million at 31 March 2008).

Fixed-line revenues also continued to show significant growth, a reflection of the continued expansion of the company's fixed line network, which has led to an 18 per cent quarter on quarter increase in subscribers to 0.22 million (Q1 0.18 million).

du announced in May 2008 that it had signed a construction and maintenance agreement to build the first direct, high-bandwidth optical-fibre submarine cable system from the United Kingdom to India. The Europe India Gateway (EIG) cable system, which will cost more than Dh2.57 billion (US$700 million), will significantly enhance capacity, whilst bringing considerable diversity and bandwidth into the Middle East and providing global access to operators in the region.

Du's entry into the UAE telecoms market was facilitated by the formation of the Telecommunications Regulatory Authority (TRA) in 2003. The TRA was given the task of operating a regulatory framework that would assist liberalisation and competition, in line with World Trade Organisation (WTO) requirements, at the same time enhancing, promoting and ensuring the quality of services.

Between 2002 and 2007, the number of mobile phone subscribers in the UAE grew by an annual average of 25.6 per cent, almost four times its population growth. Forecasts indicate that the UAE mobile market will increase from 7.7 million subscribers in 2007 to 9.2 million in 2008 and to 11.9 million by 2012.

These figures show that the UAE had the highest mobile phone penetration in the Arab world at the beginning of 2008: at this point the ratio was 173 subscribers to each 100 people. This is more than triple the world average of 49.3 for every 100 people. Penetration rates are expected to grow more modestly in the future and analysts believe that the UAE telecoms market is on course to record a compounded annual growth rate (CAGR) of 8.5 per cent.

At 30 per cent, the UAE also has the highest fixed-line penetration among the Arab states. However, growth in this sector has remained fairly static, although this is also predicted to increase following a new TRA directive instructing Etisalat and du to make network adaptations to the fixed-line network, which should lower the cost to consumers. This involves providing widespread access by 2009 to a technology called Carrier Pre-Selection Service (CPS) in the fixed line system. The technology has been available in the UAE since 2007, but a more widespread introduction will increase competition in the sector, reduce prices, and enable consumers to freely choose their provider of fixed line call services.

Analysts believe that the UAE telecoms market is on course to record a compounded annual growth rate of 8.5 per cent.

Internet Usage

Internet penetration is projected to continue its rapid growth (16.1 per cent CAGR since 2005). Current UAE internet penetration figures assume 2.4 users per subscription. TRA projections indicate that over the next few years growth in both users and subscriptions will be coupled with a fall in the number of users per subscription: the number of subscribers are expected to increase from 0.904 million in 2007 to 1.15 million in 2008, 1.44 million in 2009 and 2.66 million in 2012. Revenues from internet subscriptions should grow from Dh1.46 billion in 2007 to Dh1.82 billion in 2008, Dh2.19 billion in 2009 and to Dh2.95 billion by 2012. However, broadband penetration has been less than expected. In 2007, 42 per cent of total were broadband subscribers with the remainder using dial-up.

In 2007, the TRA successfully launched the Domain Administrator (.aeDA) to manage the .ae domain for which it has commenced the registration and licensing process. Additional details and information are available on the website www.aeda.ae.

In August 2008, following consultations with interested parties, the TRA issued its regulation policy on Internet Access Management (IAM) in the UAE. This sets down the criteria that must be taken into consideration by internet service providers to ensure the security of

> The TRA has instructed internet service providers in the UAE to unblock access to over 1000 websites that do not conflict with its regulatory policy.

the internet and protect end-users from websites with content that is contrary to the religious and ethical values of UAE society. The policy lists sites that provide specific instructions or methods encouraging individuals to commit unlawful acts or crimes; 'phishing' sites that aim to deceive users in order to obtain personal data such as user name and password for credit cards, or include harmful codes and information on piracy programs; websites that promote illegal drugs, pornography, gambling, as well as websites which include materials that reflect a hatred of divine religions and prophets in general; and sites that promote terrorism or support for terrorism.

The TRA has also instructed internet service providers in the country to unblock access to more than 1000 websites on the internet that do not conflict with this regulatory policy and all licensed internet service providers in the country must apply these guidelines equally to all internet users. However, the TRA has implemented some exceptions to the rules where access to certain websites may be fundamental to the workings of government bodies.

In accordance with the TRA regulations on content, du has indicated that it will now follow Etisalat's practice of filtering websites not in compliance with UAE laws through a proxy server. UAE policies and proxy server issues affect certain websites in the UAE such as the popular communications portal Skype.

THURAYA

Abu Dhabi-based Thuraya Satellite Telecommunications Company, a leading provider of cost-effective, satellite-based mobile telephone services through dual-mode handsets and satellite payphones, is majority owned by Etisalat. Thuraya empowers people in rural and remote areas as well as those at sea or beyond the reach of terrestrial networks by providing them a reliable access to voice and data communications.

The company launched a third geosynchronous satellite in January 2008: Thuraya 3 replaces the ageing Thuraya 1, while Thuraya 2 will continue to provide coverage for the Middle East, Europe, North Africa and some other markets. Thuraya 3 will bring countries of the Asia-Pacific region, including such major markets as China, Australia, Japan, Korea and Indonesia under Thuraya's footprint and extend its coverage to nearly two-thirds of the globe's population, doubling the market size and population covered by the Thuraya system. Thuraya 3 and related ground network commenced commercial operation from 9 June 2008.

ThurayaMarine, a second generation communications technology package launched in 2007, has also been signed up with specialised maritime distributors and has commenced service provisioning in the Asia-Pacific region.

YAHSAT

Al Yah Satellite Communications Company PrJsc (Yahsat), the UAE's first nationally owned satellite operator, made its debut at Cabsat 2008. Incorporated in January 2007 and supported by a US$1.7 billion investment from parent company Mubadala, Yahsat will develop, procure, own and operate hybrid satellite systems based on market requirements and future applications. The Abu Dhabi-based company will provide innovative solutions for government and commercial communications in the Middle East, Africa, Europe and South-West Asia.

Yahsat signed an agreement with Arianespace to launch the Yahsat 1A satellite in the second half of 2010. The satellite is currently being manufactured by the consortium of EADS Astrium and Thales Alenia Space. Another agreement was signed with International Launch Services (ILS) to launch the Yahsat 1B satellite in first half of 2011. The launch of this satellite will enable Yahsat to offer a satellite broadband service 'Yahclick' throughout the satellite's range.

In addition, Yahsat signed an agreement with the UAE Armed Forces to provide secure satellite communications in the UAE for a 15-year period. As part of the turnkey contract Yahsat will also supply the ground terminals and gateway infrastructure and will be responsible for satellite network services.

POSTAL SERVICES

Emirates Postal Corporation (EPC) was formed in 2001 following restructuring of the UAE General Postal Authority. Since then, a major change in the corporation's business model and operational strategies, including the introduction of integrated IT systems, automated sorting centres and agreements with international postal authorities, as well as the addition of new business streams in cargo

Yahsat, the UAE's first nationally owned satellite operator, will provide innovative solutions for government and commercial communications in the Middle East, Africa, Europe and South-West Asia.

Emirates Post continues to pursue a successful diversification strategy, acquiring new businesses and forming new alliances.

and logistics, financial services, direct marketing, mail fulfilment and other areas, has resulted in a remarkable turnaround in the company's fortunes. A holding company, Emirates Post Group, oversees a rapidly expanding family of subsidiaries that now includes Emirates Post, the postal corporation, Empost, the UAE's national courier company, the Electronic Documentation Centre, Emirates Marketing and Promotions, and the Wall Street Exchange Centre.

Emirates Post Group's strategic operations plan for the coming three year was formally approved in March 2008 outlining its vision for expansion and diversification, and highlighting its mission to emerge as a model for federal organisations by adopting innovative business practices.

Emirates Post declared a record net profit of Dh190 million for the year 2007, an increase of 20 per cent over the previous year, reflecting the group's continuing pursuit of business diversification, new alliances and acquisitions. Among the highlights of 2007 was the Memorandum of Understanding signed with Noor Islamic Bank to launch banking services for the low-income segment. In addition, Emirates Post and its subsidiary Wall Street began disbursing workers salaries through post offices and mobile units. Emirates Post Holding Group also plans to launch postal business centres across the UAE and GCC in partnership with leading business groups.

Al Ain International Airport has been selected as the main hub for the international courier and cargo business Empost, launched in 2007. Plans are to acquire 50 aircraft by 2012 in order to expand the service. The scheduled freighter operations, which will be implemented in four phases, will network with major cities in the Indian subcontinent, Middle East and Europe by the end of 2008.

At the twenty-fourth Universal Postal Union (UPU) Congress, the UAE was re-elected to the 40-member Council of Administration (CA) and was elected to the 40-member Postal Operations Council (POC) for 2009 to 2012, reflecting the important role that it has been playing in the Union.

The UAE is founded on the belief that the real wealth of the country is its people and, in particular, the younger generation.

There is a deep awareness in the UAE that sustained economic growth can only be achieved by investment in social development.

SOCIAL DEVELOPMENT

THERE IS A DEEP AWARENESS IN THE UAE that the only guarantee of sustained development is continuous investment in education, health and social services, with the provision of meaningful employment for all. But it is also clear that money alone is not the answer, particularly since billions of dirhams have already been spent on these sectors. Therefore, UAE Federal Government strategy has put renewed emphasis on quality, focusing on best practices in the delivery of all aspects of social development in the UAE.

This is the theme also of the Abu Dhabi Executive Council Policy Agenda: key elements of the emirate's vision for the development of social and human resources describe a society characterised by the provision of world-class services, where individuals (both national and expatriate) are valued and their unique skills and contributions are ethically leveraged toward achieving a better quality of life for all.

Dubai Strategic Plan 2015 also concurs with these sentiments, stressing that strategic success requires social development to complement and parallel economic development, and that having an effective social infrastructure is the key to reaching higher levels of sustained economic growth.

Although there are challenges ahead and much remains to be done in the area of social development, there is no doubt that UAE society is already very happy with its lot: the UN Human Development Index ranks the UAE at thirty-ninth place out of 177 countries, and at twenty-eighth the UAE earned the highest ranking of all Arab states in the 2008 Legatum Prosperity Index, which measures not just wealth but also well-being in terms of happiness, health and fulfilment in over 100 countries worldwide.

www.uaeinteract.com/socialdevelopment

POPULATION

The UAE population increased by a staggering 74.8 per cent between 1995 and 2005, the date of the last census. This is one of the highest population growth rates in the world. Estimated by the Ministry of the Economy (MoE) at 4.488 million in 2007, the population is expected to increase by 6.12 per cent to reach 4.76 million at the end of 2008 and by 6.31 per cent to 5.06 million at the end of 2009.

The ratio of nationals to non-nationals remains high: a breakdown of the 2007 figures indicates that there were 864,000 UAE nationals and 3.62 million expatriates in the country in 2007, the national population increasing by 2.9 per cent over 2006, while the corresponding figure for expatriates was 6.9 per cent. The local population is forecast to rise by 3.2 per cent in 2008 and 3.4 per cent in 2009, whilst the expatriate population will increase by 6.8 per cent in 2008 and 6.9 per cent in 2009.

In addition, males continue to outnumber females because the majority of the thousands of immigrants that the UAE welcomes each year are men: the figures show that there were 3.08 million males and 1.4 million females in the country at the end of 2007. This will rise to 3.28 million males and 1.47 million females in 2008 and 3.5 million males and 1.58 million females in 2009.

The higher growth rate in the expatriate population means that expatriates will constitute 81.2 per cent of the total in 2008 and 81.7 per cent in 2009. However, even though UAE nationals comprise a small percentage of the total population, their numbers have actually doubled in the past 15 years.

Abu Dhabi was the most populated emirate in the UAE at the end of 2007, with a total of 1.493 million people. Dubai was second, with around 1.478 million, followed by Sharjah, with nearly 882,000. Umm al-Qaiwain was the least populated, with around 52,000 inhabitants. Dubai's population is forecast to rise to 1.59 million in 2008 and 1.722 million in 2009, while Abu Dhabi's is estimated at 1.55 million in 2008 and 1.62 million in 2009.

Despite its significant population growth rate, the UAE's per capita income has more than doubled from around Dh76,600 in 2006 to Dh162,000 in 2007 because nominal gross domestic product rocketed from Dh624 billion to Dh729 billion in the same period. Per capita income is forecast to rise further in 2008.

POPULATION BY GENDER AND EMIRATE 2006–2007* (in thousands)

Emirates	Males		Females		Total	
	2006	2007	2006	2007	2006	2007
■ Abu Dhabi	945	982	485	511	1,430	1,493
■ Dubai	1,032	1,121	340	357	1,372	1,478
■ Sharjah	539	581	282	301	821	882
■ Ajman	135	144	77	80	212	224
■ Umm al-Qaiwain	31	32	19	20	50	52
■ Ra's al-Khaimah	132	138	82	84	214	222
■ Fujairah	81	86	49	51	130	137
Total	**2,895**	**3,084**	**1,334**	**1,404**	**4,229**	**4,488**

Source: Ministry of Economy   * Preliminary estimates

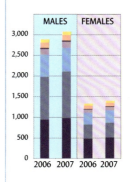

www.uaeinteract.com/population

POPULATION BY GENDER AND AGE GROUP 2006–2007 (in thousands)

		2005			2006			2007	
Age group	Male	Female	Total	Male	Female	Total	Male	Female	Total
Under 15	416,317	384,254	800,571	427,779	393,746	821,525	450,233	413,658	862,991
15–39	1,753,709	714,819	2,48,528	1,810,437	733,797	2,544,234	1,935,658	722,203	2,708,861
40–59	595,832	177,218	773,050	615,451	181,949	797,400	654,709	191,607	846,316
Over 60	40,294	23,984	64,278	41,333	24,508	65,841	43,300	25,532	68,832
Total	2,806,152	1,300,275	4,106,427	2,895,000	1,334,000	4,229,000	3,084,000	1,404,000	4,488,000

Source: UAE Central Bank Annual Report   * Mid-year estimates

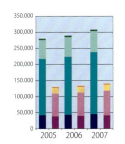

NATIONAL IDENTITY

Despite the large influx of immigrants and the demographic imbalances that ensue, the UAE continues to be a tolerant, open caring society that cherishes its religious and traditional roots. Nevertheless, there is a renewed focus in the country on the need to nurture a strong national identity.

A national identity study conducted in 2008 by the Ministry of Culture, Youth and Community Development in association with local universities and an international consultant underlined the role a strong national identity plays in sustainable development. The study, which took one year and covered the age group between 18 and 60 years in all emirates, explored weaknesses in the national identity structure and attempts to devise effective solutions. In particular, the study highlighted the vital role of the media in inculcating and infusing the spirit of loyalty and belonging, and translation of these principles in daily life practice in terms of productivity and good behaviour. The final goal is to nurture a generation who firmly believes in national identity, prudent leadership, Arab culture, Islamic faith and a shared history and heritage.

The Ministries of Presidential Affairs, Cabinet Affairs and Culture are coordinating mechanisms for implementing the study.

EIDA

The Emirates Identity Authority (EIDA), which was established in 2004, is responsible for the Population Register Programme, a centralised database of all UAE nationals and residents. Registration with the agency is compulsory for all ages.

In addition, all nationals and professional expatriates are required to obtain an identity card (ID) by the end of 2008. ID cards will be mandatory for expatriate residents by 2010. The new IDs will be multi-purpose smart cards, which will replace e-signature card, labour cards, etc. Emiratis and professional expatriates without identity cards will not be able to avail of services from government, semi-government and possibly even some private organisations from the beginning of 2009, and all expatriates in the country will be required to produce a national identity card for governmental, semi-governmental and private transactions by the end of 2010. An ID card for under 15s is not mandatory, but registration for under 15s is compulsory

About 5000 EIDA registration centres countrywide are ready to receive applications from the public. By law, it is incumbent on companies, not employees, to pay all the charges and fees related to the issuing of identity cards. Companies will be offered an incentive package to register their workers as soon as possible. Companies and individuals that are not compliant will not be able to complete any application at government offices without the IDs.

The task of registering and issuing identity cards to about 5 million people by 2010 will cost in the region of Dh202 million (US$55 million). Information on registration can be obtained from www.emiratesid.ae.

> All nationals and professional expatriates were required to obtain a national identity card by the end of 2008.

LABOUR

The UAE Ministry of Economy (MoE) has estimated that the unemployment rate will rise from nearly 3.45 per cent in 2007 to about 3.71 per cent in 2008 and 3.86 per cent in 2009.

The figures showed the workforce accounted for around 63.2 per cent of the UAE's total population of 4.488 million in 2007. This will increase slightly to 63.8 per cent of the 4.765 million population in 2008 and 64.4 per cent of the population of 5.066 million in 2009.

National Employment

Expatriates currently hold 99 per cent of jobs in the private sector and 91 per cent of positions in the government. As the economy grows, there is a risk that nationals will make up a progressively smaller

Saqr Ghobash, UAE Minister of Labour participating in the Global Forum on Migration and Development in Manila .

EMPLOYEES BY ECONOMIC SECTOR 2005–2007

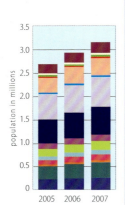

Sectors	2005	2006*	2007**
Non-financial enterprises sector	**2,111,332**	**2,286,572**	**2,466,294**
Agriculture, livestock & fisheries	193,044	209,066	225,499
Extractive industries	38,694	41,906	45,199
Crude oil & natural gas	33,200	35,956	38,783
Quarries	5,494	5,950	6,418
Manufacturing industries	336,585	364,521	393,173
Water, gas & electricity	34,207	37,046	39,958
Contruction & building	534,398	578,753	624,242
Wholesale/retail trade & maintenance	502,427	544,129	586,897
Restaurants & hotels	116,615	126,294	136,220
Transportation, storage & communication	162,768	176,278	190,000
Real estate & business services	77,858	84,320	91
Social & private services	114,736	124.259	134,026
Financial services	**31,015**	**33,589**	**36,229**
Government services	**286,105**	**309,851**	**334,207**
Household	222,506	240,975	259,916
TOTAL	**2,650,958**	**2,870,987**	**3,096.645**

Source: Ministry of Economy   * Prelim nary data   ** Estimates

More than 800,000 jobs are created each year in the UAE and most of them are provided by the private sector.

percentage of employees in the UAE. If trends continue, by 2009, UAE nationals will account for less than 8 per cent of the workforce and for less than 4 per cent by 2020.

More than 800,000 jobs are created each year in the UAE and most of them are provided by the private sector. However, up to 10 per cent of employed nationals resign each year due to problems in the workplace. Common reasons for discontent include low wages in the private sector; lack of training and development opportunities; negative stereotyping of locals; and a lack of trust between employees and employers.

It is generally accepted that there is a need for additional policies to guarantee a more significant representation of UAE nationals across the country's labour force, particularly the private sector. Accordingly, emiratisation of the workforce is a key focus of government policy and a growing number of companies in the UAE are taking measures to increase the number of nationals in their employment. The challenge is to foster a larger pool of qualified and trained UAE nationals who are fully equipped to take up responsibilities in the workplace.

Programmes undertaken in 2008 in pursuit of this goal include the launching by ershaad, the national recruitment initiative, of its website www.ershaad.ae and recruitment guide in April 2008. UAE nationals looking for jobs are invited to visit the website and register their resumes online for free. Companies in the UAE who are seeking high calibre UAE nationals are also invited to register.

In October 2008, the Abu Dhabi Systems and Information Committee (ADSIC), the information and communication technology (ICT) arm of Abu Dhabi government, launched the Jobs Abu Dhabi virtual job market, www.Jobs.abudhabi.ae. The latter is available in Arabic, English and French, creating a forum for both employers and jobseekers at home and abroad to connect and fulfil their respective employment needs.

Tanmia, the UAE's National Human Resource Development and Employment Authority, is one of the organisations that has been given a mandate to develop human resources in the UAE, at the same time maximising employment opportunities for UAE nationals and promoting emiratisation.

Tanmia's many duties include the provision of training and career guidance to ensure that there is a suitably qualified pool of national jobseekers. In addition, Tanmia organises seminars on the importance of emiratisation and works with leading institutions such as Emirates University and Dubai Industrial Academy, to further their goals.

Supported by GCC governments, Tanmia is also initiating a Gulf Network that aims to reduce unemployment among nationals of the GCC countries, where the unemployment rate averages 6 to 7 per cent among GCC nationals, despite the fact that these countries provide 15 to 17 million job opportunities for foreign nationals.

The UAE intends to give priority to UAE nationals and any remaining jobs will be offered to GCC nationals, then to Arab nationals. The programme will be a long-term one and initiating it now will mean that, 12 years hence, more jobs will be available for GCC nationals in all of these countries. The hope is that the Gulf Network will eventually become an Arab network where any unemployed national in the Arab region will be able to find jobs in the private sector.

In addition, Tanmia is focusing on increasing employment of nationals in the government sector and to this end has signed an MoU with the Ministry for Development of the Governmental Sector whereby Tanmia will provide the ministry with access to its database of registered jobseekers. The two parties will also cooperate with each

It is generally accepted that there is a need for additional policies to guarantee a more significant representation of UAE nationals in the labour force.

other to jointly organise special training programmes and seminars aimed at equipping UAE national jobseekers with the necessary skill sets that will allow them to perform to their potential in the workplace.

Other governmental bodies, such as the Abu Dhabi Emiratisation Council, are also actively pursuing an emiratisation strategy, including opening up employment opportunities for UAE nationals and providing on-job skills training.

LABOUR RIGHTS

> For the UAE, respect for labour rights is a matter of both fundamental morality and economic self-interest.

For the UAE, respect for labour rights is a matter of both fundamental morality and economic self-interest. It is also a matter of accountability, a responsibility that the UAE welcomes and accepts.

The Ministry of Labour issued a detailed labour progress report in 2007 highlighting the UAE's respect for labour rights and the challenges being posed to the labour-rights regime by the economic boom and demographic structure changes in the UAE.

As a member of the International Labour Organisation (ILO), the Arab Labour Organisation (ALO), and other labour-focused multilateral organisations, the report stresses that the UAE deals transparently and objectively with all its international labour obligations. And that it views reasoned and rational internal and external criticism as constructive and helpful.

The report provides a synopsis of the positive changes that the UAE is making to manage, enhance, and broaden the laws and policies needed to provide a nationwide system of labour rights. It also outlines and clarifies specific measures that have been undertaken and that are being undertaken by the UAE Government. As with any complex society, new challenges and new problems are constantly arising, especially as demographics change. The report is both a progress assessment and a blueprint for ongoing action.

> In 2007, 122,000 facilities were inspected by the labour ministry personnel, resulting in penalties for 8588 violations related to working conditions and workers' rights.

As the UAE Government acknowledges, much more needs to be done to enforce labour laws and to fully protect the rights of workers in the country. The report points out that current progress needs to be viewed in this context. In particular, the expatriate labour force in the UAE is exceptionally large and culturally diverse, accounting for more than 90 per cent of the private sector labour force. Ministry of Labour records indicate that a total of 3,113,000 foreign workers are employed by approximately 260,000 establishments. Meeting the challenges presented by such numbers takes diligence, time, and both fiscal and management resources.

The UAE labour progress report underlines the country's full engagement in providing quality labour rights. Moreover, the report illustrates that there is unequivocal commitment to enhancing the existing legal framework to mandate and support labour rights throughout the UAE. It also highlights the evolution of an enforcement regime that is able and willing to take the many steps needed to defend labour rights for all who work in the UAE

The report points out that the UAE is, nonetheless, committed to preserving its national identity, to further the interests of those who live and work in the country, and to continue economic growth at all levels. The UAE Government continues to administer the UAE labour environment in compliance with international law and international labour standards and the private sector understands that all laws in the UAE are being and will continue to be strictly enforced. By harmonising all of these components, the UAE intends to be a model for all countries in the GCC region and beyond.

In October 2008 the UAE Government took the initiative, in consultation with other GCC member states, to propose to the Governments of India and the Philippines, the setting up of a pilot project to survey and document best practices in the management of the temporary contractual employment cycle.

Forum on Migrant Labour

Engagement and dialogue with countries of origin of migrant labour in a spirit of shared responsibility and partnership is a key aspect of government strategy to find solutions to labour market challenges both domestically and internationally. The process was clearly outlined by Saqr Ghobash, UAE Minister of Labour, in his address to the Opening Plenary Session of the Global Forum on Migration and Development in Manila on 29 October 2008:

www.uaeinteract.com/employment

Almost 3 million Asian contract workers leave their countries every year to seek employment around the world. A large majority opts for employment in the Gulf States. In 2007, there were several million of these workers in the UAE, working in sectors as diverse as hospitality, health care, technology, the oil and gas industry, financial services and construction. As the numbers of these workers grow and the sectors in which they work become more diversified, their impact is increasingly felt at national, regional and global levels. In brief, contractual workers contribute significantly to the development of both their countries of origin and those where they work, improving, at the same time, their own economic situation and that of their families.

For those benefits to be fully realised, however, labour mobility needs to be effectively managed through the formulation of appropriate legal and policy frameworks, through the development of administrative structures and through on-going capacity building.

In the past, progress towards these objectives has been seriously hampered by the fact that countries of origin and destination often had separate agendas as well as different – and not infrequently, conflicting – priorities for action.

It is precisely for this reason that the UAE has attached such importance in recent years to improving dialogue with individual countries of origin and seeking the establishment of broader consultations at the multilateral level.

In September 2005, the UAE, together with other Gulf States, attended on an informal basis the third Ministerial Consultations on Overseas Employment and Contractual Labour for Countries of Origin in Asia, more commonly known as the Colombo Process, There, participants discussed the evolution of patterns of labour mobility in the region over the last decade as well as a wide range of policy issues and recommendations including:

- Increasing cooperation between countries of origin and destination;
- Optimising the benefits of organised labour flows, including the development of new markets, increasing remittance flows through formal channels and enhancing their impact on development;
- Ensuring the welfare and well-being of vulnerable overseas workers, especially women; and
- Building institutional capacity and inter-ministerial coordination to meet the challenges posed by labour mobility.

In the light of these recommendations, the UAE took the initiative of hosting earlier this year a two-day Ministerial consultation in Abu Dhabi that brought together twenty countries of origin and destination in Asia alongside leading international and regional organisations.

The discussions noted that temporary contractual labour was a well-established concept in Asia, but acknowledged that processes of globalisation, involving the freer movement of capital, the greater integration of economies and technological advances, provided a context in which there is increasing competition to boost economic growth and productivity through labour mobility at all skill levels. In this connection, the Ministers considered that the best social and economic outcomes would be achieved through the promotion and implementation of transparent policies, through the institution of fair and efficient recruitment and employment practices and through the provision of good living and working conditions.

The participating Ministers agreed to a declaration of principles now known as the Abu Dhabi Declaration. The Declaration stresses that countries of origin, countries of destination and, most importantly, the workers themselves benefit when workers' rights are effectively recognised and respected.

The Abu Dhabi Declaration underlines, in particular, that countries of origin benefit when workers are able to use their remittances to enhance their families' living conditions and to improve the educational status of their children, and to return home with skills and capital that contribute to the development of their own countries. The Declaration goes on to propose the creation of four key partnerships between countries of origin and destination with a view to:

- Enhancing the knowledge base on essential policy and programme components, such as labour market trends, skills profiles and remittance flows;
- Building capacity for the effective matching of labour demand and supply;
- Preventing illegal recruitment practices and promoting welfare and protection measures for contractual workers; and
- Developing a framework for a comprehensive approach to managing temporary contractual mobility, covering the four phases of labour mobility, namely recruitment and pre-departure preparation in the country of origin; installation and employment in the country of destination; preparation for return; and return and reintegration in the community of origin.

Given the consonance between these partnership objectives and the well-articulated goals of the Philippine Chairmanship of this second Global Forum on Migration and Development, the UAE took the decision to join the GFMD Steering Committee and actively participate in the discussions that helped frame the agenda and work programme for this Conference in Manila.

In parallel with this, the UAE Government took the initiative, in consultation with other GCC member states, to propose to the Governments of India and the Philippines the setting up of a pilot project to survey and document best practices in the management of the temporary contractual employment cycle. The three governments have now agreed to collaborate towards the development of such a pilot project with expert input from the Arab Labour Organisation, the International Labour Organisation and the International Organisation on Migration.

The overall goal of the project is, to put it simply, to test a range of practical measures that will serve to improve the quality of life and work of contractual workers. In more specific terms, the project seeks first of all to improve the quality of recruitment, induction and other pre-deployment processes, and then to provide the workers with decent working and living conditions during their temporary contractual employment and residency in the host country. Two important innovations complete the picture :the preparation of temporary contractual workers for return to their country of origin; and the facilitation of their ultimate return to and reintegration into their home communities. All of this is to be undertaken in a spirit of shared responsibility and partnership.

The project will leverage the introduction in the UAE of new policy guidelines and enforceable measures that ensure the protection of wages, the provision of adequate work and living conditions, access to avenues of legal redress, and the upholding of fundamental human rights.

We are confident that valuable lessons will be learnt from this experience. Ultimately we hope that we might be able to draw from it the substance of a draft comprehensive regional framework for cooperation among Asian countries of origin and destination that will demonstrate lessons learned and best practices in the effective administration of the full temporary contractual employment cycle. The formulation of this future framework for regional cooperation was a key recommendation of the Abu Dhabi Dialogue.

www.uaeinteract.com/employment

The UAE is acting on every front of its four-pillar strategy: legislation, enforcement, victim support, bilateral agreements and international cooperation. Simultaneously, the UAE will continue to cooperate with all appropriate regional and international law enforcement officials to stem this crime.

HUMAN TRAFFICKING

The problem of human trafficking afflicts the UAE just as it does almost every other country in the world. Nevertheless, the UAE is firmly against the exploitation of human beings for any purposes and against the coercive, illegal and inhumane treatment of any individual. Indeed, the first annual report released by the UAE National Committee to Combat Human Trafficking in mid-2008 stressed that the UAE is committed to doing everything in its power to help stop human trafficking wherever it occurs and to aggressively interdict those who are responsible for it with the toughest possible penalties.

'Combating Human Trafficking in the UAE 2007' highlighted the country's stand on the crime, the efforts to counter it, the obstacles and challenges it has encountered, as well as plans for the future. The report, released ahead of the UAE's participation at the UN General Assembly debate on trafficking in New York, focused on the measures taken since Federal Law 51 came into force. The 16-article law, effective since November 2006, spells out stiff penalties against traffickers ranging from one year to life imprisonment and fines of Dh100,000 and Dh1 million.

According to the report, at least ten allegations of human trafficking-related infringements of the new law were registered by the end of 2007. There were also convictions in at least five cases during this period, with the convicted receiving jail terms ranging from three to ten years for committing, aiding or abetting human trafficking.

The country's resolve to fight human trafficking at home and abroad in collaboration with international partners remains central to its counter-trafficking strategy. HH General Sheikh Mohammad bin Zayed Al Nahyan, Crown Prince of Abu Dhabi and Deputy Supreme Commander of the UAE Armed Forces, has cemented this resolve with a generous donation to the UN.GIFT to establish an international network to fight this crime.

In parallel to the UAE's tough stand on anyone convicted of trafficking, the report also documented measures that reflect the UAE's concern about the victims of this crime and their physical and emotional well-being. The report outlined the progress that the UAE has achieved with regards to the victim support network, noting the important work carried out by the Dubai Foundation for Women and Children and the new shelter in Abu Dhabi for victims of trafficking.

Specific measures associated with the UAE's comprehensive four-pillar action plan (legislation, enforcement, victim support, bilateral agreements and international partnerships) were elaborated on in the report. The report concluded by emphasising that 'the UAE has achieved much in a short period of time, but realises that much more needs to be done to combat the challenge. The country is committed to serving as an active member of the international community, as well as a model for change in the region and takes these responsibilities seriously'.

HUMAN RIGHTS REPORT

The 'UAE National Human Rights Report', which was presented to the UN Human Rights Council on 4 December 2008 under the framework of its Universal Periodic Review procedures, outlines the efforts made by the UAE in the field of human rights observance.

The report, which was prepared by a committee comprising representatives from various ministries and government institutions, with the participation of representatives from civil society and non-government organisations (NGOs), concludes that the UAE is committed to continuing its work to preserve what has already been accomplished in the field of human rights, and will continue to work diligently to improve on its record by following the best international practices in this field, at the same time identifying some of the challenges facing the country in this field, including the following:

- Providing more mechanisms to protect human rights, keeping up with national and international developments, and updating laws and systems;

- Meeting the state's expectations with regards to building national capabilities and deepening efforts for education on human rights and basic freedoms through a national plan.

- Striving to regulate the relationship between employers and workers in framework that preserves dignity and rights, and is in harmony with international standards, especially with regards to domestic help.

- Despite what has been accomplished for women, the larger challenge is increasing the empowerment of women's role in society, increasing opportunities for involvement in a number of fields based on their skills and abilities, supporting their

'With a deep aspiration to improve, the UAE is keen on tackling human rights issues head on. This aspiration stems from our own cultural heritage and religious values that enshrine justice, equality and tolerance... The government is also aware that respecting human rights in accordance with international human rights charters and customs is a priority, and we look towards meeting this priority at all levels.'

www.uaeinteract.com/humanrights

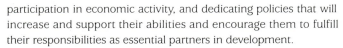

participation in economic activity, and dedicating policies that will increase and support their abilities and encourage them to fulfill their responsibilities as essential partners in development.

- Working to confront human trafficking crimes by reviewing the best international practices in the field, working to update and improve the state's legislature in accordance with international standards, working to establish institutions and agencies to confront human trafficking crimes, and working to support the foundations of international cooperation with international organisations and institutions.

A dedicated link was established on the Ministry of State for Federal National Council Affairs website (www.mfnca.ae) where the public could view outlines of the report and express their views and make suggestions – an initiative that reflects the committee's commitment to maintaining accuracy and transparency in preparing the report.

> The UAE is studying the establishment of a national human rights commission in the country, in line with the Paris Principles. The Government is also seeking to enhance cooperation with the Human Rights Council.

SOCIAL RESPONSIBILITY

The UN Global Compact GCC Network was formed in 2008 in Dubai to assist enlightened regional companies seeking practical solutions to contemporary problems related to globalisation, sustainable development and corporate responsibility. UAE companies are joining this growing worldwide movement encouraging businesses to adopt core values in the areas of human rights, labour standards, the environment and corruption, in accordance with the UN Global Compact, the world's largest voluntary corporate citizenship initiative.

An example of the corporate social responsibility principles being put into practice in the UAE is the MoU signed in August 2008 between the UAE Ministry of Social Affairs and telecom operator du to establish a comprehensive web portal of non-governmental organisations (NGOs) in the country. Besides acting as a comprehensive source of factual information on all the NGOs in the UAE, the proposed web portal will showcase the work of each organisation. It will also facilitate volunteering in the UAE by presenting all the available opportunities on one platform.

In recognition of the role that NGOs play in forging links between the public and private sector, the Ministry of Social Affairs is also

collaborating with Sharjah Tatweer Forum in several initiatives, including arranging a conference and exhibition for NGOs. Participants included organisations from the private sector, governmental and public sector, academia, civil society, international organisations such as the United Nations, and various individuals who are active in NGO work.

To further enhance the work of NGOs, the Community Development Authority (CDA) was recently set up in Dubai to act as an umbrella for social service organisations and to promote national identity by empowering UAE nationals, thereby enhancing social cohesion. CDA, which is implementing the social objectives of the Dubai government as highlighted in the Dubai Strategic Plan 2015, is tasked with instituting a legal framework under which the NGOs would fall.

EMIRATES FOUNDATION

Emirates Foundation, a government-backed philanthropic organisation, was established in 2005. Following a period of consolidation in 2007, the foundation is now entering an expansionist phase. In particular, it has researched and planned a series of 50 new initiatives for the period 2008/09 within its six core areas of operation – education, science and technology, arts and culture, social development, the environment and public awareness.

ExxonMobil has made a donation of US$5 million to the work of the Emirates Foundation over the three-year period from 2008 to 2010.

Emirates Foundation has called upon the private sector to actively participate in its new strategic philanthropic programmes for the benefit of communities throughout the UAE. At the foundation's unique donors' recognition meeting in September 2007, the Abu Dhabi government announced that it would match all private sector donations to Emirates Foundation up to that date (some Dh300 million), as well as meeting the foundation's future administrative expenses.

In 2007 the foundation launched the Tatween Initiative (localisation in English) to empower young nationals. Its declared aim is to unlock local talent through self-development and self-motivation, thereby equipping young Emiratis with the right workplace skills to flourish in the growing UAE private sector. Eight initial Tatween projects were announced by BP, Shell, Microsoft, Rolls Royce, International Power, DLA Piper, Jumeirah, the British Council and Gems Education.

The projects cover career guidance counselling; youth leadership development, industry and academic summer schools, career resource centres, internships in the private sector, empowering women in

www.uaeinteract.com/emiratesfoundation

Takatof is a voluntary social programme that was developed by the Emirates Foundation to create a culture of volunteering throughout the UAE.

The Mohammed bin Rashid Programme for Leadership Development is an innovative leadership programme aimed at nurturing national leaders who are willing and able to promote sustainable development in the UAE.

the workplace, entrepreneurship and innovation, and vocational training awareness.

The Tawteen projects are not job creation schemes in themselves. However, they are designed to directly assist Emiratis in overcoming the social and cultural obstacles that hinder personal development, while opening the door to thousands of employment opportunities in the UAE private sector.

In particular, the Tawteen Youth Leadership Project focuses on unlocking youth leadership potential in the UAE. In one of its first endeavours, selected groups of young Emiratis participated in intense leadership and team building activities in the mountains of Ra's al-Khaimah. The programmes help the youth to acquire self-confidence, skills and the right mind-set to succeed as tomorrow's leaders. Private sector partners involved in the camps are BP and Aldar Properties. Young Emiratis from the Emirates Foundation's Takatof Programme have been trained as team leaders for the camps, and they gain valuable experience in facilitation, team management and motivation.

Takatof ('shoulder to shoulder') a voluntary social programme, was developed by the Emirates Foundation to create a culture of volunteering throughout the UAE, mobilising volunteers to help those in need. In 2008, Takatof volunteers from UAE assisted their counterparts in Morocco in community projects renovating hospitals, orphanages and schools in disadvantaged areas and helping to clean up beaches.

In August 2008, Emirates Foundation launched a Dh2.5 million grant programme in support of non-governmental organisations involved in social and educational activities. Funds can be used for training, improved services, new programmes, project expansion, institutional strengthening, analysis and other activities that contribute to the effectiveness and sustainability of the organisation. The maximum amount of funding for each submission is Dh500,000 over a two-year period.

The project is designed so that non-governmental organisations with the right expertise can benefit the most from funding in order to improve and expand the work that they are doing.

Leadership Development

The Mohammed bin Rashid Programme for Leadership Development (MBRPLD) is an innovative leadership programme aimed at developing national leaders who are willing and able to promote the sustainable development of the UAE. In summer 2008 candidates of its Young

Leaders Programme participated in international study tours in France and the United States. Held under the theme 'Dubai Opening', programme candidates met high-ranking officials and interacted with renowned lecturers and speakers.

Participants were exposed to highly enriching discussions and interaction with prominent and experienced leaders, enhancing their experience and expertise in handling various leadership issues and boosting their capacity to promote the Dubai Strategic Plan 2015.

ABU DHABI AWARDS

The Abu Dhabi Awards recognise those individuals who have made a positive contribution to the community through their generosity and kindness, honouring the legacy of the late Sheikh Zayed bin Sultan Al Nahyan.

Since its inception in 2005, the Abu Dhabi Awards have generated more than 93,000 nominations which have recognised more than 13,000 individuals for performing selfless acts of goodness that benefit the people of Abu Dhabi. There are no specific award categories – anyone who has performed an act of kindness, no matter how big or small can be nominated.

In order to reach as many people as possible the 2008 campaign designed a dynamic new website www.abudhabiawards.ae. featuring 'The Wall of Goodness' and a student-generated Facebook group.

Voting for the
Abu Dhabi Awards.

The 2008 Abu Dhabi Awards Ambassadors include past recipients such as the inspirational Mrs Farida Siddiqui, a notable social activist and volunteer for a range of charitable organisations including the Red Crescent Society, and Emad Mohammed Saad, an Abu Dhabi Municipality engineer who is active in several NGOs and has spearheaded successful environmental awareness programmes in schools and other educational institutions.

SOCIAL SERVICES

No matter how prosperous the society, the vulnerable will always be in need of assistance and the provision of social services are a key component of social development. Social security benefits in the form of financial assistance are administered by the Ministry of Social Affairs. In recent years, the social care net has been widened to include additional categories of potential recipients.

www.uaeinteract.com/welfare

There has been a rise in the number of assistance cases from 33,500 in 2006 to nearly 38,000 in 2008, with beneficiaries receiving assistance of Dh2.2 billion. Cases involving the elderly accounted for 36.9 per cent of the total in 2007, whilst divorcees constituted 13.3 per cent; medical disability cases represented 10.4 per cent and those experiencing poverty represented 10.5 per cent.

Practical help is offered by the network of ministry-supported social centres run by the General Women's Union (see section below on Women). But the stars of the social care system are the 33 mentally handicapped care centres (government, private and local) serving 3339 individuals. In addition to education, professional training and rehabilitation, these centres offer medical treatment and enable the handicapped to integrate into the community.

As well as to the assistance outlined above UAE citizens are eligible for free or subsidised housing and housing programmes such as the Zayed Housing Programme (ZHP) give priority to the needs of deserving cases, such as widows, divorced women and people with special needs.

HOUSING

Access to modern housing is considered to be the right of every citizen. The rapid rise in population and the subsequent demands on the housing stock, coupled with a significant increase in rents, has necessitated government intervention at federal and emirate level to ensure that the housing needs of nationals are met throughout the federation in a balanced and sustainable manner.

A pilot government housing scheme, the Dh940 million Dhafra Meadows at Madinat Zayed, features 788 separate villas, 39 attached villas and 400 apartments. The project is organised around the expanded family and *fareej* (district) concept, based on the traditional organisation of Emirati settlements. Construction of villas has been divided into four phases 200 will be completed by the end of June 2009, 114 will be built in the second phase, 274 will be built for military personnel in the third phase, and the fourth phase of 200 villas will be paid for by the Sheikh Zayed Housing Programme (ZHP) at a total cost of Dh19 million.

As we have already mentioned, organisations such as ZHP are instrumental in providing homes for UAE citizens. In his address to the First Housing Conference organised by ZHP in cooperation with the United Nations Human Settlements Programme, Sheikh Hamdan bin Mubarak Al Nahyan, Minister of Public Works and Chairman of ZHP, indicated that all UAE nationals who applied for residential help from the programme up to the end of 2007 will be allocated housing by 2009. This is due in no small part to HH Sheikh Khalifa's pledge to construct 40,000 units and support the programme's budget at the beginning of 2008.

In 2008, ZHP approved 1661 grants and distributed 60 houses to UAE nationals in Al Ra'efa and Falaj Al Malla districts in Umm al-Qaiwain emirate, as well as Khatt district in Ra's al-Khaimah, at a cost of Dh30 million. The residential units were distributed to UAE nationals whose salaries exceed Dh10, 000 and who have the ability to repay loans.

In addition, the Mohammed bin Rashid Housing Establishment (MBRHE) has begun construction work on a Dh3 billion housing project in the Al Barsha area of Dubai. The move represents phase one of the 252 housing-unit-project, which will be executed in two phases over a two-year period as part of a plan to construct 2300 housing units in the emirate. The MRHE grants three types of loans to UAE nationals: housing loans for building of private houses; the granting of Dh750,000 loan facilities for purchasing houses (completed or uncompleted) for personal use; and the granting of a maximum loan facility of Dh300,000 for expansion of a private house.

The MRHE has also drawn up a plan through which it will be granting 150 loans per month to a tune of 1800 loans per year and it has endorsed the building of 114 residential units costing Dh185 million for UAE nationals at Sha'biyat in Al Quoz. The new residential units will replace old buildings, which are to be demolished.

SOCIAL WELFARE ORGANISATIONS

A wide array of governmental and non-governmental charitable organisations are involved in social welfare programmes in the UAE.

In addition to its international humanitarian activities (see section on Foreign Aid), the UAE Red Crescent Authority (RCA) is the largest charitable organisation in the country administering a wide array of social, economic, health and educational programmes. The Red Crescent is also involved in the administration of charitable health initiatives at home and abroad (see Foreign Aid and the section on Health) in conjunction with organisations such as the Emirates World Heart Group and 'Generous Hands' campaign.

A wide array of governmental and non-governmental charitable organisations are involved in social welfare programmes in the UAE.

Roughly 70 per cent of funds distributed by The Sheikh Zayed bin Sultan Al Nahyan Charitable and Humanitarian Foundation go to projects to benefit communities within the UAE.

The Khalifa bin Zayed Charity Foundation is also very active in the UAE and during the month of Ramadan, the foundation distributed food to 1.2 million people in the country, focusing on people with limited resources in various emirates.

Eighty per cent of the Mohammed bin Rashid Al Maktoum Charitable and Humanitarian Foundation's budget is normally allocated to projects within the UAE. The foundation's domestic programmes concentrate on education, medical treatment, food assistance, training courses and housing.

The Bait Al Khair Society provides assistance to poor students and emergency aid to those who have been hit by catastrophes. It also works with other charity organisations to ensure that the needy get the best of help.

In addition, Ajman Care Society, Sharjah City for Humanitarian Services, Umm al-Qaiwain Humanitarian Services City, the Handicapped Guardians Association and Taryam Omran Establishment for Cultural and Humanitarian Services all do sterling work with the disabled.

EDUCATION

Education is seen as the key enabler in the context of the wide range of socio-economic challenges facing the country in the decades ahead.

Education is seen as the key enabler in the context of the wide range of socio-economic challenges facing the country in the decades ahead.

At present, the UAE offers a comprehensive education to male and female students from kindergarten to university, with education for the country's citizens being provided free at all levels. There is also an extensive private education sector at primary, secondary and tertiary levels, while several thousand students of both sexes pursue courses of higher education abroad at government expense.

Despite the successes achieved in the educational field, the reality is that in a country where the national population is overwhelmingly youthful, it is imperative that the educational system is reformed to produce employable national graduates. Government strategy is now focusing on improving education standards, decentralisation of the educational system and the more active involvement of the private sector in the delivery of high-quality education being key

The UAE is reforming its educational system in order to produce employable national graduates.

components of educational policy. Government bodies, educational consultants, policy advisors and education specialists are all working to meet the challenges of transforming a centralised bureaucratic system into a student-centred learning environment, whilst bringing international best practice into play. Curricula revision, teaching standards and student performance are just some of the areas receiving attention. The goal is to produce graduates that are able to compete not only in a regional knowledge-based economy but will also be competitive players on the global stage.

In recognition of the important role of education, the UAE Cabinet allocated Dh9.706 billion or 23 per cent of its 2009 budget to this sector.

Towards Educational Excellence

A key strategy in the overhaul of the learning environment in the UAE is the pursuit of decentralised policies and practices, in particular the decentralisation of direct monitoring of education from the federal Ministry of Education to education councils. The relationship between educational committees, educational councils in each emirate and educational zones is also more clearly defined.

> The challenge is to transform a centralised bureaucratic system into a student-centred learning environment.

> More than 648,000 students were enrolled in 1259 public and private schools in 2007/08.

At the same time, the federal government has issued a new set of by-laws governing the operation and monitoring of private schools in the UAE, to ensure that every child in the country receives a quality, uniform education. The new streamlined regulations form the foundation of a system of monitoring that is focused on student achievement and continuous school improvement, replacing the old regime that was based on a static and regimented list of rules. Significant changes include requiring all private schools to become accredited to standards adopted by the Ministry of Education and creating a list of rights to give greater voice to families in their relations with private schools.

The ministry will focus its efforts on providing leadership and creating new policy initiatives to improve education while delegating direct oversight of schools to the education councils. Although the ministry still retains overall authority and responsibility for education, this delegation will increase efficiency and effectiveness of the daily operation of these schools.

Nevertheless, the ministry intends to keep tuition fees at affordable levels, and education councils in each emirate will work closely with the schools to ensure that the fees they charge are on a par with the quality of education provided by them.

Significant changes in Ministry of Education regulations require all private schools to conform with standards adopted by the ministry.

Education Councils

Education councils such as Abu Dhabi Education Council (ADEC), which was restructured in 2008 under the chairmanship of HH General Sheikh Mohammed bin Zayed Al Nahyan, are spearheading reform.

ADEC is mandated to supervise all education zones and schools in the emirate; determine, develop and implement standards that will be followed by all authorised education entities in the emirate; and develop the human resources management strategy to deliver on its vision. At the same time, ADEC will collaborate with the Ministry of Education to improve national education policies, and the Abu Dhabi government will continue to meet its existing federal funding requirements.

In 2008, three taskforces comprising local, regional and international experts were commissioned by ADEC to set a bold, new policy framework for the future education system in the emirate.

The taskforces, which report directly to Sheikh Mohammed bin Zayed, focused on the three main areas of education, P-12 education,

New curricula will be designed to meet international standards in education, at the same time preparing students for the needs of the labour market.

The UAE is committed to raising the age for compulsory education to 18 years.

vocational education, and higher education, at the same time examining examples of best practice in some of the world's most successful education systems.

The process is ongoing but it is clear that new curricula will be introduced over time. These will be designed to meet international standards and will reinforce and strengthen courses in Arabic, Islamic and social studies, and prepare students to fit labour market needs. There will be more emphasis on developing critical thinking and analytical skills and introducing vocational training. The new education model will put students at the centre of the learning process. Facilities, policies, curriculum and teachers will focus on improving the educational experience for students and preparing them for a dynamic and competitive market place. Training programmes for teachers and school administrators will be introduced to help them perform their responsibilities at an international standard and in line with curriculum and student needs. In addition, school administrators will be empowered to make decisions based on student, school and community needs. Parents will have the opportunity to partner with schools on education reform efforts and be further engaged in the education of their children.

Schools of Tomorrow

Madaris Al Ghad ('Schools of Tomorrow') is a government-sponsored pilot education initiative that will be gradually introduced to all emirates. The project was launched in 2007 with 50 schools and the necessary educational and services infrastructure is being restructured so that the project can be applied across the board with the minimum of disruption. Fourteen schools designed and built on modern architectural concepts were inaugurated in 2008 and another seven will be ready before the 2009/10 academic year.

However, the project is not just about bricks and mortar. It is, in reality, a drastic transformation in the learning life of students whereby they are encouraged to become more interactive in the classroom, their innovative skills are nurtured and new avenues are opened up in the learning process.

At the same time, the Ministry of Education supports a range of programmes throughout the Emirates to enhance the professional development of teachers, including the 'Teacher Education Programme', launched by the Institute of Applied Technology in cooperation with Cambridge University for teachers of Ra's al-Khaimah Education Zone.

Studies such as TIMSS assessment (Trends in International Mathematics and Science Study) taking place in Dubai in 2008 and PISA (Programme for International Student Assessment), which will be administered in 2009 across the UAE, are also making significant progress towards standardisation and data collection on the country's student performance.

Developments in Higher Education

The UAE has a diversified system of higher education. UAE citizens can attend government institutions free of charge, and a wide range of private institutions supplement the public sector. Ninety-five per cent of all females and 80 per cent of all males who are enrolled in the final year of secondary school apply for admission to higher education.

In the 2008/09 academic year, Sheikh Nahyan bin Mubarak Al Nahyan, Minister of Higher Education and Scientific Research, approved admissions to government universities at home and scholarships abroad for 13,315 Emiratis – 23 per cent more than the previous year's figure of 10,785. The fact that every qualified student was offered a place was facilitated by an injection of funds from the Cabinet. Without the extra funding, Ministry of Higher Education and Scientific Research projections suggested fewer than 10,000 students would have been admitted to university, leaving more than 3000 without a place.

The UAE University admitted 3355 students, the Higher Colleges of Technology 7902 and Zayed University 1558, while the government is funding 500 overseas scholarships, including 150 postgraduate students.

In a move that is aimed at permanently ending the funding shortfall, a new formula linking budgets with student numbers has been approved and is likely to take effect from the 2009/10 academic year.

In the past budgets had failed to grow in line with inflation and the increase in student population. For example, at Zayed University (ZU), the budget remained constant for six years, despite a 52 per cent increase in the number of students.

At the end of the 2007/08 academic year, ZU had more than 3300 students, in addition to 180 students from the UAE Armed Forces at the university's special branch in Sweihan, which was opened in February 2008. So far, five batches, consisting of more than 1700 students, have graduated from the university.

The UAE has in excess of 60 public and private universities and the drive to improve education across the board is a key component of UAE Government strategy.

ZU has also entered into a seven-year cooperation agreement with the Knowledge and Human Development Authority (KHDA) in relation to the establishment of Zayed International College (ZIC) in Knowledge Village, Dubai.

ZU has recently received international accreditation from the US Middle States Commission on Higher Education, the first university in the country to do so. It is generally recognised that the academic accreditation process is extremely important for educational institutions seeking to match global quality and performance standards. Indeed, proper accreditation is deemed to be critical if institutions are to answer to the demands of the local and regional job markets.

For over three decades UAEU has played a leading role in the country's development and is continuing to model its structures on best practices, particularly in the field of research.

In the meantime, the UAE University (UAEU), which for over three decades has played a leading role in the country's development, is continuing to model its structures on best practices and international standards, both academically and administratively, particularly in the field of research. The university has supplied around 40,000 graduates to the country to date. A total of 2848 students, including 2280 females, graduated from the UAEU in 2008. In addition, the university welcomed 16,372 students for the 2008/09 academic year, out of which 3355 are freshmen. The majority of students are female.

UAEU is developing a university town on its Al Maqam campus to bring together in one place all its facilities in Al Ain, with a view to creating a more conducive educational atmosphere.

In addition to the universities, a system of Higher Colleges of Technology (HCTs) throughout the emirates offers a more technically oriented education. The HCTs' commercial arm, The Centre of Excellence for Applied Research and Training (CERT), is now the largest education provider in the region. CERT prides itself on responding quickly and effectively to current needs in the regional and international work place, providing professional development and lifelong learning opportunities for the UAE, the Gulf, and – through online training courses – to many other parts of the business world.

Private Institutions

A wide range of private universities and institutions, many accredited to or linked with international bodies, offer educational opportunities to Emiratis and other nationalities. The Ministry of Higher Education and Scientific Research is responsible for the accreditation of institutes and degrees and its website provides a comprehensive list of recognised institutes and programmes.

With two campuses in Abu Dhabi and Al Ain, over 1000 new students were accepted in the 2008/09 academic year for study at the recently established Abu Dhabi University. Over half the student body at ADU consists of 45 different nationalities.

Paris Sorbonne University, Abu Dhabi, wholly owned by ADEC, is providing educational opportunities in Abu Dhabi, in partnership with one of the world's leading academic institutions. The university awards qualifications under French regulations and in accordance with academic standards set by the Sorbonne in Paris.

Successful international partnerships have also have also been developed with Insead, one of the world's largest graduate business schools. Neither are the arts neglected, as is evidenced by the opening of a branch of the New York Film School in Abu Dhabi in February 2008.

Other notable institutions include the American Universities of Sharjah and Dubai, Sharjah University and Ajman University of Science and Technology.

Dubai Knowledge Village, a member of Tecom Investments, is running Dubai International Academic City (DIAC), the world's only free zone dedicated to international higher education. DIAC will serve as the regional base for a number of international higher education institutions, targeting students who are unable to go abroad to study.

The UAE also has several vocational and technical educational centres for those seeking practical career training. These include the Emirates Institute for Banking and Finance, the Dubai School of Government, Etisalat's colleges and university, Etihad's training centre, The Emirates Aviation College for Aerospace and Academic Studies and the Petroleum Institute (PI).

In addition, Jumeirah Group run a hospitality training school and Emaar Education has also opened a new school of hospitality management in Dubai.

Funded by the Abu Dhabi government, and operated by Tourism Development & Investment Company (TDIC), a new vocational education centre has attracted registration from hundreds of residents of Dalma Island, the second largest component in Abu Dhabi's unique Desert Islands nature-based tourism destination. The Centre is designed to prepare the population for careers resulting from the emergence of the tourism industry in the emirate's Western (Al Gharbia) Region. The Desert Islands Education Centre (DIEC) will be

> Dubai International Academic City is the world's only free zone dedicated to international higher education.

the first professional education facility to open on the heritage rich Dalma Island. Further details are available on the Dalma Island Education Centre website at www.diec.org or Desert Islands at www.desertislands.com or TDIC at www.tdic.ae

Research and Development

The Government's strategy is to create an indigenous scientific culture in order to enhance research and development in the UAE.

It is generally recognised that research and development (R&D) is an essential element in economic progress. The government's strategy is to create an indigenous scientific and research culture to enhance the level of higher education and R&D within the country. One way to achieve this is to forge partnerships in research among universities and public and private sector bodies, as well as pursue cooperation with the world's prestigious universities and institutes.

Heading the partnership agenda is the launch of a web portal to be managed in conjunction with Microsoft. The partnership campaign will also see the introduction of an entrepreneurship initiative in conjunction with the Young Achievers Injaz programme, which is expected to cater to 50,000 students by 2013. Other planned re-engineering moves include the launch of a gifted student scheme.

In addition, Emirates Foundation is breaking new ground in the UAE by offering independent research grants in the fields of science and engineering, information technology and environmental sciences. The foundation's private sector partner in this initiative is Shell Abu Dhabi, which is acting in an advisory capacity. Research projects that meet selection criteria are eligible for grants of up to Dh200,000. Project applications that included the participation and empowerment

of UAE national students are strongly encouraged. More information can be found on the Emirates Foundation website at www.emirates foundation.ae under Grants and Scholarships.

In May 2008, Emirates Foundation also announced its first grant to a non-profit organisation in the area of Science and Technology. The grant, which is aimed at making high-impact science and technology programmes more accessible to young people nationwide, has been awarded to The Arab Youth Venture Foundation (AYVF). This group delivers programmes to nurture innovation and entrepreneurial thinking among talented UAE youth, placing a priority on the fun and excitement of science.

AYVF has created four distinct STEAM (Science/Technology/Engineering/Aerospace/Maths) programmes as part of a focused effort to prepare students for future careers and the next wave of national economic development. It also has plans to engage families and the broader community to move the UAE toward its articulated goal of a knowledge-based economy.

The Petroleum Institute (PI), which is located in Abu Dhabi, was created in 2001 with the goal of establishing itself as a world-class institution specialising in engineering education and research in areas of significance to the oil and gas and the broader energy industries. The PI's sponsors and affiliates include Abu Dhabi National Oil Company (Adnoc) and four major international oil companies. Today more than 1000 young men and women are enrolled in the programmes at the PI and the institute is in the design and planning stage of a major research and technology development centre.

In September 2009, the Masdar Institute of Science and Technology (MIST) will open its new facilities at Masdar City with the intake of the first class of 100 students. Developed in cooperation with the Massachusetts Institute of Technology (MIT), MIST will emulate MIT's high standards and offer Master's and Doctorate-level degree programmes focused on the science and engineering of advanced energy and sustainability technologies.

MIST and the PI signed a collaborative agreement in 2008 that will see the two Abu Dhabi academic institutions work together to create a dynamic force in the field of energy. As part of the agreement, PI has joined the Masdar Research Network (MRN).

Emirates Institute for Advanced Science and Technology is also proving to be a fertile ground for R&D. The UAE's first earth observation satellite was developed by Satrecl in South Korea with

In September 2009, the Masdar Institute of Science and Technology (MIST) will open its new facilities at Masdar City with the intake of the first class of 100 students.

in-depth participation by UAE engineers from the EIAST and is due for launching in 2009. Dubai Sat-1 will provide the UAE with its first dedicated 'Eye in the Sky'.

Khalifa University of Science, Technology and Research (KUSTR) aims to provide a centre of excellence for learning and research, primarily in telecommunications and related disciplines. KUSTR has recently launched the Sheikh Mohammed bin Zayed Postgraduate Scholarships, which sponsors UAE nationals to obtain Masters Degrees and PhDs in telecommunications, computer science, and electronics. The programme covers all expenses and also allocates an attractive monthly salary for students and guarantees employment on graduation.

KUSTR has also entered into a cooperation agreement with National Bank of Abu Dhabi (NBAD) whereby NBAD's corporate social responsibility programme will donate Dh25 million to the University's Research and Development Centre. The initiative further cements KUSTR's research and academic efforts and enables it to implement its educational strategy.

In addition, Etisalat, British Telecom (BT) and KUSTR have announced a plan to set up a joint UAE-based centre for research and development focusing on innovation in information technology and telecommunications in the UAE and the region.

Educational Awards

The Dh3.3 million Khalifa Educational Award was established in 2007/08 to help foster an environment that spurs creativity and empowers local human resources. The award covers a variety of fields: general education, higher education, people with special needs, inventive educational programmes in the UAE, procedural researches in the UAE, and inventive educational projects and programmes at the Arab countries' level.

The second cycle of the Khalifa Award for Education was launched in Cairo in October 2008 in recognition of Egypt's substantial support for development in education in many Arab countries including the UAE. Winners will be announced in April 2009.

The second cycle of the Khalifa Award for Education was launched in Cairo in October 2008 in recognition of Egypt's substantial support for development in education in many Arab countries, including the UAE.

Literacy

The UAE has pledged to eradicate alphabetical illiteracy in seven years, thus becoming the first Arab country to attain full literacy. A recent survey showed that the illiteracy rate is on the decline in the

UAE, and is now in the region of 7 per cent. This is mainly due to programmes that combat illiteracy amongst the adult population.

Currently there are thousands of nationals pursuing formal learning at 86 adult education centres spread across the country. Many are above 50 years of age. A large number of graduates from these evening schools have enrolled for higher education at various universities.

WOMEN

The empowering of women is a key component of UAE Government strategy. This pursuit of gender equality is not just a social policy initiative, it is generally recognised that full female participation is also pivotal for sustainable economic development. Women as a comparatively untapped human capital resource have a vital contribution to make to the continued prosperity of the country.

The commitment to gender equality is enshrined in the UAE Constitution and in enabling legislation that strives to maintain the balance between modernisation, cultural heritage and Islamic beliefs.

There is no doubt that great strides have been made since the foundation of the federation in eliminating all forms of discrimination against women. On the educational level, nearly half the students registered in over 1250 schools across the UAE are girls; about 75 per cent of all students in the UAE University are women; and three out of every five students in the public higher education system are women. When one considers that just over 30 years ago, only 29 women in the UAE held university degrees, it is possible to appreciate how much progress has been made in a very short space of time.

Having excelled in educational attainments, women in the UAE account for 27.95 per cent of the national labour force, marking an annual growth rate of 3.5 per cent between 1985 and 2005. Indeed women occupy 66 per cent of public-sector jobs, 30 per cent of which are leadership and decision-making posts. Participation in the government sector is not just in traditional areas such as health care and education: UAE women have also joined the police, military and airforce (the first four female women pilots to serve in the UAE airforce graduated from Khalifa Aviation College in January 2008).

Women are also represented in the legislative, executive and judiciary: the new Cabinet, appointed in late 2007, includes four

There is no doubt that great strides have been made since the foundation of the federation in eliminating all forms of discrimination against women.

women ministers, and women occupy 22 per cent of the seats in the Federal National Council. Women constitute 20 per cent of the diplomatic corps and two women were appointed as ambassadors in 2008. In addition, the law governing judicial appointments was amended in 2008 to permit women judges to be appointed in the UAE and the first female judge was appointed in Abu Dhabi in 2008.

Government Initiatives

Women's organisations in the UAE have played a vital role in representing and organising the women's movement and promoting women in the workplace, family and community.

Women's organisations such as the General Women's Union (GWU), which was established in 1975 under the leadership of HH Sheikha Fatima bint Mubarak with the full support of the Government, have played a vital role in representing and organising the women's movement and promoting women in the workplace, family and community. As is outlined below, the GWU's work is ongoing.

The Government also continues to make the necessary efforts to mainstream and promote gender equality and justice in all government institutions and it has been responsible for a number of initiatives directly concerned with women's and children's affairs, including the Family Development Foundation, which was set up in 2006 under the presidency of HH Sheikha Fatima bint Mubarak to develop and monitor implementation of women's advancement strategies. The foundation recently signed a Memorandum of Understanding with the United Nations Development Fund for Women to strengthen the foundation's capacities and update the National Strategy for Women.

As stressed by the UAE Permanent Ambassador to the UN during the fifty-second session of the Commission on the Status of Women and to the special session of the General Assembly entitled 'Women 2000: Gender Equality, Development and Peace for the 21st' Century'.

The UAE is committed to implementing the recommendations and the outcomes of all the international conferences and summits on women, including the Beijing plan of action and the outcome of the 23rd special session of the General Assembly, motivated by a conviction that implementing these recommendations is an imperative requirement to reach the internationally agreed development goals. Therefore, the UAE was very keen on joining the regional and international conventions on women and the family, such as the Convention on the Elimination of all forms of Discrimination Against Women (CEDAW). In addition the UAE is party to nine international treaties on working conditions for women, working hours and equal pay.

The UAE urges for the continuation of the international efforts to enhance international political and financial support for millions of women in the developing countries who are suffering from poverty, serious diseases and armed conflicts, so that they can improve their living conditions to comply with the principles of the UN Charter, human rights, the recommendations of the Millennium declaration and the Beijing plan of action.

GWU

The GWU has been working hard for the past 33 years to further the emancipation of Emirati women in accordance with Islamic values and Arab traditions. Funded by the government, the GWU has its own charter and is empowered to represent the women of the UAE in discussions with ministries and other government departments and institutions. It also has the responsibility of suggesting new laws or amending existing legislation. The GWU conducts its own research into matters of interest to women and is central to government policy in this area. In fact, the GWU was instrumental in the launch of the UAE National Strategy on the Advancement of Women, the objective of which is to enhance the role of women in economic, social, media, education, labour, culture as well as political fields. The GWU also represents the government at home and abroad on issues relating to the development of women.

The General Women's Union has been working hard for the past 33 years to further the emancipation of Emirati women in accordance with Islamic values and Arab traditions.

www.uaeinteract.com/women

In March 2006, the GWU, in partnership with UNDP UAE (www.undporg.ae), embarked on an intensive outreach programme to engage the public and private sectors in effective gender mainstreaming. This project's main goal is to build the capacity of the GWU, to enable the organisation to more effectively contribute to gender empowerment and sustainable development efforts in the UAE. Enhancing the GWU's capabilities, especially in the area of gender mainstreaming, will enable the organisation to successfully implement the National Strategy for the Advancement of Women in the UAE, as well as effectively monitor and follow-up on commitments made by the UAE Government with regards to CEDAW as well as other relevant conventions and international agreements.

Training has been provided to 26 government and non-governmental entities for the purpose of facilitating the incorporation of a gender-sensitive dimension into their policies and plans. Gender-sensitising dialogue sessions are also being provided to private sector management, particularly in the oil and gas, banking and financial industries. The GWU is also part of a newly established international network for cooperation in gender development efforts.

DWE

Contributing to policy-making and legislation that will enhance the role of Emirati women in society and encourage them to become a driving force in development is at the core of the Dubai Women Establishment's strategy for 2008 to 2012. The goal of the strategy, which contains a five-pronged approach, is to find a balance between work and home life, provide continuous opportunities for women in training and work, nurture leadership, and enhance the image of UAE national women.

The strategy focuses on the adoption of national development policies to increase the contribution of Emirati women to the economy, the launching of national programmes that help these women reach leadership positions, as well as introducing economic policies to enable women to work from home.

The objective is to introduce new policies and support services that remove barriers towards women's progression and growth in the workplace, especially in the private sector, and an increase in the number of women returning to work after starting a family.

DWE is committed to helping women tap opportunities in all domains while seeking new horizons. Increased acknowledgment of

Contributing to policy-making and legislation that will enhance the role of Emirati women in society and encourage them to become a driving force in development is at the core of the Dubai Women Establishment's strategy.

the contributions and accomplishments of women, improved visibility of role models and mentors and increased inspiration and motivation to encourage women to reach their full potential will help in achieving this.

One of the difficulties faced in implementing strategy is the lack of hard statistical evidence on which to base initiatives. Efforts are being made across the board to remedy this and DWE has signed a strategic co-operation agreement with the Dubai Statistics Centre (DSC) to share crucial data that will further the goals of both organisations to provide better understanding on the status of UAE women. Statistics will help identify real challenges the UAE working women face in their day-to-day life and will facilitate the implementation of appropriate solutions.

As part of its efforts to ensure Emirati women play a key role not only in the local arena but throughout the Gulf region, the DWE has initiated several women-centric programmes with the active participation of private and public sector organisations. In particular, it recently signed a memorandum of understanding with the Mohammed bin Rashid Programme for Leadership Development to formulate programmes for training and developing Emirati leaders.

Private Sector

Although the UAE has made great strides in its efforts to empower women, the Government considers this as a 'work in progress' and hopes to enable women to achieve even greater heights in the years ahead. In particular, women require support and encouragement to take up positions in the private sector.

The fact that there are so few women working in the private sector has costs for both society and the economy. A report, 'Growing Beyond Oil' by Gulf Investment Corporation (GIC) in Kuwait, argues that national women remain a major untapped resource in the GCC that could be better exploited. In the GIC report, gender equality in the labour force was cited as a key recommendation for GCC countries as they crept towards the post-oil era. The report concluded that policies like the ones adopted in the UAE – bolstering educational institutions and funding emiratisation programmes – are the way forward.

The perception is that women tend to gravitate towards professions in the services sector, banking and information technology, where there is a combination of interpersonal interaction and flexibility

Many Emirati women pioneers have succeeded in breaking down barriers, both in terms of entering careers that were previously considered to be the domain of men and reaching the very top of their chosen professions.

that allows them to stay home and raise families, if they choose to do so. This is supported by the fact that there is an increasing number of female investment bankers, financial fund managers, and portfolio managers. Programmes that take these factors into account will help correct the UAE's labour imbalance.

But while the public sector has focused on providing facilities and benefits for working women, convincing the private sector in the UAE to adapt work practices to accommodate women is a little more difficult. Similar problems occur in other jurisdictions, but it is increasingly evident that correcting them here is crucial for the region in the long run.

However, getting more women to work in the private sector is only one side of the equality equation. The other – enabling women to break through the 'glass ceiling' and achieve executive positions – is just as problematic. A report in May from 'The National Investor', an investment bank in Abu Dhabi, in conjunction with the corporate governance institute, Hawkamah, found that women occupied just 1.5 per cent of corporate board seats in the GCC. In the UAE, the figure was about 0.8 per cent.

Nevertheless, in the UAE, many of the key pieces already seem to be in place and it may be only a matter of time before women begin to assume positions of power in greater numbers.

Breaking Barriers

Despite the difficulties, there are many Emirati women pioneers who have succeeded in breaking down barriers, both in terms of entering careers that were previously considered to be the domain of men and reaching the very top of their chosen professions.

Sheikha Lubna Al Qasimi, the UAE Minister of Foreign Trade, is one of five women in the Middle East considered by the US-based business magazine 'Forbes' in 2007 to be among the world's 100 most powerful women. Prior to her appointment to the Cabinet, Sheikha Lubna had made a name for herself in the private sector as CEO of Tejari, a leading B2B marketplace in the emerging markets.

Chief executive of Dubai's Economic Zones World and Jebel Ali Free Zone Authority Salma Hareb topped the 2008 'Forbes Arabia' list of the 50 most powerful Arab businesswomen. Hareb became the first woman in the Middle East and North Africa to head a free zone in September 2005 when she became the boss of Jafza. All in all, the UAE has eight businesswomen on the list.

Etihad Airways first ever Emirati female cadet pilots are high flyers in another category. Heralded in a recently published book 'The 100 Greatest Women in Aviation', which was launched at the 2008 Farnborough International Airshow, UK, these are 'the female aviators of the future' who are 'making their own name in flying'.

Women in Investment

It is estimated that investments run by women amount to Dh12.5 billion (about US$4 billion) and women finance 32 per cent of the transactions of the financial and banking sector.

There are a number of support systems in place to encourage women to take a more active role in investment in the UAE. For example, to promote private investment by women, the UAE Businesswomen Council (UAEBC), a nationwide network of business, professional and academic women, was set up in 2002 with the assistance of the UAE Federation of Chambers of Commerce and Industry.

Forsa, part of Dubai World, is a new investment company for women that focuses on investment opportunities in real estate, retail and services segments in the MENA region. Its vision is to empower women and enable them to lead in a competitive economy. Forsa and the Mohammed bin Rashid Establishment for Young Business Leaders, recently signed a Memorandum of Understanding (MoU) designed to promote value-added investment opportunities for women entrepreneurs in the country. Under the terms of the MoU, the Mohammed bin Rashid Establishment will promote Forsa as the preferred strategic partner among its members and facilitate alliance opportunities for investment between Forsa and the young entrepreneurs. Forsa will offer smart capital to fund start-up companies and play a key role in adding further value and realising the true growth potential of portfolio companies.

Conferences

The dialogue is ongoing: in 2008, the UAE hosted, for the first time, an Arab-West group of young people focusing on women's issues. This was held under the patronage of HH Sheikha Fatima bint Mubarak as part of the 'Arab Youth Dialogue' strategy initiated in 2005 with the aim of developing a constructive discourse on resolving women's issues and protecting their rights.

Arab First Ladies attending the Arab Women's Organisation conference in Abu Dhabi in November 2008.

The Third Women as Global Leaders Conference 2008 was held in March, also under the patronage of Sheikha Fatima. Organised by Zayed University, the international student conference brought together eminent women personalities whose leadership role was crucial in shaping the modern world with participants from over 85 countries and from all sectors including education, government, and nongovernmental organisations. The conference focused on women's emergent and current leadership roles across the globe as well as the practice of educating students for and about leadership.

The Second Arab Women's Organisation conference took place in Abu Dhabi in November. Launched in March 2003, the AWO seeks to achieve women's empowerment in the Arab World and enhance their role within the family and society.

Sheikha Fatima became chairwoman of the AWO in 2007 and donated US$1 million to the organisation. In addition, Sheikha Fatima has donated money for the launching of a communication network among Arab women.

At the second AWO conference Sheikha Fatima announced a media strategy for Arab women to enable and promote their role in society and also launched a network to support the diaspora of Arab women worldwide.

Social Assistance

Although educational opportunities have transformed the status of women in the UAE, in any society there will be those who for one reason or another remain disadvantaged. As already outlined, the Ministry of Social Affairs is responsible for paying welfare assistance to those in need, including widows and divorced women. It also makes specific allocations to the women's organisations in the country.

To assist women who cannot work away from their families, the Government established the Programme for Productive Families, which seeks to improve the finances of limited income families and transform them from dependent families to contributing ones.

As a vital part of those efforts, the Ministry of Social Affairs is responsible for the management of the network of social development centre, run by the GWU which were set up with the idea of contributing to the social and economic development of Emirati women, especially in rural areas. Ten social development centres offer advice in a variety of social and domestic situations and are responsible for the first stage assessment of eligibility to receive welfare assistance (see section on Social Welfare).

Of direct assistance to women at home are the courses offered in domestic skills with nurseries provided to the children of women who wish to attend. The centres are also involved in the work of adult literacy centres, which are run in collaboration with the Ministry of Education.

In addition, the centres help women to take a more active role in society. Recreational and social activities are organised while the centres are also very active in preserving traditional heritage and handicrafts practiced by UAE women.

Heritage work groups have been established in which women continue the making of traditional handicrafts that are then sold to the public, thus providing additional income for the makers. The centres also offer simple vocational training and regular lectures on topics pertaining to culture, religion and health.

Elsewhere, the Handicrafts Centre, part of the GWU, is attempting to preserve traditional Emirati handicrafts and promote them in a way that will guarantee their survival in the long run and will meet the rising demand by visitors and residents of Abu Dhabi for quality products. This also serves the purpose of acquainting tourists with the value and history of traditional products in the UAE.

The Dubai Shelter for Women and Children was established to provide support and psychological care to all women, both nationals and expatriates, who are victims of human trafficking, domestic violence, family neglect, employer abuse and other social problems. A similar shelter has been established in Abu Dhabi by the UAE Red Crescent Authority.

HEALTH

The UAE has a comprehensive health service that delivers a high standard of health care to the population. Pre-natal and post-natal care is on a par with the world's most developed countries and healthcare provision is universal. As a consequence, life expectancy at birth in the UAE, at 78.5 years, has reached levels similar to those in Europe and North America.

www.uaeinteract.com/health

Rapid advancement in healthcare facilities in the UAE drastically reduced infant mortality to about eight per thousand births in 2008 and raised the average life expectancy age to 77 years for men and 80 years for women.

According to World Health Organisation (WHO) statistics, the UAE is ranked forty-fourth in the world in terms of health care. The aim now is to meet the challenges of the twenty-first century and develop a system for the country and the region that is at par with the world's best.

In particular, the needs of a rapidly expanding population coupled with the increased costs of equipping and operating healthcare facilities are all driving a demand for more healthcare expenditure. In the light of these trends and the government's overall reassessment of its role as a provider of services, new models of private and public sector collaboration are emerging in healthcare provision, with government focusing on policy formation and regulation.

Health Strategy

In pursuit of government strategy to coordinate and implement a coherent healthcare policy throughout the Emirates, a national Health Council was established in July 2008. Chaired by Health Minister Humaid Mohammed Obaid Al Qatami, the council comprises representatives from the Ministry of Health (MoH), the Health Authority–Abu Dhabi (HAAD), Dubai Health Authority (DHA), Dubai Healthcare City (DHCC), the medical services sectors of the Interior Ministry, the Armed Forces and the private health sector. The new council is entrusted with the task of coordinating efforts by federal and local healthcare authorities, as well as the public and private healthcare delivery sector, to ensure an integrated service and improve the standards of health care in the country.

The council will also coordinate with the Ministry of Higher Education and Scientific Research on the drawing up of educational policies for the study of medicine and health sciences in the UAE and abroad. The two bodies will share information, work together to enhance scientific research, and assist health programmes, activities and services in a way that will help to achieve the country's general health policy.

The council is also mandated to assist cooperation between the UAE, regional and international health bodies and it will give advice and express its views on matters related to health insurance nationwide. In summary, the overall objective of the Health Council is to orchestrate the ongoing development of an accessible, comprehensive, sustainable, and fully integrated cycle of care for the population of the UAE.

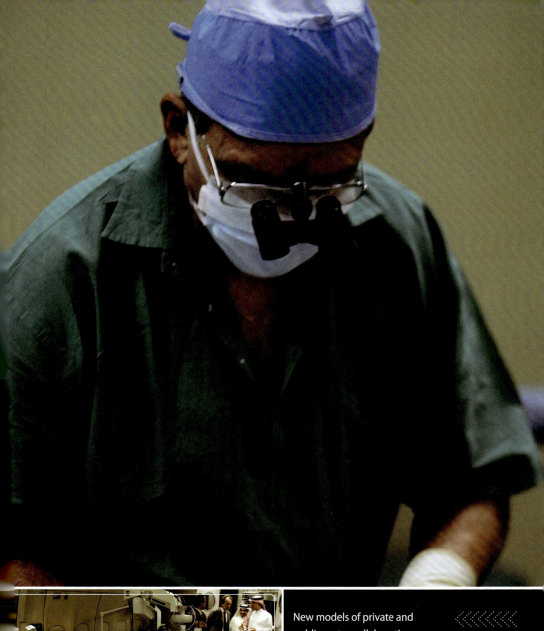

New models of private and public sector collaboration are emerging in healthcare provision in the UAE.

The MoH has unveiled a five-year health strategy for the public health sector in the northern emirates, which, unlike Abu Dhabi and Dubai, do not have separate healthcare authorities.

Planning Ahead

In February 2008, the MoH unveiled a five-year health strategy for the public health sector in the northern emirates, which fall under its purview and which, unlike Abu Dhabi and Dubai, do not have separate healthcare authorities. The strategy focuses on unifying healthcare policy and improving access to healthcare services at reasonable cost, at the same time reducing dependence on overseas treatment. The ministry plans to add three hospitals to the current 14, and 29 primary healthcare centres to the current 86. Nine were scheduled to open in 2008.

HAAD announced its five-year strategic plan in May 2008, addressing 12 priorities based on the government's vision for the health system of Abu Dhabi emirate and the comprehensively analysed needs of the population.

The demand for high-quality health services in the emirate is increasing very rapidly. As we have already seen, the population is rising steeply, the birth rate is amongst the highest in the world and more people are reaching old-age than ever before. Simultaneously, people with lifestyle associated risk factors, serious diseases, and accident related afflictions, are increasing.

Abu Dhabi, through the medium of Abu Dhabi Health Services Company (SEHA), is already responding to the changing demands in the healthcare sector. SEHA is an independent, public company launched in December 2007 to manage and develop activities in public hospitals and clinics in Abu Dhabi. SEHA currently manages eight hospital systems totalling 14 facilities, 2472 licensed beds, more than 55 Primary Health Clinics and 14,350 employees and is attracting international hospitals to manage healthcare facilities, as well as investing heavily in medical infrastructure and technology, at all times applying internationally acclaimed standards.

HEALTH INSURANCE

The introduction of mandatory health insurance in Abu Dhabi for expatriates and their dependents over two years ago was a major driver in reform of healthcare policy. Abu Dhabi nationals were brought under the scheme from 1 June 2008 and Dubai followed suit for its government employees. Eventually, under federal law, every Emirati and expatriate in the country will be covered by compulsory health insurance under a unified mandatory scheme. This will mean everybody living in the northern emirates will be covered by the same rules as elsewhere in the country and benefit from the same access to health care. The challenge is to make sure the hospitals and healthcare providers, insurers, the Government and employers work together to ensure that the transition is successful. Progress has already been made on the establishment of a federal health insurance authority to regulate the industry across the UAE.

Since its formation in 2006, the National Insurance Company, Daman, held exclusive rights to provide health insurance for expatriates and their dependents working in many government and semi-government institutions in the UAE. However, following an amendment introduced in 2008 by the Abu Dhabi Executive Council to the executive regulations of Law No 23 of 2005, Daman's exclusive status has been rescinded and other registered insurance companies are eligible to provide health insurance to all government employees, in direct competition with Daman. The decree has levelled the playing field between insurance companies and it is hoped that the increased competition will lead to a reduction in costs.

The resolution also brought new groups of beneficiaries under the ambit of the basic health insurance plan (BHIP) while the total salary bracket was also changed on the recommendation of HAAD.

Employers and sponsors are obliged to ensure that their employees and dependents who are working or residing in the Emirate of Abu Dhabi are covered by valid health insurance at all times. Health insurance policies must be renewed every year and trade licences, work visas and resident visas will not be issued or renewed without the employer submitting evidence of health insurance subscription for his employees for the previous period.

From the beginning of May 2008, Dubai Health Authority (DHA) introduced a comprehensive health insurance scheme for government employees and their dependents, including all UAE nationals as well as expatriate residents. The scheme will be extended to all residents of Dubai from 1 January 2009.

Employers will contribute the majority of the funding provided through a flat rate to the Health Benefits Contribution (HBC) pool, paid on behalf of their employees. Only authorised insurance companies will distribute health insurance schemes incorporating the new funding system.

Commencing January 2009, everyone residing in the emirate or holding a Dubai residence visa will be required to register with a public

> The introduction of mandatory health insurance in Abu Dhabi was a major driver in reform of healthcare policy.

Kidney transplant patient at Zayed Hospital.

Keyhole heart surgery at Zayed Hospital

or private outpatient clinic of their choice (subject to availability). They will then be issued with a health card that will give them access to essential health care within Dubai only. Those requiring healthcare facilities in any other emirate, once the system is in place, will have to bear the cost until the federal insurance system is in operation.

UAE nationals will continue to receive existing levels of cover and service, which means the government will bear all their healthcare expenses. The entire registration process for Dubai has to be completed within a year. However, current insurance schemes being held by companies will remain in place until all Dubai employees/residents are registered. The DHA transition programme will be introduced over a four-year period, completing in 2012, with the DHA health funding process being fully implemented by 2015.

Insurance for Travellers

Proof of health insurance is mandatory to acquire a UAE visitor's visa from 1 August 2008 under the newly implemented visa regulations. In response, Daman has launched a series of plans to facilitate visit visa application procedures. Daman's visitor insurance plans are accepted by the Federal Department of Naturalisation and Residence and satisfy entry requirements at all airports in UAE. However, holders of international health insurance policies are not required to obtain local insurance policies when applying for entry permits.

The Department of Naturalisation and Residency in Dubai (DNRD) also revealed details of health insurance plans for visitors, following the conclusion of an agreement with two insurance companies; Oman and Aman.

HEALTH SURVEYS

Preventive strategies are a formidable weapon in any public health policy and the UAE is no exception. But it is important to base policy on clear statistical data. With this in mind the Ministry of Health (MoH) conducted the first comprehensive international health survey in December 2008. The survey covered 5000 families (both expatriates and citizens) and 1000 individuals (workers) from all over the country, gathering information regarding their health status and financial capacities. MoH is also carrying out a comprehensive countrywide field study on the spread of lifestyle diseases.

CANCER

The UAE is in the process of opening a unified cancer centre that will collect and collate information in an attempt to find ways to combat the disease, focusing on prevention as well as treatment.

Information to date indicates that cancer rates are on the rise in the UAE and in many cases late diagnosis and treatment lead to medical complications and death, the most common cancers being breast cancer, prostate cancer, colorectal and skin cancers.

Breast cancer is one of the biggest killers of women in the UAE and is often diagnosed during later stages of the disease. The health issues surrounding breast cancer in the UAE were highlighted in 2007 with the launch of the US–UAE Partnership for Breast Cancer Awareness and Research, under the patronage of Sheikha Fatima.

Between 2003 and 2006, almost as many women were diagnosed with breast cancer as with all the other types of cancer combined, according to the National Cancer Registry. The disease also accounts for 22.8 per cent of the total number of diagnosed cases of cancer in the UAE, making it the country's most common cancer. The young age at which women are developing breast cancer is of particular concern to doctors: many women are being diagnosed with breast cancer in their teens and twenties and the average age at which breast cancer is being diagnosed among Emiratis is between 40 and 45, which is ten years younger than in Europe. It is estimated also that only 30 per cent of women with breast cancer in the country are diagnosed in the early stages of the disease, when the chances of a cure are greatly increased.

In an effort to address these issues, the national screening centre for women was officially opened in Abu Dhabi in 2008. Its major tasks include educating people about the importance of self-examination at an early age, and overcoming taboos associated with the disease.

Another highly positive move was the launch in January 2008 of the first mobile mammography screening unit in the UAE at Tawam Hospital in Al Ain, in affiliation with Johns Hopkins Medicine, which manages Tawam. The mobile unit provides screening mammograms and breast health education to rural women in their own communities. Tawam also has a complete support team at its dedicated state-of-the-art Breast Care Centre in Al Ain, which is a regional first.

The service is already proving to be a success, with treatment being given to many women who might not have received it, and

The UAE is in the process of opening a unified cancer centre that will collect and collate information in an attempt to find ways to combat the disease.

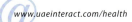 www.uaeinteract.com/health

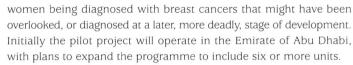

Between 2003 and 2006, almost as many women were diagnosed with breast cancer as with all the other types of cancer combined.

women being diagnosed with breast cancers that might have been overlooked, or diagnosed at a later, more deadly, stage of development. Initially the pilot project will operate in the Emirate of Abu Dhabi, with plans to expand the programme to include six or more units.

The MoH has also unveiled what it hopes will become a national cervical cancer screening campaign. Cervical cancer is the second most fatal type of cancer for women worldwide and the picture in the UAE is no different. The MoH and the Emirates Medical Association are collaborating to create an organisation that raises awareness of the disease, and the main function of the Emirates Cervicare Network is to encourage women and, in particular, Emirati women, to have an annual cervical smear test. The process is often less about overcoming cultural barriers than it is about education.

Efforts are also being made to improve treatment facilities and Mubadala Healthcare announced that it has broken ground on a state-of-the-art medical molecular imaging centre at the Tawam campus in Al Ain. that will vastly improve diagnostic imaging in the region and contribute to more efficient treatment for patients.

Scheduled for completion in 2009, the new centre will offer revolutionary diagnostic imaging systems that significantly improve the early detection and tracking of cancer, cardiovascular and neurological diseases with accuracy far exceeding conventional medical imaging.

Patients throughout the region who currently have to travel abroad for this kind of procedure will soon be able to benefit from the very latest international technological advances without leaving the UAE.

CARDIOVASCULAR DISEASE

In the UAE screening for cardiovascular diseases was carried out as part of World Heart Federation's World Heart Day 2008 campaign, part of a worldwide screening initiative. According to a study published in the 'New England Journal of Medicine', cardiovascular diseases (CVD) account for 31.4 per cent of deaths in Dubai and 28 per cent of deaths in the UAE.

While genetic factors and the incidence of diabetes have a role to play in heart disease, the problem is mostly caused by rapidly changing lifestyles, poor eating habits, lack of exercise and living and working in a stressful environment.

As with cancer prevention and treatment, government strategy is focusing on health education programmes alongside the development of centres of excellence for treatment.

The Abu Dhabi-based Sheikh Khalifa Medical Centre (SKMC), which is managed by Cleveland Clinic, is a case in point. The hospital's Department of Cardiac Sciences is an ultra-modern and all-inclusive centre of excellence that provides cardiac services and specialties, including non-invasive cardiology, interventional cardiology, electrophysiology, and cardiac surgery. SKMC is installing a new ambient experience cardiac catheter laboratory, which will add to its already high profile in adult interventional cardiology by improving efficiency and patient comfort, and it officially opened a heart resuscitation section in August 2008.

DIABETES

Diabetes is a condition currently affecting an estimated one in five people in the UAE. Again health awareness campaigns are a major tool in prevention. 'Diabetes Knowledge Action' is the award-winning public health awareness campaign orchestrated by Imperial College London Diabetes Centre (ICLDC), under the patronage of Sheikha Fatima and in partnership with Emirates Foundation.

The awareness campaign has organised a number of activities to highlight the positive effects of exercise in helping to combat the debilitating disease, including a Ramadan seven-a-side football tournament held in Abu Dhabi, dubbed 'I Play Sports'. Ten corporate community teams representing each of the sponsor companies plus ICLDC and Takatof Volunteers participated in the corporate community event. The message is that regular exercise can help protect against diabetes and it is important to lead at least a moderately active lifestyle. For those who are unable to play team sports, just 30-minutes of exercise, five days a week, will significantly help in the fight against diabetes.

SMOKING

The UAE enthusiastically embraced the global war against smoking on 'World No Tobacco Day' in June by announcing that it would target youth, implement smoking restrictions and set up clinics to assist smokers to kick the habit. There is a recognition that smoking is embedded in local culture and that there is a need to change the

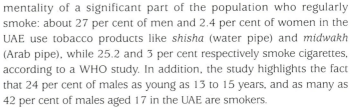

Research on diabetes in the UAE suggests that the disease will cost an estimated Dh10 billion by 2020 if the condition is not treated.

mentality of a significant part of the population who regularly smoke: about 27 per cent of men and 2.4 per cent of women in the UAE use tobacco products like *shisha* (water pipe) and *midwakh* (Arab pipe), while 25.2 and 3 per cent respectively smoke cigarettes, according to a WHO study. In addition, the study highlights the fact that 24 per cent of males as young as 13 to 15 years, and as many as 42 per cent of males aged 17 in the UAE are smokers.

The MoH has already set up several quit-smoking clinics in the Emirates and has plans to establish two clinics every year. But the MoH are concerned that people are not focusing sufficiently on the health risks associated with smoking, particularly young people.

The UAE has also been working on a federal law regulating tobacco and its uses, content and sale, in accordance with the World Health Organisation (WHO) Framework Convention of Tobacco Control (FCTC). The law, which will prohibit tobacco use in enclosed areas and public places, has been delayed since 2006 but could be implemented by the end of 2008.

Dubai has implemented several tobacco-control initiatives, outlawing smoking in enclosed public spaces and banning sale of tobacco products to those under the age of 20. Sharjah has also banned smoking at designated public places from 1 June 2008. Smoking in governmental institutions and department offices has been banned in Sharjah since 2000 and a ban on *shisha* smoking in coffee shops has also been implemented in the emirate.

The MoH will include questions on tobacco use in its comprehensive country-wide survey in association with WHO and is also considering a *shisha*-specific study. Recent research on *shisha* smoking has found more and more evidence that the Middle Eastern pastime is as dangerous, if not more dangerous than cigarette-smoking.

NEW WEBSITES

Mubadala Healthcare has launched the initial phase of Minhaal (Arabic for 'the source'), the first web portal in the Arab world to offer healthcare information in both English and Arabic languages. The web portal (www.minhaal.ae) primarily serves the UAE, but will also be an important source of knowledge for all Arabic speaking people. Minhaal has been created by Mubadala Healthcare as a way to help educate and raise awareness about health issues amongst Arabic speakers, and provide related prevention and treatment information that will empower people to make informed choices about their own health and well-being.

Minhaal provides reliable content through syndication agreements with international online resources, such as WebMD. Content is endorsed by an advisory board that presently includes representatives from HAAD and medical physicians from the Mubadala Healthcare network.

DHA launched a new website in July 2008 to provide information on its ongoing transition programme. The DHA website provides a single point of reference for information on the strategic review of the healthcare sector in Dubai. In addition to the website, the DHA is promoting the DHA online community initiative. Linked to the DHA website, this will provide an interactive public platform for invited participants to engage with the health agenda and debate some of the key health issues and concerns currently facing Dubai. DHA website can be accessed at www.dha.gov.ae.

A new website, www.minhaal.ae has been created to help educate and raise awareness about health issues amongst Arabic speakers.

NEW FACILITIES

A wide range of top-class medical facilities are under construction in the UAE. In the year in which Dr Marian Kennedy, one of the founders in 1960 of the Oasis Hospital in Al Ain, passed away, a new 200-bed facility is being built at the hospital's location to meet the demands of the twenty-first century. Although equipped with the latest technology, the new hospital will continue with the same philosophy as that of its founders. The new facilities will also enhance steps presently under way to establish Oasis Hospital as a centre for training in midwifery and other medical teaching, including an international residency programme

The official groundbreaking ceremony of the innovative Cleveland Clinic Abu Dhabi (CCAD) was held in January 2008 by Mubadala and Cleveland Clinic USA. The world-class, 360-bed (scalable to 490), multi- specialty facility which is located on Al Sowwah Island, across from the Abu Dhabi Mall, is scheduled to welcome its first patients in early 2011.

Cleveland Clinic Abu Dhabi is one of a number of initiatives led by Mubadala Healthcare, the division of Mubadala dedicated to investment in strategic, high value and economically sustainable projects that enhance the private healthcare infrastructure of Abu Dhabi and the UAE.

www.uaeinteract.com/health

The Cleveland Clinic Abu Dhabi will be a unique extension of the USA model, providing a spectrum of speciality healthcare services for the UAE and the region.

CCAD will be a unique extension of the Cleveland Clinic model, providing a spectrum of specialty services that are designed to cater to the healthcare requirements of Abu Dhabi and the region. One of the objectives of CCAD is to address the needs of patients currently travelling abroad for treatment. Like its counterpart in the United States, CCAD will be a physician-led medical facility served by US-trained and board-certified physicians. It will provide a number of career opportunities, and the medical professionals will receive ongoing training directly from Cleveland Clinic.

Mubadala Healthcare also entered into an agreement in September 2008 with Wooridul Spine Hospital of the Republic of Korea to establish a spine centre in Abu Dhabi, the first such centre to address the significant prevalence of spine and lower back injuries in the region. Scheduled for completion by the end of 2010, the Abu Dhabi Spine Centre will treat low-acuity spine injury patients, based on minimally invasive treatment principles. The centre will cover spine disease prevention, diagnosis, testing, treatment, physiotherapy and rehabilitation for inpatients and outpatients throughout the region and patients who currently have to travel abroad will benefit from the highest international standards of care in Abu Dhabi

The new centre will be located in Arzanah, the mixed-used development surrounding Zayed Stadium, alongside other Mubadala Healthcare facilities – the Abu Dhabi Knee and Sports Medicine Centre and the Arzanah Medical and Diagnostic Centre. Mubadala Healthcare also signed a memorandum of understanding with Aldar Properties in June to explore the development of new healthcare facilities at Aldar developments in the UAE.

United Eastern Medical Services (UEM), an Abu Dhabi-based privately owned healthcare development and investment company, is building a new state-of-the-art 160-bed women and children's hospital in Abu Dhabi. Umm Al-Emarat Hospital or 'Mother of the Emirates' is UEM's flagship project with which it hopes to set new standards in architecture and healthcare delivery throughout the region.

Dubai Healthcare City (DHCC), Dubai's new healthcare sector free zone, is part of the Dubai government's efforts to develop medical facilities that will attract patients to Dubai from the wider region. Work is currently under way on a 400-bed University Hospital that will open its doors to patients in 2011. The city's first teaching hospital, which will function as the main tertiary care facility within DHCC, is part of the Dh4 billion Mohammed bin Rashid Al Maktoum Academic Medical Centre, which includes the Harvard Medical School Dubai Centre (HMSDC), Dubai Harvard Foundation for Medical Research, Maktoum Harvard Library and Jumeirah Creekside Park Hotel. Harvard Medical School is providing its expertise in setting up the facilities and will support teaching and training of doctors. The hospital is expected to attract medical graduates looking for work and career training in the Gulf.

A HELPING HAND

In its quest to provide a high quality, technologically advanced health service for the region, the UAE has not forgotten that there are people both at home and abroad who are in dire need of medical services and are unable to afford them. A fruitful relationship has developed between public-private partnerships and not-for-profit organisations to address this issue. Some of these programmes have already been highlighted in the section on Foreign Aid.

'Hands of Charity', a humanitarian initiative launched by Deputy Prime Minister HH Sheikh Hamdan bin Zayed Al Nahyan, signed an agreement in June with the Washington-based Children's National Medical Centre to work together to implement medical programmes for treatment of children suffering from birth disorders and carry out research aimed at combating chronic, contagious and congenital diseases found among children in the region. The initiative is under the patronage of the Chairwoman of the Family Development Foundation, HH Sheikha Fatima bint Mubarak.

The 'Generous Heart Initiative', a health partnership between the Red Crescent Authority (RCA), chaired by Deputy Prime Minister HH Sheikh Hamdan bin Zayed Al Nahyan, and the Emirates World Heart Group (EWHG), was launched in July 2008 to provide medicine and perform surgery on underprivileged patients suffering from heart diseases. Hundreds of patients have been treated so far and curative, surgical and preventive programmes were maximised during the holy month of Ramadan.

The mobile cardiac centre is screening hundreds of heart patients inside and outside the country and a significant number of national patients have undergone open-heart surgery, many of whom could

Dubai Healthcare City is part of the government's efforts to develop medical facilities that will attract patients to Dubai from abroad.

not afford to bear the high costs of the surgery, which could reach up to Dh100,000. Operations were conducted at Al Noor hospital in Abu Dhabi and Welcare hospital in Dubai.

The RCA-backed EWHG is also working with the Zayed Charity Initiative for community development on the first-ever programme in the Middle East for endoscopy-based open-heart surgery for poor cardiac patients. The programme was announced at the open-heart surgeons' forum hosted by EWHG. The forum was convened in the UAE for the first time and sought to create a proper scientific environment for exchanging expertise between heart centres in the UAE and other countries.

Dubai Hospital is treating hundreds of visually impaired people from over 14 countries as part of the 'Noor Dubai' initiative, which was announced on 3 September by HH Sheikh Mohammed bin Rashid Al Maktoum, Vice-President and Prime Minister of the UAE and Ruler of Dubai. The aim of the initiative is to provide health services to at least one million people suffering from treatable blindness and visual impairment in developing countries on a local, regional, and international scale.

DISEASE CONTROL

Most infectious diseases like malaria, measles and poliomyelitis that were once endemic in the UAE have been eradicated.

The UAE began its malaria eradication efforts in 1972, culminating in a nation-wide campaign and programme of action in 1977. By 1985, the campaign led to a sharp drop of 70 per cent in malaria cases. Malaria was eradicated by 1998, and not a single case has been reported since then. However, the situation continued to be monitored by WHO experts until the country was formally declared to be malaria-free in 2007.

Health screening is a crucial aspect of preventive medicine and the UAE has a head start in developing a comprehensive model of treatment. Cases of tuberculosis in UAE are few and far between and the rate of the spread of the disease in the UAE is the lowest in the region and the east Mediterranean zone. However, some of the immigrants entering the UAE come from countries with a TB occurrence rate of 60 per 100,000 people. As a result of this and other possible risks from contagious diseases such as HIV AIDS,

Hepatitis B, Hepatitis C, leprosy, TB and syphilis – MoH has amended the regulations on mandatory screening tests for all expatriates applying for visas to live, study or work for a period of not less than six months in the UAE.

The Preventive Medicine Department of the Ministry of Health, Abu Dhabi Health Authority and Dubai Health Authority are the only authorities permitted to conduct the medical tests.

Hundreds of visually impaired children from over 14 countries are being treated as part of the Noor Dubai initiative.

BLOOD

The UAE celebrated World Blood Donor Day 2008 in June at Emirates Palace Hotel in Abu Dhabi. The UAE is the first Arab country and the fifth worldwide to host the event which was held under the theme

Strict rules and regulations for the control of blood transfusions have been introduced for all government and private health facilities throughout the Emirates.

'Giving Blood Regularly'. World Blood Donor Day 2008 had three broad objectives: creating greater public awareness of the necessity of regular and voluntary donations; highlighting the fact that the need for voluntary non-remunerated blood donation is continuous; and emphasising that the health and safety of blood donors is an important issue.

A WHO report issued at the end of World Blood Donation Week praised the UAE and China for their exemplary blood donation services: the two countries boast a 100 per cent disease-free blood donation scheme.

The government set up the national blood transfusion programme in 1990 and has worked hard in the meantime to foster a culture that would ensure 100 per cent voluntary and free blood donation. The UAE was the first country in the region to have stopped the importation of blood in 1984 following the discovery of HIV/AIDS and other contagious viruses.

In July 2008, the Federal Cabinet approved a system for regulating blood transfusion throughout the Emirates. The mechanism, which was developed by the MoH, made it mandatory for all government and private health facilities at federal and local level to implement strict rules and regulations so as to ensure high standards of safety for patients in need of blood.

COUNTERFEIT MEDICINES

A new national centre for control and monitoring of counterfeit medicines is being set up in Dubai under the authority of the MoH's Pharmaceutical Control Department. The body will be made up of representatives of health, customs and other relevant authorities. As part of the project a common registry for medicines will be created in order to unify the process. A central committee has commenced devising benchmarks and standards required to set up the centre. The centre's mandate includes raising awareness among the public about the proper use of medicines under drug control regulations and the project demands constructive cooperation between federal and local agencies to ensure its success.

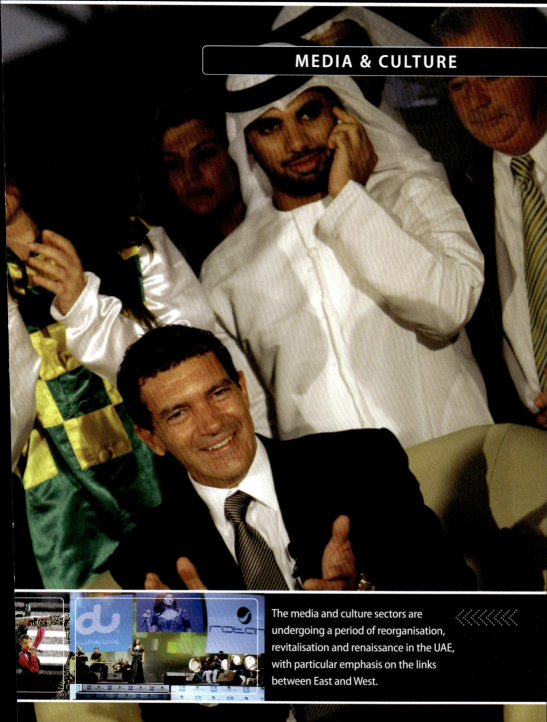

The media and culture sectors are undergoing a period of reorganisation, revitalisation and renaissance in the UAE, with particular emphasis on the links between East and West.

MEDIA & CULTURE

THE MEDIA AND CULTURE SECTORS ARE UNDERGOING a period of reorganisation, revitalisation and renaissance in the UAE, with particular emphasis on investment in world-class resources, introducing international best practices into all areas of activity, stimulating and encouraging local participation, and at the same time forging bridges between East and West. In particular, the Abu Dhabi 2030 vision seeks to establish the emirate as a regional centre for culture with a global capital city as its hub.

The Abu Dhabi 2030 vision seeks to establish the emirate as a regional centre for culture with a global capital city as its hub.

NMC

Following a period of government restructuring in 2006, the National Media Council (NMC) was established to oversee media development in the UAE and to support media initiatives. All jurisdictions and responsibilities concerning media affairs that previously fell under the dissolved Ministry of Information and Culture were transferred to the NMC. In particular, the core media bodies of the old ministry, in the form of the Press and Publications Department, the External Information Department and the Emirates News Agency (WAM), are now under the authority of the NMC.

One of the NMC's primary tasks is to issue media licences, including the licensing of media personnel and companies and the publication of newspapers, magazines, periodicals and books in free zones. The NMC has the power to cancel or suspend media licences if the holders are in violation of attached conditions.

Labour Minister Saqr Ghobash is Chairman of the NMC, which is governed by an executive committee and a dedicated board of directors. The organisational structure of the NMC was re-examined in 2008, leading to the redefinition of its three main sections: media activities; the news agency and the external information department; and institutional services and support units. In addition, Michael Garin, a highly respected media industry executive for nearly 40 years, CEO of Central European Media Enterprises (NASDAQ: CETV), was appointed to the board of the NMC in 2008 to assist the board in meeting the challenges ahead.

EMIRATES NEWS AGENCY

Emirates News Agency (WAM or *Wakalat Anba'a al-Emarat*) began operations in 1976. Since mid-2006 it has been under the authority of the National Media Council. The agency transmits news on national, regional and Arab affairs and is a widely respected source for international media. WAM is a member of the Group of Arab Gulf Cooperation Council news agencies, the Federation of Arab News Agencies (FANA), the Islamic News Agencies Union, the Pool of Non-Aligned News Agencies and the Organisation of Asia-Pacific News Agencies (OANA). Its headquarters is in the UAE capital, Abu Dhabi, with other offices in Dubai, Sharjah, Ajman, Umm al-Qaiwain, Ra's al-Khaimah, Fujairah, Al Ain and Madinat Zayed.

WAM maintains a team of around 25 reporters outside the UAE, with offices in the Arab cities of Cairo, Beirut, Rabat, Riyadh, Damascus, Sanaa, Algiers, Jerusalem, Gaza, Khartoum, Amman, Baghdad and Tunis. Other offices and reporters are located in London, Paris, Brussels, Geneva, Moscow, Washington, New York, Tehran, Islamabad, New Delhi, Istanbul and Canberra. The agency also operates a website (www.wam.ae) with services in both Arabic and English.

Since it was established, WAM has kept abreast of changes in technology and now distributes its news and picture services by satellite and internet, both locally and internationally. Over 90 per cent of its photographs are available in digital format, which has helped both to improve efficiency and to cut costs.

WAM provides daily news coverage of official and other events throughout the UAE and is one of the key sources of information for all media establishments in the country.

WAM provides daily news coverage of official and other events throughout the UAE and is one of the key sources of information for all media establishments in the country. It provides coverage of around 85 to 90 per cent of official activities at home and abroad. In addition, WAM plays an important role in documenting development in the UAE, and in providing information to researchers and others.

WAM receives the transmissions of 30 Arab, Gulf and international news agencies and has cooperation and news exchange agreements with 20 Arab, Asian and international news agencies, part of an effort to strengthen collaboration between the media of the UAE and other countries.

Meanwhile, WAM, via a central news portal run by IPS, relays daily news in English, Spanish, French, Portuguese and Swahili languages to over 1000 newspapers and 2000 broadcast stations worldwide. The current figures show that over 6000 media institutions from 97

countries subscribe to WAM, an achievement made possible by the news exchange cooperation agreement between WAM and Inter Press Service (IPS). The IPS news portal can be accessed on www.ipsnews.net, while WAM's daily English news as well as selected news service in Spanish, Portuguese, Swahili and Japanese languages are relayed over the internet.

WAM organises regular training workshops as part of a long-term strategy for building the professional capacities of its editors and those working for other media outlets.

UAEINTERACT

UAE Interact (www.uaeinteract.com), supported by the National Media Council, has been in continuous operation for 13 years and was one of the first Internet sites to carry daily news stories on the UAE. All items posted to the website are categorised by subject area and archived, with the result that the site contains a substantial database of searchable articles on the UAE going back as far as 1997. The site presents news and information in eleven languages, Arabic, English, Russian, Japanese, Mandarin Chinese, Korean, Spanish, French, German, Italian and Portuguese. All sections are updated

Chairman of the UAE Journalists' Union, Mohammed Yussef, receives the Arab Media Creativity Award from Prime Minister of Kuwait Sheikh Nasser Al Mohammed Al Sabah (left) and Secretary General of the Arab Media Forum Mahdi Al Khamis (centre).

regularly and they contain a wide range of comprehensive information on the country, together with popular films and other downloadable resources such as digital files of the UAE *Yearbook*. UAE Interact is consistently listed by Google as one of the top websites on the UAE.

ABU DHABI MEDIA COMPANY

Abu Dhabi Media Company (ADMC), set up in June 2007 to revitalise the media industry in the UAE's capital, has already established itself as a leading multi-platform media and entertainment provider in the MENA area. ADMC was created as a public joint stock company from the assets of Emirates Media Incorporated. It employs 1100 people across its operating units, which include, television, radio, publishing, digital media, distribution, and printing.

> ADMC has negotiated a series of investment initiatives with Hollywood giants that are destined to establish its position as a global media company, at the same time nurturing and promoting indigenous media.

ADMC owns and operates Abu Dhabi TV, Abu Dhabi Sports Channel, Emirates TV, Abu Dhabi Radio, Emarat FM Radio, Holy Quran Radio, and Sawt Al Musiqa; *Al Ittihad, The National* and *Al Mal* newspapers; *Zahrat Al Khaleej, Al Super* and *Majid* magazines, as well as other businesses, including United Printing Press.

As outlined in Economic Development, ADMC has also fostered a series of investment initiatives with Hollywood giants that are destined to establish its position as a global media company, at the same time nurturing and promoting indigenous media. These include the creation of two film funds with Warner Brothers and the formation of the film financing subsidiary, imagenation abu dhabi, that plans to spend more than US$1 billion (Dh3.67 billion) developing, financing and producing as many as 40 feature films over the next five years (see below). ADMC has also formed a joint venture with Arvato Middle East Sales, a subsidiary of Bertelsmann, the German-based media company, to create the digital media brand Getmo.

CEO Edward Borgerding, former Executive Vice President of Walt Disney International, was hired in March 2008 to head the newly re-branded ADMC.

PRINT MEDIA

The UAE is the regional centre of the print, publishing and advertising industries, with a growth rate of 15 to 20 per cent expected year-on-year.

ADMC launched two newspapers in 2008: a quality daily broadsheet *The National* published its first issue on 20 April 2008, whilst *Al Mal,*

The entertainment industry is thriving in the UAE, with poetry, dance and music extravaganzas staged throughout the country but especially in Abu Dhabi and Dubai.

WORLD EXPOS

The UAE's participation at Expo 2008, held in Zaragoza, Spain, was crowned by winning the organisers' gold medal for content and design. Seen by almost a million visitors the UAE exhibition was created around a series of films that revealed the story of the UAE's rapid development and its efforts to solve issues of water supply in one of the driest places on earth! In a shift away from more traditional approaches to displaying the country, the story-driven 2008 exhibition on the UAE, adhering to the 'Water and Sustainability' Expo theme, highlighted the UAE's modern approach to solving developmental challenges such as water supply and sustainable energy. In a speech accepting the gold award on behalf of the UAE Government, Minister of Labour, Saqr Ghobash, dedicated the accolade to the UAE's President, Sheikh Khalifa bin Zayed Al Nahyan, and reaffirmed the UAE's commitment to maintaining its participation in World Expositions.

'A pavilion like no other', is how the imaginative and appealing structure for the United Arab Emirates' pavilion was described by Saqr Ghobash at the official launch of the country's participation at Expo 2010 – the largest ever World Exposition event, scheduled to open on 1 May 2010 in Shanghai. Inspired by one of the country's most evocative natural landscapes, the precipitous sand-dunes of the UAE's legendary deserts, the building is a triumph of form and function, harmonising nature and architecture to create a fascinating structure that commands attention and reminds visitors of the Expo 2010 theme: 'Better City, Better Life'.

Designed by Foster + Partners, one of the world's leading architectural teams, the building will be the first ever truly recyclable Expo pavilion. Following completion of Expo the building will be dismantled and moved to a more permanent location, thus gaining maximum value from the extensive planning, design and construction that is involved in Expo participation.

The building's strong appeal lies not just in its unusual organic form but also in the reflective nature of its outer covering, helping to recreate the changing patterns and colours of the UAE's natural and urban environments. Diffused light penetrates the building during the day and spectacularly illuminates the pavilion by night. Also in keeping with the theme of Expo 2010, the building will demonstrate a number of innovative environmental strategies, including the UAE's ambitious sustainable agenda programme. The unique pavilion is considered as a beacon for such principles, its high-tech form an expression of the passive environmental measures it employs.

Shaped by the wind, a natural dune appears rough on the side that bears the full force of the wind, and smooth on the surface that collects the sand after it has been tipped over the ridge. The design seeks to replicate this, deflecting the Shanghai winds and protecting the smooth, leeward side. The curve of the dune responds to the arc of the sun and is orientated towards the north, with the solid shell forms protecting against the direct glare from the south and allowing indirect light to enter the habitable areas via a complex series of louvres.

The slopes rise to 20 metres in height to enclose the exhibition spaces within and arched entrances protected by canopies shelter visitors as they queue to enter the building. The outer finish is rosy gold-coloured stainless steel designed to shimmer in the changing light.

The UAE pavilion is located in the eastern section of the Expo site, south of the river and within easy reach of the Chinese pavilion on the opposite side of the main thoroughfare. It is approached via an entrance along the south ring road, across the elevated Expo walkway and is oriented to address a public square in the north-east corner of the site.

Situated on largest plot size (6000 square metres) available to Expo participants, 'The Dunes', as the building has become known, has a footprint of 3452 square metres and encloses a total of approximately 3900 square metres of exhibition space, information areas, and other facilities.

The overall installation is a celebration of city living in the UAE – the swiftness with which the nation has built modern cities and, with the resources that they are investing in sustainable technology, their global leadership in helping us all to live better in the cities of tomorrow.

Visitors will approach The Dunes by a walkway, which follows a stream of water towards the entrance. Proverbs and quotations along the route will gradually immerse people into the ideas and themes of the exhibition. Entering the pavilion, visitors will be presented with a short film, taking them from the birth of the UAE to today. Next they will enter a large space where reactive technology and AV is used to present the daily lives of an Emirati family. From there, moving into a large, darkened theatre space, visitors will be taken on a simulated 'dream journey' to the UAE, showcasing its many magnificent attractions.

The final area of the pavilion provides visitors with a wide range of information on the country. After leaving the building they will find comfortable, shaded seating where they can relax and contemplate.

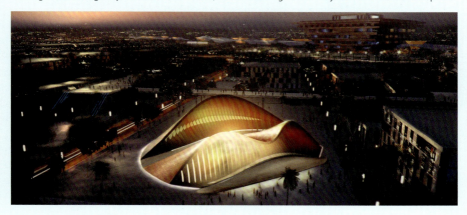

Advertising spending in the UAE increased by 47 per cent in the first half of the year from US$655 million (Dh2.41 billion) in 2007 to Dh3.41 billion (US$929 million) in the first six months of 2008, according to statistics compiled by the Pan Arab Research Centre.

the UAE's first Arabic language weekly financial newspaper, was launched on 23 June.

ADMC appointed former London *Daily Telegraph* editor Martin Newland to head *The National*. Newland has hired 175 journalists, including 40 home news reporters and 25 foreign correspondents to ensure that the paper meets international standards.

The 48-page tabloid *Al Mal* focuses on business and financial developments in the Gulf region, with particular emphasis on the UAE, filling a niche for comprehensive financial analysis.

Two of the oldest papers in the country, *Gulf News* and *Khaleej Times*, celebrated their thirtieth anniversaries in 2008. Following the launch of the country's first tabloid *7Days*, three years ago, there has been an upsurge in new newspapers. *7Days* was followed by *Xpress and Emirates Today* – now reborn as *Emirates Business*. One of the driving forces behind this development is that the UAE's newspapers are taking the major share of print media advertising. Ad-spend in the UAE has increased from Dh3.19 billion (US$869 million) in 2005 to Dh4.77 billion (US$1.3 billion) in 2007 – the highest in the Middle East, according to the 2007 Advertising Spend Report issued by the Pan-Arab Research Centre. Of this, around two thirds went to Arabic and English-language newspapers. Market analysts estimate that the UAE's print advertising expenditure will rise to Dh8.8 billion (US$2.4 billion) in 2009.

Dubai Press Club

Despite the upsurge in print media, there is a general awareness that journalism in the region requires assistance to develop. Dubai Press Club is one of the organisations that have been established to help local journalists, male and female, hone their skills. Since 1999, the club has sought to establish itself as a centre of journalistic excellence and a meeting-place for local, regional and international media. The club is now a well-established forum for journalists and media professionals to debate, discuss and deliberate upon issues of relevance to daily life.

Dubai Press Club has also endeavoured to play a vital role in the growth of the regional media industry through the launch of unique initiatives such as the Arab Media Forum and Arab Journalism Awards.

The seventh Arab Media Forum, which was held from 23 to 24 of April 2008, provided a platform for two days of intensive deliberations on the impact of new technologies on the media. It brought together over 600 local, regional and international media and 50 industry experts under the theme 'Bridging Arab Media Through Technology'.

The Arab Journalism Awards were presented by HH Sheikh Mohammed bin Rashid Al Maktoum, Vice President and Prime Minister of the UAE and Ruler of Dubai, at the closing ceremony of the forum. Comprising 12 different categories and special honours, the prestigious awards recognised excellence in Arab journalism. Makram Mohammed Ahmad received the 'Media Personality of the Year' award for 2008 and special awards were presented to the relatives of deceased Iraqi journalists, Shihab Al Tamimi and Ahmad Al Rabei.

In September 2008, Dubai Press Club in association with the UAE Journalists Union celebrated the first anniversary of a decree issued on 25 September 2007 by Sheikh Mohammed bin Rashid Al Maktoum prohibiting the imprisonment of journalists for media-related offences. The decree, which ended the criminalisation of press offences, greatly enhanced freedom of the press in the region, encouraging open and independent journalism and was praised locally and internationally, particularly by the Arab Journalists Union and the International Federation of Journalists.

This prohibition on the imprisonment of journalists is also contained in the new federal Media Law, which is a revision of the 1980 federal Press and Publications Law. The new law, due to be gazetted in early 2009, also states that there shall not be prior censorship of any media outlets in the country, recognising that a free press is a basic building block of a free society.

A prohibition on the imprisonment of journalists for media-related offences is reiterated in the new federal Media Law, which is due to be gazetted in early 2009.

MEDIA ZONES

The year 2008 saw the launch of a new 'Arab-centric' media free zone in Abu Dhabi, another milestone in pursuit of Abu Dhabi emirate's strategy to become a creative hub for the media, as well as for arts and culture. Set up by the Abu Dhabi Media Free Zone Authority, twofour54 (geographical coordinates of Abu Dhabi) was launched on 12 October 2008 with the aim of becoming a centre of excellence for Arabic content creation. A temporary campus for the media park is located near Khalifa Park. A permanent 200,000 square metre media park containing production studios and post production suites, as well as transmission services for local regional and international film,

Twofour54, Abu Dhabi's new 'Arab-centric' media free zone, was launched in October 2008 with the aim of becoming a centre of excellence for Arabic content creation.

Characters from the popular UAE cartoon Freej.

broadcasting, digital publishing and music industries, will be constructed by 2013 in the Mina Zayed area.

Dubai's Tecom Business Parks brings under its ambit media-related clusters such as Dubai Internet City, Dubai Media City, Dubai Studio City and International Media Production Zone

The first media cluster, Dubai Internet City (DIC), opened in October 2000 and has consistently recorded higher year-on-year performance, registering a growth rate of 33 per cent in 2007. DIC was quickly followed by Dubai Media City, a dedicated media centre boasting the largest media community in the region. DMC grew by 40 per cent in 2007. Dubai Studio City, which facilitates all aspects of film, TV and radio production, also strives to participate in initiatives that help strengthen the film industry in Dubai. Its relationship with Manhattan Film Academy has brought world-class industry experts to the emirate, to the benefit of the young UAE film-making community.

Fujairah Creative City, a media free zone that was established in 2007 under the auspices of the Fujairah Culture and Media Authority, will be completed in 2009 with the cost of the first phase running to Dh201.85 million (US$55 million). Dunya Fujairah TV was the first channel to start operations from the city, which also has a network of FM radio stations targeting foreign communities in the UAE. Twenty-four new satellite TV channels went on air from Creative City at the end of 2007 and the beginning of 2008, raising the total number of operating channels from the city to 37. The 4000 square metre Creative City will have seven zones for radio, TV, press, technology, a media-training academy, theatre and cinema.

All UAE media free zones are subject to UAE media-licensing regulations as operated by the NMC and all media activities in free zones must comply with relevant UAE laws and regulations.

Ibda'a Awards

Ibda'a Media Student Awards were initiated by Dubai Media City in association with the International Advertising Association in 2001 to encourage creativity and excellence in media studies regionally and globally. Prizes include internships with global media companies. The 2007 edition of Ibda'a attracted over 2200 entries from more than 21 countries, including Egypt, India, Iran, Lebanon, Pakistan, the Philippines, the UK and UAE.

In recognition of the changing face of technology, the seventh Ibda'a Media Student Awards on 29 November 2008 featured the introduction of a new 'mobile film' category, honouring the best short film captured through a mobile phone. Other award categories include journalism (non-news), radio, animation, graphic arts, analogue photography, digital photography, print advertising, TV advertising, film/TV feature, TV documentary and mobile film (www.ibdaa-awards.ae).

TELEVISION

Abu Dhabi TV, the broadcasting branch of ADMC, launched a new channel 'Plus One' in 2008. New programmes were also commissioned for Abu Dhabi Sports Channel and Emirates TV, including a new reality contest, 'Ton of Cash'. Billed as the largest scale reality TV show in the Arab world, 'Ton of Cash' was shot on location in the UAE and Oman over 60 days.

Qatari poet Khalil Al Shebrami Al Tamimi (centre), winner of Dh1 million in the 'Millions Poet' TV contest with UAE Foreign Minister Sheikh Abdullah bin Zayed Al Nahayan and Sheikh Ahmed bin Mohammed bin Rashid Al Maktoum.

Homegrown TV production firms are gearing up to face the challenge from abroad and are in fact producing some of the most successful programmes in the region. For example, 'Prince of Poets' has become one of the most watched TV shows in the Arab world.

'Prince of Poets' was developed in association with the Abu Dhabi Authority for Culture and Heritage (ADACH) to take classical poetry to the masses. The same production company is also behind 'Millions Poet', a live pan-Arab poetry contest. Both programmes tap into the popularity of poetry in the region and prove that a blend of heritage and modern technology can be extremely successful.

'Millions Poet' was one of the programmes that won three gold and two silver medals for the UAE at the tenth Gulf Radio and TV Production Festival held in Bahrain. The UAE took part in the festival for the first time in 2008 under the umbrella of the National Media Council. The second gold went to 'Step', a popular talk show, also produced by Abu Dhabi TV, and the third was awarded to 'Vitamin', an awareness programme produced by Dubai TV. A religious programme entitled 'Good Morning' produced by Abu Dhabi Radio and 'Windows of Stones' produced by Sharjah TV won silver medals.

Noor Dubai, a new free-to-air community television channel, commenced broadcasting at the beginning of Ramadan in 2008. The station, owned by Arab Media Group and transmitted through Arabsat and Nilesat, is a logical progression of the popular Noor

Highly successful televised pan-Arab poetry contests tap into the popularity of poetry in the region and prove that a blend of heritage and modern technology can be extremely successful.

Najwa Karam performs at a grand ceremony in Beirut on 1 November 2008 to launch the UAE-based pan-Arab satellite music channel 'Al-Dafrah'.

Radio station. The channel encourages and facilitates positive and constructive discussions on current social, environmental, religious and humanitarian themes that are impacting on the UAE, highlighting both the continuity and change between generations in this rapidly evolving society.

DUBAI CULTURE AND ART AUTHORITY

The Dubai Culture and Arts Authority (DCAA) was launched in 2008 with a mandate to create a rich environment for Emirati heritage, visual arts, theatre, music, literature and poetry. Various initiatives undertaken by the DCAA are outlined below.

ADACH

Abu Dhabi Authority for Culture and Heritage (ADACH), which was established in 2005, is a government organisation with far-sighted aspirations – to harness the pride of the people of the UAE through the development of its cultural heritage, and to be the leading cultural development organisation in the region. Internationally it is contributing to the strengthening of intercultural dialogue by nurturing projects that encourage the sharing of cultural traditions and experience.

ADACH has a holistic vision of culture, which embraces both tangible and intangible heritage. It is committing all its resources to the preservation of architectural and archaeological assets as well as to the development of Emirati and international arts, music, literature and cinema.

ADACH is pursuing a number of initiatives in arts and culture, detailed below, that reflect its vision for the cultural development of Abu Dhabi. It has also taken over existing facilities in Abu Dhabi, including the popular arts and library facilities at the Cultural Foundation, which it intends to develop. Together, the initiatives constitute a programme rich in symbolism and importance to the people of the UAE, and provide a unique representation of what Abu Dhabi has to offer the rest of the world.

ADACH organises a range of cultural exhibitions throughout the year.

FILM

In the wake of global economic upheaval, American and European film executives have turned to the Gulf in search of new sources of film financing. As we saw in the chapter on Economic Development,

the result is that Emirati film-makers are the beneficiaries of an extraordinarily rapid build-up in the infrastructure and funding needed to support a local film industry. The number of films made each year in the UAE is rising continuously. Thus last year there were over 160 shorts produced, and in the last three years, three feature films came to fruition, with others in various stages of production. It seems that this is only the beginning.

In 2008 Participant Media of Los Angeles, the maker of thought-provoking films such as the award-winning environmental film 'An Inconvenient Truth', teamed up with ADMC's imagenation abu dhabi to create a US$250 million (Dh917.5 million) fund to finance 15 to 18 films in the next five years. This fund will facilitate the making of films that not only entertain, but also raise awareness of issues and inspire social change. Participant will take the lead in developing the films, as well as overseeing production and arranging worldwide distribution. The company will establish an office in Abu Dhabi.

Imagenation has also formed an alliance with National Geographic Entertainment, best-known for producing the award-winning 'March of the Penguins', to produce ten to 15 films costing US$100 million over the next five years. Each film will have a budget of between US$5 million and US$60 million. The aim is to make movies 'that focus on people's relationship to the world, their environment and each other.'

Legendary Hollywood actress Jane Fonda receiving a lifetime achievement award at the Middle East International Film Festival in Abu Dhabi.

The Circle

ADACH established The
Circle in 2007, an
initiative devoted to
the production,
financing and
encouragement of
film-making talent in
the Middle East.

In recognition of the significant role films can play in promoting the culture and heritage of the UAE and the region, ADACH established The Circle in 2007. The initiative is devoted to the production, financing and encouragement of film-making talent in the Middle East. ADACH, in association with the world-renowned New York Film Academy, also established a film and acting school in 2008 that is devoted to developing the film industry in the UAE. New York Film Academy – Abu Dhabi will assist ADACH to foster and support regional artistic talent and to create an environment conducive to strong cultural and artistic expression.

Throughout the year, a variety of programmes are organised by The Circle, informing local investors of financing structures, showcasing new artists, improving the skills of Emirati and Middle East film-makers and facilitating production collaborations.

Circle Film Labs, also known as Adasa, is a year-round effort devoted to nurturing and growing the skills of emerging Emirati film-makers. Adasa provides a unique opportunity to preserve Emirati culture by creating local stories that can be filmed and shared with the world.

The Circle hosted a conference parallel to the Middle East International Film Festival (see below) that enabled young film-makers to interact with renowned producers and directors from around the world. In turn, The Circle Conference launched the Shasha Grant – an international US$100,000 screenwriting contest designed to identify, develop and launch the career of an up-and-coming film-maker; and the Cloeween Connection, which will spotlight 15 emerging directors in the region and facilitate collaborations on their next films through the Producers Circle.

Interactive Media Circle included discussion panels and an exhibition focused on the introduction of new media technology. The combination of cutting-edge exhibits and advanced interactive experiences was designed to promote Abu Dhabi as a prime destination for new media production in the Middle East.

MEIFF

In recognition of the role that cinema plays in contemporary culture, ADACH organised the second Middle East International Film Festival (MEIFF), from 10 to 19 October 2008 in Abu Dhabi.

This year prize money for the prestigious Black Pearl Awards was increased to more than US$1 million, giving MEIFF its own unique personality within the film festivals of the world. The awards were the culmination of ten action-packed days of cinema, with 152 movies and 186 screenings shown in five Abu Dhabi venues. A total of 76 feature films and 34 short films from over 35 countries competed for the awards.

In addition to a wide range of acclaimed international feature and documentary films, including several made in the UAE and elsewhere on environmental issues, the organisers ran a special event in partnership with the Paris-based socially conscious Cinema Verité to pay tribute to the Oscar winning actress Jane Fonda.

MEIFF also launched the 'Most' initiative during the festival in conjunction with The Saban Center for Middle Eastern Policy at The Brookings Institute in Washington. 'Most', 'Muslims on Screen and Television', will become a cultural resource providing valuable information about Islam and Muslims for the US entertainment community. Its aim is to meet the critical need for increased understanding and accurate representation on both sides.

In addition MEIFF hosted the Arab Film Industry Research Circle covering the current situation of Arab cinema in the Levant, Egypt, the Gulf and North Africa, and ran a symposium on women in the entertainment industry.

The second Middle East International Film Festival provided ten action-packed days of high-quality cinema at a number of venues throughout Abu Dhabi, including the spectacular Emirates Palace Hotel.

DIFF

The fifth edition of the popular Dubai International Film Festival (DIFF) was held from 11 to 18 December 2008, building on 2007 when the festival experienced record-breaking figures in industry and press registration, audience attendance and films from around the world. DIFF continues to deliver innovative and universally important programming, in line with the festival's mandate to foster intercultural dialogue. New to DIFF in 2008, animation was included as a special category in the 'Out of Competition' offerings. 'Cultural Bridge, Meeting Minds', 'Celebration of Indian Cinema' and 'Cinema for Children' and 'Rhythm and Reels' continued in their roles to showcase the best in international cinema. 'The Day After Peace' was chosen to head the 'Rhythm and Reels' line-up for 2008 and the screening was followed by performances from local and international artists, uniting around the most fundamental issue that humanity faces.

Emirati director Abdullah
Hassan Ahmed, winner of the
best short film at the
Gulf Film Festival.

In addition, the Dubai Film Market provides a platform to trade film content locally, in line with the festival's commitment to stimulate regional and international film production and trade.

Other Film Festivals

In April 2008, Dubai hosted the inaugural Gulf Film Festival (GFF) dedicated to films produced in the region. 'When The People Spoke', a film about the face-off between moderates and fundamentalists over women's rights won the best documentary prize at GFF, whilst Iraqi film-maker Mohammad al-Daradji's debut feature *Ahlaam (Dreams)* won the top prize.

Under the patronage of the DCAA, supported by AMG and DIFF, and hosted by Dubai Knowledge Village, 'Documentary Voices: Pulling Focus', the region's first-ever film festival focusing exclusively on documentaries premiered in Dubai in July 2008.

About 20 thought-provoking documentary films depicting various themes, including music, politics, war, peace, and faith, were screened and critically reviewed during the event. The documentaries were top-quality productions sourced from Arab countries, the US and Iran. DCAA recognises that documentaries have created some of the most compelling perspectives of life and society in today's world and see the festival as an opportunity to raise the profile of documentary film-making in the UAE.

Arts Grants

Organisations such as the Emirates Foundation are also fostering indigenous artistic talent. This year, 25 Emirati writers and artists were awarded grants under the Emirates Foundation arts grants programme for visual arts, theatre, music, literature and film. The recipients in the latest round of awards include film-makers, writers and poets.

An Emirates Foundation-funded production, 'Bint Mariam', was awarded second prize at GFF and second place in the short film category at the Arab Film Festival in Rotterdam. 'Bint Mariam' ('Mariam's Daughter'), which was filmed in 2008 in Ra's al-Khaimah, is directed by local film-maker Saeed Salmeen Al Murry.

BOOKS

The number of books published in Arabic, both original works and translations, is far less than in other regions and languages.

Translation, in particular, has been identified as a way to enhance knowledge transfer to the Arab world. At the same time translation is seen as a key tool to foster intercultural dialogue.

'Kalima' is a major initiative launched by ADACH that funds the translation, printing and distribution of foreign literature into Arabic. Every year, Kalima selects 100 renowned titles of classic, contemporary and modern writing from around the globe and translates them into Arabic for widespread distribution throughout the Arab world.

The Mohammed bin Rashid Al Maktoum Foundation through its 'Tarjem' programme, which was launched in February 2008, is pursuing an ambitious target of translating more than 1000 books in three years, to stimulate high quality translation of the world's bestsellers from various languages into Arabic. Topics range from business administration and environment to literature, including Nobel Prize winner Doris Lessing's *Memories of a Survivor* and former US Vice-President Al Gore's *An Inconvenient Truth*.

'Kalima' is a major translation initiative launched by ADACH that funds the translation, printing and distribution of foreign literature into Arabic.

The foundation is also publishing the world's first comprehensive *Arabic Narrative Encyclopaedia*, exploring, analysing and documenting the Arabic literary genre.

Abu Dhabi International Book Fair

The Abu Dhabi International Book Fair is probably the Middle East's fastest growing book fair. Held from 11 to 16 March in 2008, 482 exhibitors from 42 countries attended the eighteenth fair, a 25 per cent growth in space, with around 600,000 titles from 400 global publishers on display. The addition of new venues for events and a large range of services to exhibitors, visitors and the press at the state-of the art Abu Dhabi National Exhibition Centre, in addition to a strict adherence to copyright standards, ensured that the fair achieved a high level of professionalism. The fair is organised by Kitab, a joint venture between ADACH and the Frankfurt Book Fair.

Sheikh Zayed Book Awards

The Sheikh Zayed Book Awards recognise significant contributions to Arabic culture in nine diverse categories and are designed to help foster scholarship and creative development in Arabic culture. Former Moroccan Minister and Ambassador to the United States, Mohammed

Benaissa was named 'Cultural Personality of the Year' at the 2008 Sheikh Zayed Book Award for his unique contribution to Arabic culture, walking away with a prize of Dh1 million (US$272,000). Winners in six other categories were also celebrated for their achievements in fostering cultural development in the Arab World, each receiving Dh750,000.

The Sheikh Zayed Book Awards secretariat also organises seminars in Europe and elsewhere to spread awareness about the award and to encourage translation of literature, at the same time building connections between Arab and other cultures. For more information click on www.zayedaward.com.

The aim of the Sheikh Zayed Book Awards, which were established in October 2006 in memory of the late Sheikh Zayed bin Sultan Al Nahyan, is to foster scholarship and creativity, creating an environment to celebrate achievements in Arab culture and to showcase contributions to international literature and the arts.

ECSSR

The ECSSR, founded in 1994 in Abu Dhabi, is an independent institution dedicated to the promotion of academic research and empirical enquiry. ECSSR serves as a focal point for scholarship on political, strategic, military, environmental, economic and social issues pertinent to the UAE, the Gulf and the greater Middle East through the sponsorship of research and studies conducted by scholars from around the globe.

The core of its work lies in identifying and analysing issues of vital significance, predicting future trends and devising management strategies to cope with such issues. As well as maintaining and training its own staff of researchers, it hosts conferences, symposia, workshops and lecture series renowned for the eminence of the participants and the quality of their content and influence.

The ECSSR's publishing activities have made it a major source of specialised scholarly publications in the region. As well as publishing monographs in its *International Studies Series*, it also publishes the proceedings of conferences, symposia and lectures in *Emirates Occasional Papers* (an English series) and *Strategic Studies* (an Arabic series) In addition to these and other publications, ECSSR translates into Arabic works of importance to the centre and its audience, both regionally and globally.

Publications during 2008 include the following: two books, *Arabian Gulf Security, Internal and External Challenges; China, India and the United States: Competition for Energy Resources,* edited by ECSSR; '*Indo-Iranian Relations and the Arab Prism*' by P. R. Kumaraswamy in the *Emirates Occasional Papers* series; *From Militants to Politicians: Atavist*

Islam and the Concept of Democratic Peace by James Wylie in *Emirates Lecture Series*; *Two Visions of US Foreign Policy: Republican and Democrat* by Rudolph W. Giuliani, John Edwards in *International Studies*; *The Experience of the UAE in Studying Public Opinion* by Ahmad Mahmoud Al Astal in *Strategic Studies*; and *Iran's Potential to Develop Nuclear Weapons Technology and Materials* by John Large in *Emirates Lecture Series* – Arabic. Log on to www.ecssr.ac.ae for more information.

MUSIC

ADACH is committed to presenting the finest performing arts from around the world to the broadest possible audience and music features strongly in these plans.

Abu Dhabi Music and Arts Festival has brought major classical concerts to Abu Dhabi each spring and the Al Ain Festival, which is held under the patronage of Foreign Minister HH Sheikh Abdullah bin Zayed Al Nahyan, has continued to delight music lovers for the past eight years. The Al Ain Classical Music Festival 2008 was expanded from its traditional three-day event into an 11-day celebration, taking in productions in both Al Ain and Abu Dhabi.

Al Ain staged the region's first Arabic performance of Mozart's celebrated opera *Don Giovanni* in 2008, combining the libretto, music and theatre talents of both Europe and the Middle East. This was a universal production, produced in cooperation with Milan's celebrated Accademia Teatro alla Scala, a theme reflected in the cosmopolitan mix of the attending audience.

In 2008 another initiative by ADACH added a new dimension to the music scene. Abu Dhabi Classics, a blend of classic, symphony, jazz and ethnic music, will run from 24 October 2008 to 7 May 2009. Music lovers are being given the opportunity to celebrate weekly live concerts of some of the world's most gifted musicians who represent the best that the contemporary performing arts scene has to offer. The selection is based not only on international recognition, but also on the basis that the artists in question have chosen to specialise in an integration of music styles, a fusion of sounds, instruments and influences. Apart from great music performed by world-renowned artists and orchestras from all parts of the world, Abu Dhabi Classics is also focusing on music education, especially in the form of workshops for school children.

World music is a central feature of Abu Dhabi Classics.

In Dubai, the Dubai Event Management Corporation's partnership with New York's Metropolitan Opera will bring to Dubai the Met's innovative series of live opera transmission filmed in HD and presented with multi-channel, surround-sound audio. Dubai joins a network of 28 countries and 850 movie theatres and performing arts centres staging some of the critically acclaimed series of live high-definition performances.

THEATRE

The curtain rose on 10 August 2008 on the Dubai Festival for Youth Theatre, an event that seeks to celebrate young theatre talent in the UAE. Over ten days, the festival, organised under the auspices of the DCAA at the premises of the Cultural and Scientific Association, provided a rare treat for theatre lovers, presenting a new play in Arabic every night. The plays, featuring local and regional themes, were written and directed by some of the well-known names in the region. The organisers of the Youth Theatre Festival hope that such initiatives will provide an opportunity for young nationals to develop their skills and talent and to possibly identify theatre as a career opportunity.

ART

Artparis Abu Dhabi, organised in partnership with ADACH and TDIC at Emirates Palace Hotel, is widely recognised as the region's leading modern and contemporary art fair. Notable works exhibited included pieces from Alexander Calder, Andy Warhol, Damien Hirst, Henri Matisse, Pablo Picasso and Paul Cezanne.

Supported by ADACH, ArtParis Abu Dhabi returned to Abu Dhabi from 18 to 21 November 2008, reasserting the capital's position as meeting point for contemporary art in the region. Both the first successful ArtParis Abu Dhabi in 2007 and the 2008 exhibition placed an emphasis on promoting Arab artists, young talent and contemporary art. A total of 700 artists, representing 22 countries participated in ArtParis Abu Dhabi, with 58 galleries exhibiting, including 14 specialising in the Arab world.

Earlier in the year, Artscape, a new series of informal, cultural events was launched in Abu Dhabi with the first Artscape Picasso held on 28 August 2008 at the Cultural Foundation. English and Arabic speakers enjoyed an evening celebrating the work of Pablo Picasso and modern art-related themes in an informal manner through a multi-art form programme, including films, live music, literature, a live painting studio, art-related games, and an arts lounge.

Artparis Abu Dhabi and the Artscape series are organised by Tourism Development and Investment Company (TDIC), and supported by ADACH. TDIC's public programme is laying the groundwork for the opening of the Cultural District on Saadiyat Island.

TDIC's extensive cultural programme is laying the groundwork for the opening of the Cultural District on Saadiyat Island.

Art Dubai

The 2008 edition of the DIFC-sponsored Art Dubai took place from 19 to 22 March with 37 international and regional galleries exhibiting. As well as its commercial aspect, Art Dubai endeavours to provide a range of educational opportunities. The new three-day discussion platform, DIFC Global Art Forum, also brought an international group of over 40 artists, curators, dealers, museum directors, critics and academics together for three days to focus on issues affecting art and the arts community, with the Middle East as a primary focus.

DIFC's 'Season of Arts', a celebration of all forms of artistic disciplines, from visual to performing and musical to interactive expression, also took place in March 2008. The 16-day event, which coincided with Art Dubai, brought together a selection of diverse up-and-coming and renowned Middle Eastern and Western artists, film-makers, musicians, and dancers. The eclectic line-up of events included contemporary art exhibitions, large-scale, interactive installations, film screenings and live musical performances. DIFC also hosts a series of on-going exhibitions that run independently throughout the year.

Dubai International Financial Centre's 'Season of Arts' is a celebration of all forms of artistic disciplines, from visual to performing and musical to interactive expression.

MUSEUMS

The UAE has a wide array of museums, both traditional and modern. Building on this cultural heritage, Abu Dhabi is investing heavily in cultural development. Nowhere is this more evident than on Saadiyat Island, which, as we have already seen, TDIC is transforming into an international cultural, leisure and residential destination. Saadiyat

Island's Cultural District will house the largest single cluster of world-class cultural assets. These include the Louvre Abu Dhabi, designed by Jean Nouvel; the Sheikh Zayed National Museum to be designed by the UK's Foster + Partners under the direction of Lord Norman Foster; the Guggenheim Abu Dhabi contemporary arts museum, the world's largest Guggenheim and the only one in the Middle East, which has been conceptualised by Frank Gehry; a performing arts centre designed by Zaha Hadid, a maritime museum with concept design by Tadao Ando and a number of arts pavilions.

A major new museum for the UAE Armed Forces is also being planned, which will trace the history of weapons and warfare in the region since prehistoric times.

The first of the institutions, the Sheikh Zayed National Museum, the Guggenheim Abu Dhabi Museum and the Louvre Abu Dhabi are scheduled to open between 2012 and 2014. Bruno Maquart, former Director of Centre Pompidou, is the Executive Director of the French Museums Agency, which is steering development of the Louvre Abu Dhabi. Under a 30-year operating agreement, Abu Dhabi will pay EUR400 million for the Louvre brand name and for hundreds of artworks loaned from the Paris museums for periods of between six months and two years. The agreement also covers a multitude of operational issues, including individual proposals to theme the Louvre Abu Dhabi's exhibition halls and guidelines for exhibitions to be mounted in the museum.

The deal is part of a broader EUR1 billion cooperation agreement with the French Museums Agency that will see artworks travel from Paris to the Gulf when the branch opens in 2012. Exhibits will come from the Louvre and other Paris museums, including the Musée d'Orsay and the Centre Pompidou. The intention is to not just to focus on Western art, but to establish a dialogue between West and East, between North and South.

Concept designs for all the Cultural District assets are currently on show in a fascinating exhibition that is open daily to the public in Abu Dhabi's Emirates Palace Hotel.

Sheikh Sultan bin Tahnoun Al Nahyan, Chairman of the ADTA, Bruno Macquart, Director of Agence France-Museums, and French Culture Minister Christine Albanel. The French Minister was on an official visit to the UAE to attend the signing of an agreement between Agence France-Museums and the ADTA.

Khor Dubai Project

The Khor Dubai Project, which was launched in March 2008 under the umbrella of DCAA, will see construction of libraries, theatres, art galleries, cultural institutes, an opera house and more than ten thematic museums at sites throughout Dubai. The project will include the world's first museum devoted to the Prophet Mohammed. The joint public-private sector project will celebrate Dubai's cultural diversity and showcase the emirate's rich past, dynamic present and promising future.

Dubai's first Museum of Middle East Modern Art was announced in June 2008. Dubai Properties Group (a member of Dubai Holding) is the developer of the new museum, which has been designed by world-renowned architects, UN Studio, and of Dubai's Culture Village. The latter will be located on 3.716 million square metres of land in the historic district of Al-Jadaf. In addition to the Museum of Middle East Modern Art, the Dh50 billion (US$13.6 billion) project will include an amphitheatre for live performances and international cultural festivals, an exhibition hall and smaller museums displaying local and international art, as well as a shipyard for traditional dhow builders. It will also include residential, commercial and retail zones.

Historic Buildings

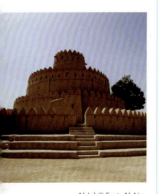

Al Jahili Fort, Al Ain.

ADACH has renewed its efforts to preserve and restore historic buildings in Al Ain City, a major cultural and tourist destination in the UAE. The projects include the restoration of Al Jahili Fort, which dates back to 1898 and is one of the most important historical landmarks in the city, and the House of Hamad bin Hadi Al Darmaki. The Fort will host a new visitor information centre, a temporary exhibition gallery, a permanent exhibition on the explorer, Mubarak bin London (Sir Wilfred Thesiger), and a walk-through audio-visual installation on the history and development of Al Ain.

Spearheaded by ADACH, Abu Dhabi's oldest building is set to become a cultural heart for the country. Following a multi-million dirham makeover, Qasr Al Hosn, also known as the White Fort, will become a repository and museum, as well as a symbol of the nation.

Dubai's Architectural Heritage Department, which now falls under the auspices of the DCAA, is responsible for preserving and maintaining historic buildings and cultural centres in the emirate, including the heritage districts in Bastakiya, Shindagha and Al Ra's where a large number of historic buildings have been successfully restored to their former glory.

Two new museums, one in Nad Al Sheba dedicated to falcons and the other in an historic building in Bastakiya showcasing Islamic coins that were in circulation in the region since the time of the Islamic caliphates, opened in the first half of 2008.

The historical district of Al Shindagha will also be home to the House of Poetry, which is being established by the Mohammed bin Rashid Al Maktoum Foundation to promote classical and contemporary Arabic poetry. It will also facilitate the interaction between Arab poets and their peers from across the globe and further the role of poetry as an effective communications tool in the pursuit of intercultural dialogue. A top priority will be to promote, research and document Nabati poetry, an indigenous form of verse unique to the Gulf region. The House of Poetry will complement the role and mission of Dubai International Poetry Festival.

The restored Al Fahidi Fort in Dubai is now a thriving interactive museum with a wide range of archaeological and ethnographic exhibits. The eighteenth century fort in Ajman, Umm al-Qaiwain Fort, Ra's al-Khaimah Fort and Fujairah Fort have also been lovingly restored and turned into fascinating museums.

Sharjah's renovation and restoration of architecturally acclaimed heritage buildings and an old souk in the Sharjah Arts Area and Sharjah Heritage Area have earned it international acclaim. Many of these fine buildings house art, Islamic and ethnographic museums run by Sharjah Museums Department, including the country's first national art gallery, and one is also home to the Emirates' Fine Art Society.

> A top priority for the new House of Poetry will be to promote, research, and document Nabati poetry, the indigenous form of verse unique to the Gulf region.

Sharjah Museums Department

Sharjah made a number of additions to its already impressive list of museums in 2008: The Sharjah Islamic Museum, depicting Arab and Islamic culture through the centuries, was opened at the beginning of June 2008 with an Islamic Artefacts Exhibition mounted in cooperation with the Berlin Islamic Museum. The new museum houses more than 5000 exquisite Islamic artefacts from all over the Islamic World, arranged according to themes over seven spacious galleries and display areas.

A Classic Cars Club and Museum housing 120 vintage American and European cars owned by HH Dr Sheikh Sultan bin Mohammed Al Qasimi, UAE Supreme Council Member and Ruler of Sharjah, was also opened in 2008. So too, was Sharjah Aquarium, which displays a host of marine species from the smallest clown fish and delicate

Restored heritage buildings are frequently used as museums.

Sharjah has 17 museums, including Sharjah Art Museum & Contemporary Arab Art, which is the largest in the Gulf with both temporary exhibitions and permanent collections by renowned artists.

seahorses to moray eels, rays and reef sharks, enabling visitors to make a journey underwater and discover the smaller marine life found in the rock pools, coral reefs, lagoons and mangroves of the UAE.

Sharjah already has a fine array of natural history centres: Sharjah Natural History and Botanical Museum, which opened in 1995, has since been recently renovated to a very high standard. The Arabian Wildlife Centre is an impressive modern zoo that displays local wildlife in their natural habitats. The nearby Breeding Centre, which is not open to the public, is focusing on the breeding of endangered Arabian species with the hope of re-introducing some of the rarer species into the wild. This is where, for the first time in the UAE, captive breeding of the Arabian leopard was achieved.

ARCHAEOLOGY REVIEW

During the annual archaeology field season in the Emirates, from autumn 2007 to spring 2008, further new light was shed on the country's ancient heritage, now known to stretch back to the Palaeolithic or Early Stone Age period, perhaps over 200,000 years ago. Fieldwork, undertaken by local departments in each emirate as well as by visiting academic teams and consultants led to the identification of many previously unrecorded sites and to the gathering, through excavation and mapping, of more information from known sites. This was supplemented by the results of scientific finds analysis undertaken both locally and at institutions abroad.

Archaeological teams have been active throughout the UAE in the winter season.

New surveys for evidence of occupation from the Palaeolithic period, only proven to exist a few years ago, were carried out by a British team in the northern emirate of Ra's al-Khaimah, in association with the local museum, and identified a number of new sites along the western foothills of the Hajar Mountains. Further work was also undertaken at the sites of Jebel Faiyah, in Sharjah, by a joint German–Sharjah team, and of Jebel Barakah, in western Abu Dhabi, by ADACH. While dating of the sites has yet to be finalised, it is evident from the Jebel Faiyah site that there were several distinct periods of occupation. Still poorly known, the Palaeolithic period in the UAE is likely to be a major focus of attention in future years as archaeologists seek to learn more about the country's oldest inhabitants.

The distribution and nature of sites from the Late Stone Age or Neolithic period, which began in the Emirates around 7500 years ago, is much better known. By this time, the UAE's inhabitants included both nomadic and settled communities, some building extensive stone houses, as on Abu Dhabi's western island of Marawah, while the pearling industry had begun and maritime trade links with Mesopotamia had been established.

The relative sophistication of the Neolithic fishing and pearling industry was the subject of investigations during the last year, at the fifth millennium BC island site of Akab, in Umm al-Qaiwain. Carried out by a French team, the work has shown that the site, first occupied around 4750 BC, was occupied continuously for over 500 years. Its inhabitants had domesticated goats, sheep and dogs, while they also hunted gazelles and wild donkeys. The main focus of the economy, however, was on the exploitation of resources from the nearby lagoon and mangroves, while they also had the skill to build boats capable of fishing in deeper waters. One interesting discovery from the latest work was that the Akab people were probably producing shell beads and fish-hooks not just for their own use but for trading with other communities in the Gulf. Pottery from Ubaid, in Mesopotamia, also indicates the extent of their commercial network.

Although the UAE's Neolithic inhabitants had domestic animals, as shown from finds at Akab and Dalma, for example, they also hunted wild animals, of which the largest was the camel, which was not domesticated until the beginning of the Iron Age.

One major discovery announced during the year was that of a collection of over 60 camel skeletons at a site in Abu Dhabi's western deserts. Although first identified several years ago, the skeletons have now been examined in detail by a team from ADACH and have been dated by the Kiel Radiocarbon Dating Laboratory in Germany, showing that they are of Neolithic date. Scattered over an area of more than 100 metres square that was once an ancient lakebed, the site is the largest discovery of ancient camel bones anywhere in the Arabian Peninsula. Further study is now under way to determine whether the camels had died naturally, or if they had been killed by Neolithic hunters.

Today, the economy of the UAE depends, to a large extent, on its export of oil and gas, which have provided the basis for its industrial development. However, as we have seen in the chapter on History, the export of raw materials is nothing new. As far back at 3000 BC, or 5000 years ago, at the beginning of the local Bronze Age, copper

Recent archaeological excavations have shed new light on the Palaeolithic or Early Stone Age period in the UAE.

Circular piece of stone on a string used in ancient times as a fishing weight.

For the first time, a major copper mining complex in the UAE is being subjected to a detailed study. Situated in Wadi Hilu, part of Sharjah, the complex is being examined by a joint German-Sharjah team.

was being mined in the UAE mountains and was being exported to Mesopotamia. One of the key Bronze Age ports, at Umm al-Nar, close to Abu Dhabi, was the site of the first archaeological excavations in 1959, or 50 years ago. Now, however, for the first time, a major copper mining complex is being subjected to a detailed study. Situated in Wadi Hilu, part of Sharjah, the complex is being examined by a joint German–Sharjah team. During fieldwork in 2007 and early 2008, one major find was a large semi-spherical copper ingot, proving that smelting had taken place at the site, while pottery at the site suggests a date in the early Bronze Age. The foundations of several buildings are also present, while there are veins of copper ore in the nearby hillsides. Further study of the site is likely to add important new information to knowledge of this earliest of the UAE's industries.

Wadi Hilu, though in the mountains, is close to another Early Bronze Age settlement, at Kalba, on the UAE's east coast. Studies of finds found at the settlement during excavations several years ago, undertaken by an archaeologist from the University of London, working with the Sharjah Directorate of Archaeology, have shown that the site was involved in a long distance trading network that reached from Mesopotamia throughout the Gulf and southern Iran and away to the Indus Valley, giving an indication of potential destinations for some of the copper from Wadi Hilu.

The task of identifying, and then excavating archaeological sites is, of course, only the beginning of a long process of further work, as the finds from the excavations are carefully studied and analysed. Another important study undertaken over the last year was an analysis of cornelian beads found, in profusion, in many of the UAE's collective graves from the Bronze Age Umm al-Nar period. Focusing on beads from graves at Hili, in Al Ain, and at Shimal and Dhayah, in Ra's al-Khaimah, the study, carried out by a doctoral student from the Sorbonne University in Paris, showed that most of the beads were produced at workshops in the Indus Valley, from where they were exported to the UAE and Oman – adding further information on the types of goods involved in the regional trade network of the time.

Moving on from the Bronze Age, a further season of work was undertaken at the important Iron Age fortified settlement at Muwailah, near Sharjah International Airport. Carried out by a team from Bryn Mawr College in the United States, in association with the Sharjah Directorate, the latest work has confirmed the extensive commercial contacts maintained by Muwailah's inhabitants, and also helped to clarify the rapid growth of the settlement in a relatively short space of time, helping to explain the chronology of Iron Age settlement throughout south-eastern Arabia.

Preliminary investigation of another Iron Age settlement was also undertaken at Wadi Madhab, in Fujairah, by a British team. The team also examined and recorded several dozen pre-Islamic graves and pottery from the mid-Islamic period, which has previously been found only rarely on the UAE's east coast. Further results from this work can be expected in future years, but the work at Madhab is, perhaps, more significant for another reason. The initial survey of the wadi that led to the identification of the sites was commissioned by a property development company as part of an initial Environmental Impact Assessment of the area, prior to commencing development. Realising the potential significance of the discoveries, the developer then financed a month-long further study of key features of the site, the first time that a commercial developer in the UAE has ever funded the excavation of archaeological sites in an area planned for development. With this precedent having been set, it is hoped that other private companies will follow suit in the years ahead. Government-controlled bodies, like Abu Dhabi's Dolphin Energy and the Abu Dhabi Company for Onshore Oil Operations (Adco) have, however, provided extensive support for archaeological work in their area of operations for several years.

Other surveys carried out throughout the country have continued to identify previously unrecorded archaeological sites, showing that, even after 50 years of work, there is still much to be discovered. One group of finds of particular significance was a series of several large, well-built stone villages in the mountains of Ra's al-Khaimah, dating to the seventeenth and eighteenth centuries. The villages are located near coastal palm groves, yet situated to allow them to be easily defended, perhaps an indication of a period of political instability.

As usual, the programme for the thirty-ninth annual Seminar for Arabian Studies, held at the British Museum in London in July, included a number of papers on topics related to UAE archaeology, covering both the place of the Emirates within a regional context and the results of individual excavation seasons. Papers presented will be published in 2009 in the *Proceedings of the Seminar for Arabian Studies* (www.arabianseminar.org.uk).

A further season of work was undertaken at the important Iron Age fortified settlement in Muwailah, Sharjah by a team from the US and preliminary investigation of another Iron Age settlement was undertaken at Wadi Madhab in Fujairah by a British team.

Early Islamic gold coin.

www.uaeinteract.com/archaeology

An Iron Age figurine of a camel, from Muwailah, in Sharjah.

The fifth in an annual series of symposia organised in Al Ain by the Zayed Centre for Heritage and History gave archaeologists the opportunity to present results from their 2007/08 work.

The fifth in an annual series of symposia organised in Al Ain in April by the Zayed Centre for Heritage and History, part of the Emirates Heritage Club, (www.zayedcenter.org.ae) gave local and visiting archaeologists the opportunity to present results from their 2007/08 work to colleagues and other interested parties, while two other conferences were held in November, that of the Archaeozoologists of Southwest Asia – International Council for Archaeozoology (ASWA-ICAZ) in Al Ain, and another on 'New Perspectives in Recording UAE History', organised by the Centre for Documentation and Research in Abu Dhabi.

In addition, two major new books on the archaeology of the Emirates were published during 2008. The first, *The Natural Environment of Jebel al-Buhais: Past and Present*, is the second in a series of the archaeology of Jebel al-Buhais, in the Emirate of Sharjah, an area best known for its major Neolithic (Late Stone Age) cemetery, but also including sites from the Bronze and Iron Ages. The second, *Emirates Heritage Volume 2*, is the proceedings of the second annual archaeological symposium held by the Zayed Centre for Heritage and History, in 2004 and of a symposium on UAE history also held that year. Papers on UAE archaeology were also published in a number of academic journals, including *Arabian Archaeology and Epigraphy* and the locally produced *Tribulus*, journal of the Emirates Natural History Group.

ENVIRONMENT & WILDLIFE

Government organisations and NGOs continue to promote the conservation of the UAE's marine and terrestrial habitats and the fauna and flora that live within them.

Over the course of the past year, long-term environmental sustainability strategies have been launched and plans have drawn up for a wider network of protected areas.

ENVIRONMENT & WILDLIFE

DURING THE COURSE OF THE LAST YEAR, EFFORTS by government, non-governmental organisations and by private individuals to promote the conservation of the UAE's marine and terrestrial habitats, and the fauna and flora that live within them have continued to grow, to meet the increasing challenges faced by the country's rapid programme of development.

These efforts have covered a wide variety of areas. One focus has been on the implementation of a tighter regulatory regime on industrial and other development activities that have an impact not only on the environment and wildlife but also on the country's human population. Long-term environmental sustainability strategies have been launched, plans have been drawn up for a wider, and much larger, network of protected areas and there has also been a continuing programme of detailed scientific research.

One much-welcomed measure in terms of regulation was the introduction of tight controls over the country's quarrying industry. Largely situated in the mountain areas of Ra's al-Khaimah and Fujairah, the quarries produce the rock and gravel used for major construction industry projects in the coastal areas, in particular in Dubai. Besides their direct impact on the mountain environment and its fauna and flora, the quarries also produce large quantities of dust that threaten the health of nearby towns and villages.

New regulations introduced by the Ministry of Environment and Water cover air quality guidelines, noise, health and safety practices and the impact on the environment of areas adjacent to quarry sites and their associated rock crushers. They also give government authorities the power to order quarries to cease work during periods when atmospheric conditions are likely to cause dust to remain suspended in the air, threatening human health. Work close to villages and towns will only be permitted during the day while tighter controls have also been imposed on the use of explosives.

Of the 80 or so quarries currently operating, a few, largely managed by international companies, are already meeting, or nearly meeting, the new guidelines, but over three quarters of the quarries will need to improve their performance substantially or will be closed down.

www.uaeinteract.com/environmentandwildlife

A major initiative during the year was the launching by EAD of the Abu Dhabi Environment Strategy 2008–2012.

Another major initiative during the year was the launching by the Environment Agency – Abu Dhabi (EAD) of the Abu Dhabi Environment Strategy 2008–2012, which lays down the environmental policy agenda for the next five years. Developed through a wide process of consultation with major stakeholders, the strategy sets a benchmark for monitoring changes over time, outlines the long-term vision, mission and goal of the emirate in terms of environmental policy and provides an action plan for the future. Two and five year targets have been identified for ten priority areas, including environmental sustainability, water resource management, air quality, hazardous materials and waste management, biodiversity management, environmental awareness, an environmental health and safety management system, and management of emergencies.

Introducing the strategy, EAD's managing director, Mohammed Al Bowardi, who is also secretary-general of the Abu Dhabi Executive Council, described it as being:

. . . our roadmap to a future in which everyone will be able to enjoy the benefit of a clean, safe and healthy environment.

Our challenge is that many still live an unsustainable lifestyle. They believe it is more convenient to postpone concern for environmental problems to a later date. But we cannot wait for a later date. We need to be strategic and act today because our environment is under pressure from a number of different directions at once.

The generation that destroys the environment may not be the one that pays the price. It is the future generations that will confront the consequences. Achieving Sustainable Development in our Emirate will take patience, commitment and persistence. It has to become a conscious and deliberate pursuit to change our mindset. It will not happen overnight.

For the first time ever, EAD has successfully satellite tracked a single adult Sooty falcon to its wintering areas in Madagascar.

As the country's development programme occupies an ever-growing proportion of the UAE's land, so too is a larger proportion of the country's territory now being scheduled for protection as national parks. In Abu Dhabi, which already has several thousand square kilometres of protected areas, both onshore and in shallow coastal waters, EAD was finalising plans at the end of the year for the formal designation of new areas that will more than double the amount of land and sea being protected in the emirate. Much is in the southern and western deserts, but another area being considered for formal protection is that of the mangroves and adjacent mudflats and

As the country's development programme expands, so too is a larger proportion of the country's territory now being scheduled for protection as national parks.

channels just to the east of Abu Dhabi Island. An important habitat for breeding fish and for birds, in particular, it is being proposed as the first of one of five new National Parks under the Abu Dhabi 2030 Strategic Plan.

In the northern emirates of Sharjah, Ra's al-Khaimah and Fujairah, areas of the Hajar Mountains are also being prepared for designation as protected areas, an important step, since the mountains are home to much of the UAE's endangered wildlife and provide key habitats. Large areas of Dubai's deserts are now also formally protected, although virtually the entire coastal zone of that emirate has now been irrevocably altered by development. That is not always a completely negative factor, however. For the first time in 2008, three species of seabirds were recorded breeding in Dubai, on undeveloped offshore islets that are part of The World project, and plans are now being proposed to set aside islets specifically to encourage further breeding.

With conservation of endangered species of wildlife continuing to be a focus of the UAE's environmental policy, Al Ain Zoo, founded in 1967 and the largest in the Middle East, has now completed the initial phases of a major overhaul, including not only substantial improvements in terms of visitor facilities but also a better standard of care for the more than 4000 individual mammals, birds and reptiles in its collection. One new focus has been on the endangered species of arid zones, both in Arabia and Africa.

Another major initiative during the year was the launching by EAD of its Environmental Sustainability Report, the first public sector report of its kind in the Arab world. Drawn up in association with other government bodies and public sector organisations, including the oil and gas industry, and based on the world's most widely accepted guidelines for sustainability reporting, the Global Reporting Initiative's G3 Guidelines, the document is an important step in helping EAD to meet various aspects of its sustainability strategy.

One of the major steps taken by EAD as part of the strategy outlined in the report will be the promotion and implementation, in co-ordination with other stakeholders, of an integrated Environment, Health and Safety Management System within three years, to link all factors related to economic growth, environmental protection, health and safety of workers, and community health. A new Abu Dhabi Sustainability Excellence Group (SEG) with representatives of

In November 2008, EAD announced that it had entered into a ten-year strategic partnership with the U.S-based research and technical services firm RTI International to assist the Emirate of Abu Dhabi in enhancing its existing environmental protection programmes.

Conservation of endangered species of wildlife continues to be a major focus of the UAE's environmental policy.

The formation of a new Mohammed bin Zayed Species Conservation Fund, which will have an initial endowment of Dh125 million, was announced in October 2008.

the major sectors in Abu Dhabi, including oil and gas, real estate and construction, large private companies and the banking sector, will work to share best practices throughout Abu Dhabi.

Recognising that conservation programmes can only be truly successful if they are multinational, the UAE was co-organiser, along with the UK, of an international conference in Abu Dhabi in late October at which a new multinational Memorandum of Understanding (MoU) was signed by 28 countries on conservation of birds of prey in Africa, Europe and Asia. The formation of a new Mohammed bin Zayed Species Conservation Fund was also announced in October. With an initial endowment of Dh125 million (US$34 million) provided by Abu Dhabi Crown Prince Sheikh Mohammed bin Zayed Al Nahyan, the fund will provide grants for small-scale projects throughout the world that are aimed at protecting individual endangered species (www.mbzspeciesconservation.org).

Scientific research into aspects of the country's environment has continued to yield good results, with work being undertaken by government agencies such as EAD, the Environment and Protected Areas Authority (EPAA) in Sharjah and the Environment Protection and Industrial Development Commission of Ra's al-Khaimah, non-governmental organisations such as the Emirates Wildlife Society and the Emirates Bird Records Committee and independent observers.

During 2008, for example, three new species were added to the UAE Bird List, bringing the total to 444, a remarkable number for such a small and arid country, while several species of reptiles, insects and molluscs new to the country were also identified. It is probable that there is much more that remains to be discovered, as investigations of the UAE's remarkable biodiversity continue.

One important initiative was the signing in February of a MoU between EAD and the Emirates Bird Records Committee (EBRC) under which the agency will maintain the EBRC database of nearly a quarter of a million records of wild birds seen throughout in the UAE since the late 1960s. To be continually updated with the addition of new records, this will provide EAD with one of the most extensive national databases of wild bird records in the Arabian Peninsula. The two will also collaborate on the preparation of the official national checklist of birds, in accordance with internationally accepted standards.

The Dubai Desert Conservation Reserve (DDCR) has been accepted as an official member of the International Union for Conservation of Nature (IUCN). The achievement marks the DDCR as the first wildlife and conservation area in the UAE to be formally declared by IUCN as a Protected Area.

New species are being discovered in the UAE as the country seeks to find a sustainable balance between development, conservation and protection of its biodiversity.

The value of scientific research is, of course, fully realised only when results are published, and several important new books on aspects of the UAE's natural history have been published during the year. Leading the way has been EAD, which launched two major publications in October, *Marine Environment and Resources of Abu Dhabi and Terrestrial Environment of Abu Dhabi*, as well as a more specialist publication on marine phyto-plankton of the Gulf. An EAD-sponsored book on the UAE's breeding birds was nearing completion at the end of the year, whilst the long-awaited Arabic edition of *The Emirates: A Natural History* will be launched in March 2009.

Another major work, volume one of *Arthropod Fauna of the UAE*, represents the first results of a detailed examination of the UAE's insects, adding several hundred species to the UAE national list, including nearly 90 species that had never previously been identified anywhere and were new to science.

Further discoveries are regularly made, as the UAE seeks to find a sustainable balance between development, conservation and protection of its biodiversity.

Sheikha Maitha holds the UAE flag as she leads the UAE team into the stadium for the opening ceremony of the twenty-ninth Olympic Games in Beijing.

U-19 CHAMPIONSHIP SAU

Emirati players celebrate after beating Uzbekistan 2–1 in their AFC Under-19 Championship final football match in Dammam, Saudi Arabia on 14 November 2008.

SPORTS & LEISURE

INVESTMENT IN SPORTING ACTIVITIES AND OUTDOOR PURSUITS is not only an important component of the UAE's strategy to attract visitors to its shores, it also features strongly in efforts to promote the country abroad.

The UAE has already established itself on the international sporting stage, hosting many of the world's major events in a wide range of sports, from horse racing to motor racing, golf, tennis, football, rugby, cricket, sailing, powerboat racing and almost every other competitive sport. These events not only attract large numbers of competitors and sports enthusiasts from around the globe to the UAE, they also see some of the country's own top sportsmen and women in action.

Sporting facilities in the UAE, already some of the best in the world, are being constantly upgraded, whilst massive new schemes, such as Dubai Sport City and Abu Dhabi Sports City, are under construction.

Aside from the international circuit events, the UAE has a healthy indigenous sporting environment with the local community taking part in a wide variety of sporting activities. Teams from throughout the seven emirates regularly compete in national leagues and cups in a multiplicity of sports that are controlled by specialised governing bodies. Top sporting venues (both indoor and outdoor) along with a favourable climate ensure that the activities continue throughout the winter season. New sporting bodies, such as the Abu Dhabi Sports Council, have been established to coordinate growth and development of local and national sports clubs. Their objective is to build a healthy society and at the same time nurture local sporting talent. Abu Dhabi Sports Council has also agreed to provide increased financial backing and financial incentives for sports clubs that are keen to promote international competitive standards.

Sports are also played at a social level and residents are able to take full advantage of the country's parks and recreational grounds where football, basketball and cricket matches are a favourite pastime, while the desert and mountain areas outside the main cities provide rough, rugged terrain for more adventurous pursuits.

UAE rally champion Mohammed bin Sulayem and Pavel Annenkov of Kazakhstan at the ceremonial start of the UAE Desert Challenge Rally in Abu Dhabi on 27 October 2008.

www.uaeinteract.com/sports

With the Arabian Gulf on its western shores and the Indian Ocean along its eastern flanks, the UAE is particularly attractive for watersports' fans. Those living on the Gulf coast are blessed with long stretches of sandy beach where residents take part in sports such as sailing, jet-skiing, surfing, swimming and kitesurfing. Snorkelling and diving are hugely popular within the region. Many residents and visitors enjoy the UAE's east coast, which also provides a wealth of exotic fish and coral.

Sport Sponsorship

International sport sponsorship, considered to be very effective brand advertising, has been used to great effect by UAE companies and government bodies, serving not only to further brand awareness but also to bring the UAE to audiences around the world.

Motorsports, with its singular global reach, is a particularly popular sport for sponsorship. Since 2007, Abu Dhabi Tourism Authority (ADTA) has had a three-year partnership with the highly successful BP-Ford World Rally Team, which includes Sheikh Khalid Al Qassimi as a driver. The addition of world rallying to Abu Dhabi's motorsports' portfolio demonstrates the emirate's pledge to become one of the world centres of motorsport excellence.

Motorsports with its singular global reach readily attracts sponsorship.

In 2008, Abu Dhabi-based Etihad Airways signed a three-year sponsorship deal with the Ferrari F1 team, the current Formula One world championship holders. Ferrari is developing a close association with Abu Dhabi, through the exciting new theme park being built on Yas Island, home to the capital's new F1 race track.

Etihad had already signed a three-year deal in December 2007 to become the title sponsor of the Formula One Abu Dhabi Grand Prix, starting with the inaugural event on Yas Island in 2009. Under the deal, the F1 race will be named the Formula One Etihad Airways Abu Dhabi Grand Prix until 2011.

Etihad Airways won the 'European Sponsorship of the Year' award in the European Sponsorship Association's business to consumer category for its imaginative sponsorship of GAA hurling in Ireland.

Etihad Airways' involvement with the Ferrari F1 team is one of a growing number of high-profile sports sponsorships for the national airline and complements existing partnerships with Chelsea Football Club, Harlequins Rugby Football Club, the All Ireland Hurling Championships and the Abu Dhabi Golf Championship.

Etihad began a partnership with Chelsea in September 2007 that has seen the airline host the inaugural Chelsea Soccer Schools in February 2008, as well as bringing current and former players out to the UAE's capital to host football clinics.

Etihad has also extended its growing array of international sports sponsorships to Australia in a five-year deal which includes the renaming of the famous Telstra Dome in Melbourne as the Etihad Stadium. The deal comes into effect on 1 March 2009, the start of the Australian Football League (AFL) season.

Abu Dhabi United Group (ADUG), controlled by HH Sheikh Mansour bin Zayed Al Nahyan, purchased UK's Manchester City Football Club in September 2008, a move that has brought a considerable amount of attention to the emirate. The team's signing hours later of Robinho, a Brazilian world star from Real Madrid, for GB£32.5 million kept the emirate in the headlines and underlined ADUG's commitment to make Manchester City the biggest club in the Premier League. Further major signings were being considered at the end of the year.

Dubai-based Emirates airline is FIFA's official partner until 2014. Other key football sponsorships by Emirates include its much-vaunted GB£100 million deal with Arsenal Football Club and sponsorship deals with Paris Saint Germain Football Club, Hamburger SV and AC Milan, The airline also announced in September 2008 that it had signed a three-year sponsorship deal with the successful Greek club, Olympiacos FC. The deal, covering the current season with options to extend the partnership for a further two years, will see the familiar Fly Emirates sign displayed at the Karaiskaki Stadium, the home of Olympiacos.

Emirates also backed the New Zealand entry and runner-up in the thirty-second America's Cup, the world's most famous yacht race. In

Visitors examine a model of the Formula One Yas Island circuit at an exhibition in Abu Dhabi.

The UAE's Ahmed Khalil receiving the Asian Football Confederation 'Youth Player of the Year' award in Shanghai on 25 November 2008.

UAE's Omar Juma Al Salfa competes in the men's first-round 200 metre race, heat 7 at the 'Bird's Nest' National Stadium during the 2008 Beijing Olympic Games.

addition, Emirates sponsors a wide range of sporting activities around the world, including horseracing, cricket, tennis, rugby, powerboat racing and golf. Emirates was also instrumental in bringing the IRB Rugby Sevens World Cup 2009 to Dubai and is the principal sponsor of the event, which will be held at The Sevens, Emirates' new state-of-the-art sports venue in Dubai.

UAE Olympic Team

Nine UAE athletes were proud to represent their country in the twenty-ninth Olympic Games in Beijing in 2008, pitching themselves against world-class sportsmen and women from over 200 countries.

Sheikha Maitha bint Mohammed bin Rashid Al Maktoum took part in the women's 67kg taekwondo event. A recipient of 'Best Arab Athlete' in 2006 and winner of the UAE's 'Best Female Sportsperson' award for two consecutive years, Sheikha Maitha was also the obvious choice to hoist the UAE's flag at the opening ceremony. Moreover, Sheikha Maitha had created history as the first Emirati woman to win an international gold medal when she received first place in the + 65kg category at the tenth Pan Arab Games in 2004, repeating her outstanding performance the following year. Amongst other achievements, Sheikha Maitha was awarded a silver medal in the + 60kg category during the 2006 Doha Asian Games. She is also the Arab, Asian and European champion in karate, kickboxing and taekwondo and the honorary President of the UAE Karate and Taekwondo Federation.

Mohammed Salem Abdulla Zahmi of UAE stands on the podium after winning the 70 kg beach body building competition at the 2008 Asian Beach Games in Bali.

Sheikh Ahmed Mohammad Hasher Al Maktoum achieved fame as the UAE's first Olympic medallist, winning gold at the Athens Olympics in the double trap shooting event. Sheikh Ahmed has also won gold medals at the 2003 and 2004 World Cups, as well as the World Shooting Championships in 2005, which was an Olympic qualifying event. He is the Athlete Ambassador for the humanitarian organisation 'Right to Play International', which brings sport and play to the lives of children affected by war, poverty and disease.

Sheikh Saeed competes in the men's skeet shooting qualification event at the Beijing Shooting Range Hall during the Olympic Games.

Sheikh Saeed Bin Maktoum Al Maktoum is the Asian and Arab Champion in skeet shooting and the patron of the national skeet shooting team. Sheikh Saeed won a bronze medal in the eleventh Asian Championship, held in Kuwait in 2007, which was an Olympic qualifying event. He also took silver at the Doha Asian Games in 2006 and gold in both the individual and the team events in the tenth Gulf Championships in Kuwait in 2007. In February 2008 Sheikh Saeed and his team-mates were awarded gold medals at the Asian Championships in India.

Sheikha Latifa bint Ahmed bin Maktoum Al Maktoum qualified for the Beijing Olympics following her win in the individual qualifying event at the seventh Qatar International Show Jumping Championships on her horse, *Kalaska de Semilly*. At the Asian Games in 2006, she came away with a bronze medal as part of the UAE team. She was also a gold medallist in the 2007 Sharjah International Jumping Championship.

Sheikh Ahmed competes in the men's trap qualification shooting event held at the Beijing Shooting Range Hall during Day 2 of the 2008 Beijing Olympic Games.

Saeed Rashed Al Qubaisi made history in Beijing as the first Emirati to represent the country in judo at the Olympics, competing in the 73kg category for men. 2007 was a particularly good year for Qubaisi as he claimed the gold medal at both the GCC Youth Championship and the Arab Championship.

Adel Khaled Abdul Ghafar competed in dinghy sailing (laser class) at Beijing, having won a silver medal in the GCC Championship in 2007 and gold in the both the European Championship and the Pan Arab Games in 2007 for the same event.

Obaid Ahmed Al Jasimi participated in the 100 metre swimming freestyle competitions, for which he has previously won gold at the 2005 and 2006 GCC Championships. Al Jasmi has also received awards in other swimming competitions, most recently the gold medal in the 100 metre medley in the GCC Championships in 2007.

www.uaeinteract.com/sports

UAE national football team line-up during the 2010 FIFA World Cup qualifier match between South Korea and the UAE at Seoul World Cup Stadium on 15 October.

Iran's defender Sattar Zare (back) stands alert as Emirati striker Ismail Matar controls the ball during their Asian zone Group 2 World Cup qualifying football match in Dubai on 19 November 2008. The match ended in a 1–1 draw.

Ali Obaid Shirook competed in the 400 metre and 400 metre hurdles. In the West Asian Games, hosted by Doha in 2005, he had won a bronze medal in both the 400 metre and the 400 metre relays. In 2007, Shirook took bronze in the 400 metre hurdle event at the Pan Arab Games in Egypt and silver in the fifteenth Arab Games in Jordan. Omar Juma Bilal Al Salfa is a talented sportsman and a rising star on the UAE's athletics scene, having won three gold medals in 2008 for the 100 metre event at the UAE National Championship and the UAE President Cup and the 200 metre event at the Youth Asian Championship.

Although none of the UAE participants came away from the Olympics with medals, they did their best for their country and work is now under way to prepare for the next Olympics in London. Sheikh Rashid bin Mohammed bin Rashid Al Maktoum, an award-winning sportsman in his own right, was elected in September 2008 for a four-year term as President of the National Olympic Committee (NOC).

Football

Like any other sporting nation, the UAE has a huge interest in football. The UAE FA was first established in 1971 and since then has dedicated its time and effort to promoting the game, organising youth programmes and improving the abilities of not only its players, but of the officials and coaches involved with its regional and national teams.

The UAE was host to the eighteenth Gulf Cup in January 2007 and it proved to be a momentous occasion as the national team managed to pull off one of its biggest achievements in football, beating Oman 1–0 to win the coveted cup for the first time in its 35-year history.

However, in 2008 the UAE's participation in the Asian World Cup final round qualifiers was not so successful. The UAE team hopes to feature more prominently in the lead up to the 2011 Asian Cup in which they were drawn in group C alongside Uzbekistan, Malaysia and India.

In the meantime, the UAE defeated an opposing bid from Australia to stage the FIFA Club World Cup in 2009 and 2010, a testament to the quality of sporting infrastructure in the country, particularly the stadiums at Zayed Sports City and the Mohammed bin Zayed Stadium, home to Al Jazira Football Club. The UAE's successful hosting of the 2003 FIFA Youth World Championship and the 2007 Gulf Cup proved that the country has the necessary experience.

At home, clubs are adopting a new professional ethos and a new Pro League, the UAE's first-ever professional season, kicked off on 14 September 2008 with the Super Cup match between league champions Al Shabab and President's cup winners Al Ahli. The 12-team Pro-League commenced on 19 September. Another division will be added to the league for the 2009/10 season.

Khalfan Al Rumaithi, who was elected president of the UAE FA for a four-year term on 28 May 2008 following the first ever elections to the UAE FA, has commented that despite the challenges ahead the UAE FA is committed to taking the game to a new level. In particular, the FA would like to see more games being played, national companies sponsoring local teams, UAE TV stations broadcasting games, and an increase in support by fans. Already, International Petroleum Investment Company (IPIC) and Borealis have signed a three-season sponsorship deal worth Dh30 million with Al Jazira.

The skills of future UAE players could certainly be enhanced by the signing of an agreement in May 2008 between Inter Milan, the Abu Dhabi Sports Council and UAE real estate developer Hydra Properties to build the only Inter Milan football academy in the region in Abu Dhabi. The academy, which will be open to children between the ages of nine and 14 years, will be based in Hydra City and will house a stadium to be built and sponsored solely by Hydra Properties. Young soccer players from all UAE clubs will have the opportunity to go to Inter Milan for part of their training.

The UAE under-16 soccer team has already made history by qualifying for the 2009 FIFA World Cup finals following its defeat of Australia 3–2 in the Asian under-16 championship quarterfinals.

Cricket

Cricket is another very popular sport in the UAE with events being organised throughout the Emirates. Sporting bodies such as Abu Dhabi Cricket Council, Dubai Cricket Council (DCC) Ajman and Sharjah Cricket Council, under the auspices of the Emirates Cricket Council, foster and encourage the development of the sport.

The magnificent new Zayed International Cricket Stadium, which was opened in 2006 in Abu Dhabi, was the venue for the three-match, one-day international series played between Pakistan and West Indies on 12, 14 and 16 November in which Pakistan took the honours.

UAE cricketer Anjad Ali jumps in the air to receive a throw as Sri Lanka cricketer Chamara Silva reaches his crease during a Group A match between Sri Lanka and the UAE for the Asia Cup at Gaddafi Stadium in Lahore on 26 June 2008.

UAE cricketers celebrate during the Group A match between Sri Lanka and the UAE for the Asia Cup at Gadaffi Stadium in Lahore.

The West Indians were playing for the first time in Abu Dhabi, but India, Pakistan and Sri Lanka have all played international cricket here before.

The impressive new Cricket Stadium being built at Dubai Sports City will be ready by February 2009. Meanwhile, in September 2008 the Pakistan Cricket Board (PCB) announced that they have signed a US$9 million three-year deal to play international one day and twenty20 matches in Dubai starting with a triangular series in April 2009.

Sharjah already has a world-class stadium and has hosted a number of one-day events and Ajman Cricket Council are planning to build new cricket grounds, including an international standard turf wicket.

Indeed the Emirates has the best cricket facilities of any Associate member of the International Cricket Conference, putting many Test-playing countries to shame. Due to the massive expatriate workforce, as well as the success of the Sharjah Cup, which put the Emirates on the global sport map in the 1980s and 1990s, cricket has a keen following in the country and the UAE team has been the most successful Asian country outside of the four Test sides on the field,

There is no lack of talent, either, as proven by the performances of players like Zahid Shah, Mohammed Tauqir, Khurram Khan and Amjad Ali at the Asia Cup, although the team itself was unsuccessful. Efforts are now being made to turn the team into a genuinely competitive force. Emiratis – indeed, full-time homegrown players of any nationality – are considered to be the key to progression of the game and competition at international level, and the UAE has committed to picking a quota of four Emirati players in every squad. At the same time, Emirates Cricket Board is setting up scholarship schemes for talented youngsters.

Tennis

Plans to nurture a UAE tennis champion are being supported by Tennis Emirates, the governing body for the sport in the UAE. Training programmes have been established and in the next ten to 15 years, the UAE hopes to develop players of international standard. Tournaments, such as the annual Tennis Championship at Abu Dhabi International Tennis Complex, part of Zayed Sports City, are staged throughout the UAE with the aim of seeking out both new and undernourished talent.

In the meantime, the UAE consistently attracts the leading tennis players in the world to compete in international tournaments staged here. Dubai Duty Free first hosted the men's tournament in 1993, and since then the competition has grown to be one of the most popular events on the ATP Tour. For the past five years former world number one Roger Federer has dominated, winning four in-a-row. On the women's side, the now-retired Justine Henin also won the singles crown four times. However, in 2008, neither player managed to reach the finals with American Andy Roddick taking his debut title in the Gulf region, while Russian Elena Dementieva became the new champion in the women's tournament.

Elena Dementieva of Russia receives the trophy after defeating Svetlana Kuznetsova of Russia in the final of the WTA Barclays Dubai Tennis Championships at the Dubai Tennis Stadium on 1 March 2008.

2009 will see several changes with the ATP and WTA moving in to restructure both the men's and women's competitions. Having run as an ATP International Series Gold event from 1998, the men's tournament will be one of the ten '500' status tournaments on tour, while the women's competition will change from a WTA Tier II tournament to one of the 15 'Premier' events. Dubai will be joined by Rotterdam, Acapulco, Memphis, Barcelona, Washington DC, Beijing, Tokyo, Basel and Valencia for the new-look 2009 ATP Tour.

Camel Racing

The inhabitants of Gulf states have enjoyed a long and productive relationship with the camel, which is held in great admiration and respect. Formalising camel racing was one way of maintaining its central role in UAE life. Through camel racing, the UAE has been able to maintain the symbolic significance of the camel and, by giving it structure, has developed it into a professional sport with significant prize money. Camel racing is also a big tourist attraction throughout the winter months.

Robotic jockeys have replaced human jockeys in camel races in the UAE.

The UAE now has no less than 15 racetracks across the Emirates. Nad Al Sheba, 10 kilometres outside of Dubai, Al Wathba, 30 kilometres south-east of Abu Dhabi, and Al Ain track, which is 20 kilometres west of Al Ain, are all large, well-equipped camel tracks with high-tech facilities. Two smaller tracks are located in Sharjah, one in Ra's al-Khaimah and one in Umm al-Qaiwain. Others are spread throughout the desert areas.

Even though camel racing has become a popular pastime in the UAE, it has not been without controversy. Particularly worrying were allegations that young expatriate jockeys from south Asia and Africa

Mohammed bin Sulayem was elected to the FIA World Motor Sport Council in November 2008, the first Arab to achieve this honour. He was also named as Vice-President of the FIA for Sport by the Federation Internationale de l'Automobile.

were being kidnapped or, indeed, sold by their parents, and smuggled into the country. In 2005 the UAE took measures to clarify the prohibition on underage jockeys and improve enforcement of the law. Anyone caught using a jockey under the age of 18 or a jockey that is less than 45 kilograms in weight faces a Dh50,000 (US$13,620) fine or a three-year jail sentence, with the penalties being doubled in the case of repeated offences. With the assistance of Unicef, young camel jockeys have been repatriated to their home countries and given assistance with reintegration into their local communities.

Motor Sports

The UAE has a busy international motor sports' calendar orchestrated by the very active Automobile and Touring Club (ATCUAE). The motor year commences with the Abu Dhabi Classic, the FIA Historic Rally Championship in Abu Dhabi, a championship series that expanded from Europe into the Middle East for the first time in January 2007. The gruelling UAE Desert Challenge concludes the FIA Cross Country Rally World Cup for cars and trucks, and the FIM Cross Country Rally's World Championship for bikes later in October, whilst the Dubai International Rally rounds off the hotly contested FIA Middle East Rally Championship in November.

The UAE Desert Challenge was conceived by Mohammed bin Sulayem, President of ATCUAE, whose motorsport career goes back to the early 1980s. Bin Sulayem, who has a record 14 FIA titles to his name, is well qualified in his role having very considerable experience as a competitor and an organiser, together with unparalleled knowledge of the desert.

The seventeenth edition of the UAE Desert Challenge, commencing at Emirates Palace Hotel on 28 October 2008 and ending in Dubai on 2 November, fielded a mighty line-up of cars, bikes and trucks from the Middle East and overseas, an entry list featuring 120 drivers, co-drivers and riders from over 30 countries. The absence of some big names due to the credit crunch and the re-scheduling of the Dakar Rally did not put a damper on this year's event, which saw Qatar's Nasser Al Attiyah become the first Arab driver for 15 years to win the cross-country crown, while French rider Cyril Despres scored his fifth bikes title triumph.

The UAE National Rally Championship, organised by the Emirates Motor Sports Federation (EMSF), features six rounds throughout the Emirates, split into Desert and Saloon events. Sheikh Abdullah Al

UAE driver Yahya Al Helei and his co-driver Khalid Al Kendi drive their Nissan Patrol during preliminary super stage action in Dubai before the official start of the UAE Desert Challenge Rally.

Qasimi and co-driver Wael Marjan drove off with the prestigious Abu Dhabi Rally title in April 2008, round 4 of the National Championship and round 2 in the Saloon Class. Sheikh Abdullah, who finished second to his brother Sheikh Khalid in 2007 in Abu Dhabi, leads the Saloon Class having also triumphed in the Sharjah Rally.

As already mentioned, Sheikh Khalid plays a primary role in Abu Dhabi Tourism Authority's one-year-old partnership with the BP-Ford World Rally Team, which features strongly in the 15-event FIA World Rally Championship series.

A wide array of national and international track motor sports' competitions are held at venues such as Dubai Autodrome, including the relatively new Speedcar Series, in which drivers from various fields of motor racing, including former F1 drivers, battle it out for the prize pot of US$3 million.

However, the real Formula One is set to take the UAE by storm. As already outlined in the chapter on Infrastructure, Abu Dhabi's new world-class F1 track is rapidly taking shape on Yas Island. An extraordinary meeting of the International Automobile Federation's (FIA) World Motor Sport Council (WMSC) held in Paris in October 2008 confirmed the provisional date of 15 November 2009 for the highly anticipated Etihad Airways Abu Dhabi Grand Prix to be held at the venue. Abu Dhabi will now be the host for the grand finale of the 18-race calendar, which kicks off with the Australian GP on 29 March 2009.

The recently formed Abu Dhabi Motor Sport Management, headed by internationally renowned F1 authority Philippe Gurdjian will develop and manage F1 in the UAE.

Spanish motorcyclist Marc Coma sits on his 690cc KTM Rally bike at the ceremonial start of the UAE Desert Challenge Rally in Abu Dhabi on 27 October 2008.

Rory McIlroy of Northern Ireland hits a shot from the helipad atop the Burj al-Arab.

Golf

Immaculate greens, lush fairways, high-tech practice ranges and facility-driven clubhouses make the UAE a world-class destination for golfers, both amateur and professional. Many of the innovatively designed clubhouses are outstanding architectural landmarks in their own right, frequently basing their design on traditional aspects of UAE culture. At Abu Dhabi Golf Club, one of the emirate's most distinctive golf courses, the clubhouse is in the shape of a falcon swooping down on a golf ball. Emirates Golf Club, although built from thoroughly modern materials such as white concrete and gleaming glass, has managed to create a series of cool, tent-like structures lying low to the ground, redolent of a vanished era. Meanwhile, the clubhouse at Dubai Creek Golf and Yacht Club evokes the gently billowing sails of a stately dhow and that at Jebel Ali Hotel and Golf Resort the prow of a ship overlooking the Arabian Gulf.

At least ten new golf courses are under construction, many being designed by world-famous professionals. The legendary Gary Player is responsible for the signature golf course on Saadiyat Island; The Tiger Woods Dubai is the first-ever course in which the world-famous golfer has had a design input and just one of five themed courses in Dubailand's Golf City; and Sergio Garcia has joined forces with Greg Norman and Pete Dye to design the Wild Golf Course, the fourth elementally themed course in the multi-billion dirham, award-winning Jumeirah Golf Estates.

It is not surprising that these prestigious golf courses are the venues for a series of the world's top events on the global golfing calendar. Abu Dhabi Tourism Authority (ADTA) runs the PGA Abu Dhabi Golf Championship at Abu Dhabi Golf Club. The club has undertaken a two-phase Dh20 million (US$5.45 million) upgrade, initially to improve the spectator and player experience for all involved in the competition, and in the long-term to deliver a world-class sporting and leisure facility to club members and tourists. The third Abu Dhabi Golf Championship in 2008 was won by German prodigy, Martin Kaymer, with Lee Stenson and Henrik Stenson as runner-ups. Abu Dhabi kick-starts what has become known as the 'Desert Swing', taking the players on to Doha and to Dubai for the Dubai Desert Classic.

Martin Kaymer featured again in the nineteenth Dubai Desert Classic, which was held at the Emirates Golf Club's superb Majlis

Martin Kaymer on the eighteenth green at the end of the final round of the 2008 Abu Dhabi Golf Championship at Abu Dhabi Golf Club.

Course at the beginning of February 2008. However, this time Tiger Woods underlined his status as the world's greatest player with a mesmerising final round performance to take the title, winning by a shot from Kaymer.

An addition to the calendar in 2009, the Dubai World Championship, will be staged in November as a climax to the new US$10 million 'Race to Dubai', a season-long competition that will replace the PGA European Tour Order of Merit. The deal will pump a staggering U$100 million (Dh367.36 million) into the Tour over the next five years. To be held annually at Jumeirah Golf Estates, the tournament will be open to the top 60 players on The Race to Dubai. Jumeirah Golf Estates will also become home to The European Tour's international headquarters from 2009.

Sheikha Latifa riding 'Kalaska De Semilly' in the Beijing Olympics showjumping competition in Hong Kong.

These high-profile events and, of course, the spread of superb courses, have played an important role in the dramatic rise in popularity of the sport since the UAE Golf Association was formed in 1995, inspiring and motivating excellence. The UGA, however, is keen to promote the game among youngsters and improve the performance of national teams. Some national teams have already done well on the regional circuit, winning the Arab Junior Championships, but to be consistently competitive they need to participate in more national and international tournaments.

Equestrian Sports

Emirates Racing Authority (ERA) is the internationally recognised body overseeing horse racing in the UAE. Races of thoroughbreds and the legendary purebred Arabians take place in many of the region's top equestrian clubs and courses, but the highlight of the season is the Dubai International Racing Carnival (DIRC), nine weeks of top-class racing.

One of the world's leading thoroughbred breeding and racing operations, Godolphin, has been a major participant in the DIRC and a huge contributor to the UAE's racing circuit. Established by the Maktoum family, Godolphin runs a state-of-the-art operation in Dubai's Al Quoz area. Younger horses are broken in at the specially designed Desert Stables with only the best-bred picked for international competition.

Recognised as the world's richest race, the US$6 million Dubai World Cup has become the favourite meeting place for the global racing

Top: Sheikh Mohammed with his horse 'New Approach' and jockey Kevin Manning after winning the Epsom Derby.
Right: Robby Albarado rides US-born horse 'Curlin' to victory in the Dubai World Cup.

fraternity. Hot favourite and US horse of the Year 2007, *Curlin*, ridden by Robby Albarado, galloped away with the 2008 Dubai World Cup.

The 2008/09 season opened at Nad Al Sheba on 6 November and the 2009 Dubai World Cup will also be held on 28 March at Nad Al Sheba, the culmination of 46 race meetings, hosted by three UAE racing clubs, the Abu Dhabi Equestrian Club, Dubai Racing Club and Jebel Ali Racecourse.

Work has also begun on the spectacular new Meydan racecourse near Nad Al Sheba which is scheduled to stage the 2010 World Cup.

Purebred Arabian racing is very popular at home in the UAE where purebred Arabian horses are prized animals with a long tradition in the desert. But concerted efforts are being made to foster and support the sport elsewhere, with the UAE promoting Arabian racing in many famous racing centres around the world during the summer months. The main aim is to dispel the myth that Arabian horses do not make good race horses.

Central to this promotion is the UAE Equestrian and Racing Federation, which sponsors a series of races for purebred Arabian horses around the globe. The federation, with the support of President HH Sheikh Khalifa bin Zayed Al Nahyan and Abu Dhabi Crown Prince General HH Sheikh Mohammed bin Zayed Al Nahyan, has been organising these races as part of the UAE President Prize series for 14 years and they have been steadily gaining in popularity. They are now a part of the flat-racing calendar and large crowds regularly turn out to witness the purebred Arabians in action.

Purebred Arabians also excel in endurance racing, a gruelling sport that is hugely popular in the UAE and one in which Emiratis shine at home and abroad. HH Sheikh Mohammed bin Rashid Al Maktoum, Vice President and Prime Minister of UAE and Ruler of Dubai, led the UAE team to win the 2008 European Endurance Championships in the UK, shortly after triumphing in the Syrian Endurance Championships. The 160 kilometre race qualified the UAE team for the World Endurance Championships in November in Malaysia, in which the UAE team took gold. Sheikh Mohammed has been leading the UAE to the world endurance meet since the 1996 championships in the United States.

UAE female riders Sheikha Latifa, Sheikha Maryam, Sheikha Futaim and Sheikha Sheikha, also triumphed in the UK during the 2008

National Bank of Dubai play Qatar Airways during the third Cartier Dubai Polo Challenge at Desert Palm Polo Ground on 28 March 2008 in Dubai.

HH Sheikh Mohammed bin Rashid Al Maktoum takes part in an endurance race in Wadi Rum, Jordan on 14 November 2008.

season and were crowned as team champions in the Women's European Open Endurance Championships, while Sheikha Latifa won the individual event.

At home, Yousuf Ahmad Al Beloushi finished ahead of Spain's Maria Alvarez Ponton in the Sheikh Maktoum bin Hamdan bin Rashid Al Maktoum Challenge 120 kilometre endurance ride at the Emirates International Endurance Village in Dubai, again winning the first and last races in the Dubai International Endurance 2007/08 season. Earlier in the year, HH Sheikh Hamdan bin Mohammad bin Rashid Al Maktoum, Crown Prince of Dubai, led a UAE sweep of the top three places in the HH The President of the United Arab Emirates Cup endurance ride.

Showjumping is another equestrian sport that features strongly on the national circuit. But Emirati riders have also triumphed abroad in this demanding field: Sheikha Latifa bint Ahmed Al Maktoum participated in the 2008 Olympic Games, whilst Sheikh Shakhbut bin Nahyan Al Nahyan won the Valkensward Show jumping Championship in Holland in August 2008.

Watersports

As mentioned in the introduction to this section, the UAE is an ideal venue for all types of competitive watersports, from traditional dhow racing to modern yacht and dinghy sailing, powerboat racing and jet-skiing.

The season for the evocative traditional dhow sailing races begins on 1 October with the first heat for the 22-foot class at Dubai International Marine Club (DIMC). Approximately 40 dhows go through eight heats in all before the overall winner is decided on points gained. Lucrative prizes are awarded for the victors in this and other competitions for the larger boats.

In May, marking the end of the season, the spectacular Sir Bu Nua'ir dhow race is living proof that the country has a firm hold on tradition. Every year since the event was started in 1991, dozens of dhows have raced along the UAE coast in a re-enactment of the sprint home by pearlers of old from the pearl banks near the island of Sir Bu Nua'ir. Local knowledge of wind and tides is a huge advantage and a younger generation of sailors, many of whom have a seafaring background, are keeping the tradition alive whilst adding their own competitive touches.

For nationals and expatriates, sailing plays a huge part in their weekend leisure activities as excellent facilities in all the emirates, including at Abu Dhabi International Marine Club (ADIMC), the Dubai Offshore Sailing Club (DOSC), Dubai International Marine Club (DIMC), Fujairah International Marine Club (FIMC), and in Sharjah, Ajman and UAQ, coupled with a good all-year-round climate, enable enthusiasts to take part in numerous activities and competitions. Established in 1988, DIMC was the first Arab organisation to be granted full membership of the Union Internationale Motonautique (UIM). The highly successful Maktoum Sailing Trophy, comprising a regatta of ten inshore races and one offshore passage race for individual yachts, held at DIMC in February is an indication of the progress made by the sport in the UAE.

Emirates Sailing School trains UAE nationals to international standards to represent the UAE in competitions abroad. Training covers all watersports but mainly focuses on attaining skills in sailing Optimists, Lasers and Toppers. In addition, the UAE National Sailing Championships are a central part of the sailing calendar. While some of the youngsters gain their first serious competitive experience outside of their local club activities in these regattas, the junior line-up also includes members of the UAE national team.

Motivation and inspiration for these young enthusiasts and their older counterparts was provided by the appearance of *Alinghi*, the

Traditional dhow races evoke the sprint home by pearlers from the pearl banks off the coast of the UAE.

winner of the thirty-second America's Cup, in UAE waters in the winter of 2006/07. Drawn by ideal meteorological and sea-conditions, *Alinghi* perfected the skills that allowed it to triumph in a closely fought final against Emirates Team New Zealand.

The Class One World Powerboat Championships first appeared in the Gulf in 1989, when the region's initial race took place off Mina Seyahi in Dubai. The UAE has since staged the championships eight times. Indeed, the UAE's powerboat Victory team is classed as the most successful in the history of the World Championships with driving legend Ali Nasser himself picking up an unprecedented 14 world titles in 13 years.

The Victory team raced hard throughout the international 2008 season in pursuit of their eighth world title in 16 years. The two-boat squad powered by team-mates Nadir bin Hendi and Mohammed Al Merri in *Victory 1* with Jean-Marc Sanchez and Abdullah Al Mehairbi in *Victory 7* performed well in initial heats before clinching the title in the penultimate round of the championship at Mina Seyahi on 6 December. *Victory 1* scored 125 points overall, with *Victory 7* in second place at 105 points and Qatar 95 in third at 81 points.

The President's Cup Formula 2000 championship powerboat race series, which extends over two weekends in March, with the first leg taking place at the Abu Dhabi Breakwater, is an important event for aspiring F1 drivers. The second and final leg is held in Sharjah. Sharjah is also home to the eighth and final round of the UIM F1 World Powerboat Championships in December.

Fujairah also looks set to become an important fixture in the Continental F2000 Championship diary, having hosted a Grand Prix in February 2008 where 18 boats from 12 nations vied for valuable points as well as a share of the prize money. The Fujairah International Marine Club (FIMC) was also chosen to be the official headquarters of the F2000 Championships as well as the executive organising committee for all championship meets.

EXHIBITIONS & EVENTS

Investment in the exhibition, events and conferences industry is yet another strand in the UAE's strategy to position itself as a global centre of tourism and trade.

 The World Future Energy Summit is one of the world's leading conferences and exhibitions on global energy policies and the development of alternative and renewable investment and infrastructure.

SUMMIT

www.wfes08.com

EXHIBITIONS & EVENTS

INVESTMENT IN THE EXHIBITIONS, EVENTS AND CONFERENCES industry is yet another strand in the UAE's strategy to position itself as a global centre of tourism and trade. In addition to providing a platform for the direct promotion of business activities, MICE (meetings, incentive, conference and exhibition) events encourage business relationships, boost economic diversity, encourage development and contribute significantly to the image of the country worldwide.

With its huge purpose-built exhibition halls and luxury hotels boasting state-of-the-art conference facilities, the UAE is at the crossroads of Europe, Asia and Africa and is uniquely positioned for access to the billions of people who live and work within just a few hours flight of the country.

Recent estimates conclude that the UAE has about half of the total covered exhibition space currently available in the Gulf Cooperation Council (GCC), but this will increase to 65 per cent by 2009. The addition of a sophisticated infrastructure, a strong economy, a secure hospitable environment and diverse leisure opportunities helps to explain why the country attracts major global events.

> The UAE is at the crossroads of Europe, Asia and Africa and is uniquely positioned for access to the billions of people who live and work within a few hours flight of the country.

EXHIBITION CENTRES

ADIEC

Abu Dhabi National Exhibition Company (ADNEC) built, owns and manages the state-of-the-art Abu Dhabi International Exhibition Centre (ADIEC), the Arabian Gulf's largest exhibition venue, which is widely regarded as one of the most modern facilities of its type in the world. The spectacular venue comprises 55,000 square metres of fully interconnected exhibition floor space spread over 12 halls, an 18,000 square metre visitor concourse, and a multi-purpose hall suitable for events ranging from huge conventions to pop concerts.

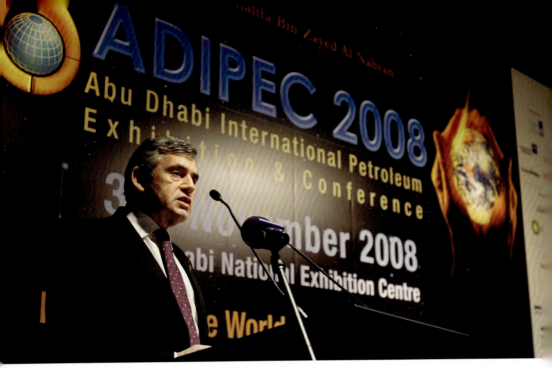

Some of the Gulf's largest and most significant international exhibitions, such as Idex, a major defence exhibition and conference, Adipec, Abu Dhabi International Petroleum Exhibition & Conference, Gulf Incentive, Business Travel and Meetings Exhibition (GIBTM) and ISNR Abu Dhabi, an international trade show focused on addressing homeland security challenges facing governments and businesses in the region, are held here.

Surrounding ADIEC is the Dh8 billion (US$2.18 billion) Capital Centre development, a fully integrated community project that is considered to be a major strategic element of Abu Dhabi's 2030 vision. Capital Centre will house a new business and residential micro-city of 23 towers, including seven hotels. On completion in early 2011, Capital Centre will also feature Capital Gate, a 35-storey signature tower, a 2.3 kilometre waterfront Marina Zone; the 'Galleria', a shopping mall with restaurants, retail outlets, and cinemas; and its own monorail.

In June 2008, Adnec commenced dredging for the marina, the first phase of which will feature a 250-metre quay wall suitable for stern mooring more than 20 yachts. This will be ready by March 2009, in time for the highly anticipated Abu Dhabi Yacht Show. ADTA and Adnec have been marketing the destination worldwide to great effect.

Adnec also recently acquired ExCeL London, the UK capital's largest exhibition venue, as part of its strategy of developing a global network of venues to serve the international exhibitions industry. The benefits to Abu Dhabi include increased international awareness of the city and the emirate, international training opportunities for UAE nationals and an opportunity to support international events. For further information on ADNEC's events and developments visit www.adnec.ae.

Abu Dhabi also has excellent meeting and conference facilities at its many five-star hotels. But the most impressive are to be found at the capital's new seven-star Emirates Palace Hotel. This has a 1200-capacity auditorium, a main ballroom that can accommodate up to 2800 people, 48 meeting rooms, six large function terraces, a media centre and business centre, all built within the heart of a beachfront hotel that stands on 100 hectares of landscaped gardens. The hotel deserves its designation as the 'most luxurious and technologically advanced meeting facility in the region'.

DWTC

At the northern end of Sheikh Zayed Road, Dubai World Trade Centre (DWTC) is the towering figurehead of a large exhibition complex that includes the adjacent Dubai International Convention and Exhibition Centre (DICEC). Built in the 1980s, DWTC was the city's first skyscraper. Today, dwarfed though it is by new buildings, it remains at the epicentre of Dubai's international trade and business industry, having hosted key conferences for over 20 years. With the number of exhibitions and meetings at the venue rising significantly, DWTC recorded 551,056 visitors to DICEC between January and June 2008, compared to 393,665 in the first six months of 2007, an increase of 40 per cent. DWTC executives were confident that they were on track to beat the records set in 2007, officially the group's 'busiest year ever.'

Construction is well under way on the first phase of the Dubai Trade Centre District project, the high-end commercial development that will create a new central business quarter at the heart of Dubai.

An international conventions facility also managed by DWTC, the Airport Expo Centre is a convenient five-minute drive from Dubai International Airport. However, extensive new exhibition facilities are being built at Jebel Ali adjacent to the new Al Maktoum International Airport. Dubai Exhibition City is destined to be an integrated commercial destination anchored by one of the world's largest exhibition centres, Dubai Exhibition Centre.

DWTC-hosted events include some of the most strategically important industry sectors such as aviation, banking and finance, and

Sheikh Mansour bin Zayed Al Nahyan at opening of Environment Exhibition.

The extensive new Dubai Exhibition City, which is under construction near Jebel Ali, is destined to be an integrated commercial destination anchored by one of the world's largest exhibition centres.

www.uaeinteract.com/exhibitions

Sharjah Book Fair at Expo Centre Sharjah.

biotech. Among the significant exhibitions that debuted this season were Aircraft Interiors Middle East, an event that targets the high-growth aviation sector in the region. Other major successes were the inaugural event for banking and finance, MEFX, organised in partnership with Dubai International Financial Centre, and the China Sourcing Fair, the premier commercial event for traders and volume buyers from the MENA region and suppliers and manufacturers from China. Many of Dubai's extensive range of luxury five-star hotels also boast impressive conference and meeting facilities that host events throughout the year, including the exotic new Atlantis Hotel on Palm Jumeirah.

Expo Centre Sharjah

Sharjah pioneered the region's exhibition industry in 1977 when it opened an exhibition complex in the emirate. Twenty-five years later, with an investment of Dh183.5 million (US$50 million), the Expo Centre Sharjah was inaugurated as the centrepiece of a larger 'Expo City'. Managed by Sharjah Chamber of Commerce and Industry (SCCI), the Expo centre is being extended and a 300-room hotel is being built that will give exhibitors and foreign delegates easy access to the venue.

The Expo Centre hosts regular specialised trade fairs, including Texpo, an annual international trade exhibition for garment machinery, textiles and accessories; the National Careers Exhibition, aimed at UAE nationals in the banking and finance sectors; the biannual Mideast Watch and Jewellery Spring and Autumn Shows; Arab Asia Trade Fair, showcasing everything from DIY products to flora and fauna and the Sharjah World Book Fair.

Expo Centre Sharjah is bordered by Al Khalid Lagoon, making it an attractive option for marine events such as the highly successful Gulf Maritime Exhibition.

Rakeen unveiled innovative designs for the new RAK Convention & Exhibition Centre at the Arabian Travel Market in 2008.

RAK Convention Centre

In an effort to increase foreign investment into the emirate, as well as boost tourism and trade, Ra's al-Khaimah investment company Rakeen unveiled a Dh1.46 billion (US$400 million) RAK Convention & Exhibition Centre on the first day of the Arabian Travel Market 2008. The innovative building will have a superior high-tech finish, using technologically advanced ceramics that have been developed by RAK Ceramics. The structure of the new exhibition centre is designed to merge with its surroundings, maintaining the majestic beauty of the sand dunes.

Ra's al-Khaimah already has a 37,400 square metre exhibition complex close to the active business centre of the city. Its calendar includes the Families Exhibition, Drinks and Food Stuffs Fair, Career and Training Fair, and Ramadan Festival.

Fujairah Exhibition Centre

The Fujairah Exhibition Centre (FEC) on the east coast covers 1080 square metres of indoor floor space, an outdoor display area, exhibition halls, management offices and service utilities. It is centrally located between both the international airport and Fujairah Trade Centre on one side and the seaport and free zone on the other. A number of internationally important exhibitions have been held at the centre since its establishment. These include Buildex, the Motor Show, the Fujairah International Agricultural Exhibition, and Fujairah International Education and Training Exhibition. FEC also hosts seasonal fairs for the general public.

EXHIBITIONS

The following is a small representative selection of the many exhibitions that take place every year in the UAE.

ABU DHABI 2008

The International Hunting and Equestrian Exhibition (Adihex), also known as Abu Dhabi 2008, is a four-day annual platform for the hunting and equine industries with a distinctive emphasis on heritage and traditional sports. The fifth edition of the exhibition took place at ADIEC from 8 to 11 October, with 526 companies from 37 countries taking part, a 22 per cent increase on 2007, underlining the local, regional and international profile that the event has achieved.

Sponsored by HH Sheikh Hamdan bin Zayed Al Nahyan, Deputy Prime Minister and President of the Emirates Falconers' Club (EFC), Abu Dhabi 2008 was organised by the EFC in cooperation with the Abu Dhabi Authority for Culture and Heritage (ADACH), Sorouh Real Estate and Abu Dhabi Sports Council.

These two camels were purchased by Sheikh Hamdan bin Mohammed bin Rashid Al Maktoum for Dh6 million (US$1.5 million) during the first day of Adihex.

HH Sheikh Mohammed bin Zayed Al Nahyan, Crown Prince of Abu Dhabi, attending Adipec.

Falconry is a major draw at Adihex. This year, hybrid falcon auctions were added to the other main attractions in the exhibition, camel and horse auctions, and a saluki dog show, encouraging animal owners to breed higher quality animals.

Adihex supports the use of farm-bred birds to protect endangered wild falcons whose capture is illegal under Cites. In order to maintain a balance between heritage and environmental protection, hybrid falcons have been introduced for hunting purposes in the UAE, and many are on offer, and are bought, during Adihex, just in time for the hunting season.

Other events that lend this show a unique atmosphere include competitions for best falconry equipment; Nabati poetry on falcons and hunting themes; best research on Arab hunting and equestrian traditions; 'Made in UAE' competitions for traditional crafts; prizes for the best Arabic coffee; as well as painting and photography competitions focusing on UAE/Gulf heritage.

ADIPEC

More than 37,000 oil experts and executives representing 89 countries gathered in Abu Dhabi from 1 to 7 November 2008 for the annual international petroleum show, one of the largest events of its kind in the world. This is hardly surprising considering the size of the emirate's hydrocarbon industry. The four-day Abu Dhabi International Petroleum Exhibition and Conference (Adipec 2008) covered nearly 85,000 square metres at ADIEC and attracted 1500 exhibitors from nearly 55 countries.

Adipec coincided with the Energy Investment Summit and Energy 2030 event, a high-level conference supported by Adnoc and the Petroleum Institute. The 2008 edition explored Abu Dhabi's 'Vision 2030' and its commitment to leading the global debate for energy resources of the future, in tandem with crucial issues affecting the environment, geo-science integration, oil and gas development cycles, drilling improvements and advances in petroleum technology.

IDEX

Since its inception in 1993, the International Defence Exhibition and Conference (Idex) has grown steadily to emerge as one of the largest and most important events for the global defence industry. Idex 2009, which runs from 22 to 26 February 2009 at ADIEC, is expected to be the largest since its launch in 1993. ADIEC's 12 halls covering 55,000 square metres will house military hardware produced by 900 top companies from 50 countries. The exhibition, co-organised by the Armed Forces, attracts high profile defence and security personnel from around the globe, the majority of whom are government representatives.

Equipment on sale includes high-precision weaponry systems, guided missiles for air defence, electronic warfare systems (C4I) and ballistic missile systems. Other items on display include naval vessels and submarines, undersea defence technology, unmanned aerial vehicles (UAV) and maritime UAVs.

Idex will feature live demonstrations on land, air and sea and Adnec's new marina facilities will facilitate participation of a broader range of naval craft and amphibious demonstrations.

Locally produced military hardware will also feature, including the Gulf's largest warship, the Baynunah class corvette, which is being built for the UAE Navy by Abu Dhabi Ship Building. In fact, at least 30 sections of the exhibition are dedicated to UAE defence services or products.

Idex is one of the most important exhibitions for the global defence industry.

In 2007, 862 companies took part in the show, with 143 delegations from more than 50 countries. Defence systems sales amounted to more than Dh2 billion (US$545 million) with the UAE's Armed Forces buying the lion's share, worth nearly Dh1.4 billion.

Idex 2009 will also incorporate the Gulf Defence Conference, which is regarded in international academic and military circles as a top forum on defence strategies and technologies.

Abu Dhabi Motor Show

Driven by strong growth in the regional and global automotive industry, Abu Dhabi International Motor Show (ADIMS), a biennial event, which took place at ADIEC from 17 to 21 December 2008, has been re-branded and re-launched. Showcased were luxury cars, high performance supercars, custom cars, executive saloons, concept and hybrid cars, sports cars, family cars and SUVs, motorcycles and quad bikes, as well as commercial vehicles such as trucks and pickups, vans and mini buses, luxury coaches, limousines, trailers and campers.

An Italian Spada TS Codatronca supercar on display in Abu Dhabi.

Launched over 20 years ago, ADIMS is one of the oldest automobile exhibitions in the Middle East. With a completely new management, a new state-of-the art venue and a new brand identity, the exhibition was the largest and most comprehensive motor show in the Middle

East in 2008. Emirates Auctions conducted an auction of cars and licence plates at ADIMS, part of the proceeds of which went to charity.

Abu Dhabi Yacht Show

Abu Dhabi is venturing into the upper echelons of global yachting with the debut Abu Dhabi Yacht Show (ADYS) scheduled for 12 to 14 March 2009. Abu Dhabi Tourism Authority (ADTA) moved to establish the emirate's superyacht credentials ahead of the event by running a destination pavilion and acting as headline sponsor for the Monaco Yacht Show, using the opportunity to present Abu Dhabi's superyacht hub proposition to the most influential audience in the sector.

A yachting event of global standing is an excellent 'fit' for Abu Dhabi, which has extensive natural marine assets and a rich maritime history: the people of Abu Dhabi have a long relationship with the sea as it was a key provider of sustenance in the past and is now a focal point for sport and relaxation.

ADYS will be held at ADIEC's new marina, which has a 250 metre quay wall for stern mooring and will be capable of berthing at least 20 superyachts of 25 metres or more in length.

World Future Energy Summit

After a hugely successful inaugural event in January 2008, the World Future Energy Summit (WFES) is set to become one of the world's leading conferences and exhibitions on global energy policies and the development of alternative and renewable investment and infrastructure. WFES attracted heads of state, numerous energy and environment ministers, and CEOs of companies from 77 countries, 220 exhibiting companies and over 11,000 visitors over three days. Accolades accorded the 2008 edition include 'Best Launch Event' from the prestigious Association of Event Organisers Excellence awards and the 'Best Congress in the Middle East' award from the Middle East Event Industry Awards.

The programme for WFES 2009 encompasses a wide range of themes, including energy policy, investment and funding, green buildings, clean transport, solar, wind, biofuels, ocean power, geothermal, nuclear, waste to energy, fuel cells, carbon management, and environmental strategy. With over 15,000 attendees expected in 2009, the summit will be the largest meeting of influential figures within the renewable energy industry. The exhibition has been

HH Sheikh Mohammed bin Zayed Al Nahyan, Abu Dhabi Crown Prince, tours the Masdar Energy Initiative Exhibition with US President George W. Bush, Secretary of State Condoleezza Rice and US Ambassador Michele Sison.

extended to cover over 20,000 square metres and will include a series of new feature areas to encourage networking and interaction within this global community. There will also be a range of social events, including the Zayed Future Energy Prize ceremony and dinner.

Cityscape Abu Dhabi

Cityscape Abu Dhabi, held from 13 to 16 May 2008 at ADIEC, was an international property investment and development event, focusing on all aspects of the property development cycle in this booming market. The exhibition attracted regional and international investors, property developers, leading architects and designers to an annual forum that celebrates the very best in real estate, architecture, urban planning and design.

Over 50,000 participants attended Cityscape Abu Dhabi 2008 and billions of dirhams worth of property deals were done. An additional fourth day was added to the show to meet the extremely high level of demand from visitors.

The Cityscape brand is a global one and stretches to seven destinations in three continents, but because of the expanded facilities provided by ADIEC, Cityscape Abu Dhabi 2009 will be the largest event in the range.

Mecom

The second edition of the Middle East Communications Exhibition and Conference, held at ADIEC from 26 to 28 May 2008, was one of the largest dedicated business-to-business networking platforms for the communications industry in the Middle East. With over 100 exhibitors offering the latest and most innovative products and technology in the communications industry, Mecom provided a unique opportunity for communication professionals to interact and connect with industry counterparts and competitors. The three-day event featured a concurrent conference programme offering over 60 topics and seven tracks that address the latest trends and best practices for the communications sector. Over 50 telecom industry leaders attending the conference shared, discussed, explored, and found solutions for the issues facing the telecommunication industry today. Mecom is officially supported by the UAE Telecommunications Regulatory Authority and Dubai Internet City.

www.uaeinteract.com/exhibitions

Najah Education Conference

Najah 2008 (19–21 October at ADIEC) was the most comprehensive education, training and careers event ever to be held in the UAE. Specifically created to service the needs of all three distinct sectors in one focused environment, Najah, an annual event, provides tailored solutions to each visitor's needs, based on extensive research with key visitor focus groups. However, Najah is much more than an exhibition. The event featured numerous activities for visitors, including job profiling, careers advice, over 100 'topic specific' seminars and the region's largest high-level strategic educational conference. It also showcased many leading UAE companies seeking to recruit.

Power Generation & Water Middle East 2008

This annual exhibition (26–28 Oct 2008 at ADIEC) provides an ideal platform for companies involved in the power generation, energy and water sectors to exhibit their products, services and solutions, at the same time enabling them to conduct and evaluate business opportunities with targeted key decision-makers in a market that is expanding exponentially. The exhibition serves as a comprehensive showcase for the regional and international power generation, energy and water industries.

Abu Dhabi Medical Congress 2008

The Abu Dhabi Medical Congress, held in 2008 from 26 to 28 October at ADIEC, brings together healthcare manufacturers, wholesalers, dealers and distributors, providing key contacts and information on the major topics affecting the healthcare industry today.

Roadex/Railex

Held in 2008 from 23 to 25 November at ADIEC, Roadex/Railex focuses on all aspects of the transport industry, including infrastructure, traffic management, rescue services, safety and parking, global traffic engineering, highway maintenance, road railway and metro technology, interiors, bridge, road and tunnel construction, transport IT, street furniture, barrier systems, signage and SatNav/GIS.

Environment 2009

Environment 2009, which will take place from 19 to 21 January 2009 at ADIEC, will be the fifth highly successful edition since the event was

ADNEC hosted three new exhibitions in December 2009: Fashion Expo Arabia, Shoe and Leather Fair Middle East and Optical Exhibition, the only trade exhibition for the optical industry in Abu Dhabi

first held in 2001. Organised in conjunction with the Environment Agency – Abu Dhabi (EAD), Environment 2009 will focus on energy, water, waste, air and land management issues. This is a particularly relevant topic at present as MENA countries are expected to invest Dh16.5 billion to Dh22 billion (US$4.5–US$6 billion) annually on freshwater projects over the next ten years.

Participants will include governmental organisations dealing with environmental matters from the MENA countries (Middle East and North Africa) and the rest of the world.

Environment 2009 will focus on energy, water, waste, air and land management issues, all topics that are vitally important to the development of the region.

Gitex

Twenty-eight years old in 2008, Gulf Information Technology Exhibition (Gitex) or Gitex Technology Week, as it is now called, is one of the three biggest exhibitions of its kind in the world. Gitex Technology Week 2008, running from 19 to 23 October at DICEC, featured three dedicated industry events: Gitex Business Solutions, Gulfcomms, and Consumer Electronics. Also held in conjunction with Gitex Technology Week were Global Conference, Gitex Majlis, and Gadget Glam 2008. In addition, the week-long Gitex Shopper at Airport Expo, which was open to the public, showcased the latest in games, audio and digital technology.

Gitex continues to attract companies from leading technology hubs around the world, who recognise the unique opportunities for expansion and further growth that the Middle East markets offer. The 2008 edition welcomed 3300 exhibitors from 82 countries spread out over 64,000 square metres, including 30 country pavilions, with attendance figures around 130,000.

The UAE Government had a strong presence at Gitex 2008, with six UAE ministries showcasing their electronic platforms, applications and e-services, enhancing public awareness of government efforts to provide a highly effective and enabling electronic work environment.

Gitex Technology Week also hosted some of the year's most high-profile launches, with consumer electronics companies in particular seeking to demonstrate their commitment to the Middle East market by making the event a key platform for new technology. Innovation was also on display in the world of electronic gaming, with the inaugural Gitex Digital Game World. A series of developer workshops were also held, with specific emphasis on supporting the development of original Arabic games and software.

Dubai International Boat Show

Powerboats line up at Dubai International Boat Show.

Held at the Dubai International Marine Club at Mina Seyahi, Dubai International Boat Show (DIBS) welcomed over 800 exhibitors from nearly 50 countries in 2008, including up to 400 boats, the highest number since the show was launched in 1992. Companies from every part of the industry, from boat-builders through to marine equipment, suppliers and service providers, showcased their latest products and services, providing a unique opportunity to see some of the world's most exclusive and luxurious super yachts lined up next to speedy sport cruisers, powerful motorboats and other desirable craft.

Dubai Motor Show

The biennial Middle East International Motor Show at DICEC targets the buoyant automobile market. Attended by hordes of automobile enthusiasts and prospective buyers, international vehicle manufactures display their wares, including fleets of off-road vehicles, concept cars, high-performance sports cars, custom-built automobiles and motorcycles. Manufacturers participating include BMW, Mercedes-Benz, Volkswagen, Lamborghini, Jaguar, Rolls-Royce, Suzuki and Land Rover, to name but a few.

Dubai Airshow

Billed as the world's third largest aerospace exhibition, the biennial Dubai Airshow, which celebrated its tenth anniversary in 2007, will be staged in 2009 at the Dubai World Central aviation city in Jebel Ali. The new Dubai Airshow site will cover 425,000 square metres, double the size of its former venue at Airport Expo Dubai, and will be housed in a semi-permanent structure for its first outing before moving to a permanent facility for 2011.

Dubai Airshow 2007 hosted 850 exhibitors and 11 national pavilions representing 50 countries: 45,420 visitors attended, 10,000 more than in 2005, and over 140 aircraft were displayed. In addition, the show also saw over Dh550 billion (US$150 billion) worth of orders placed during its five days and now holds the record for the largest amount of deals ever concluded at one event.

Arabian Travel Market

The Arabian Travel Market (ATM) is universally recognised as the leading travel industry event for the Middle East and pan-Arab region, another rapidly expanding economic sector. The fifteenth edition of ATM ran from 6 to 9 May 2008 at DICEC and was open to the public on the last day. The four-day event welcomed 14,046 visitors representing 114 countries, including 119 hosted buyers from the premium leisure industry, golf and MICE sectors.

Uniting key market players from six continents, this event comprises four days of intensive business meetings, a diverse seminar and education programme, press conferences and social networking opportunities. Large-scale UAE tourism projects were on display, whilst airlines, tourism organisations, hotels, tour operators and individual countries showcased their holiday attractions to boost visitor numbers. Four days of seminars, press conferences, meetings and networking opportunities during ATM 2008 kept globetrotters up-to-date with the latest destinations and industry trends.

Seven-time F1 World Champion Michael Schumacher inspects the model of a tower that will carry his name. The tower will be built on Reem Island in Abu Dhabi.

Cityscape Dubai

Cityscape Dubai is another major business-to-business real estate investment and development event in the Cityscape global brand. Held from 8 to 11 October 2008, the seventh Cityscape Dubai attracted over 60,000 real estate professionals from more than 120

Visitors examine the model of a proposed 'new city' at the opening of Cityscape 2008.

countries across the globe, including a record number of regional and international investors, property developers, governmental and development authorities, leading architects, designers, consultants and senior professionals involved in the property industry, providing an annual forum that celebrates the very best in real estate, architecture, urban planning and design from around the world.

Although the credit crunch was affecting markets across Europe and the US, the Middle East remained an attractive proposition for regional and international investors with experts predicting resilience and continued growth in the sector.

Five conferences, seminars and workshops running alongside the exhibition enabled delegates to thrash out strategies, investment and development opportunities as well as debate macroeconomic conditions, financing options, real estate marketing and branding.